FOUNDATIONS OF PEACE AND FREEDOM
The Ecology of a Peaceful World

By the same Editor:
ALTERNATIVES TO WAR AND VIOLENCE

FOUNDATIONS OF PEACE AND FREEDOM

The Ecology of a Peaceful World

Edited by
TED DUNN

Christopher Davies
Swansea

172·4

First published 1975 by
Christopher Davies (Publishers) Ltd
4/5 Thomas Row
Swansea SA1 1NJ

ISBN 0 7154 0130 0

*Printed in Wales by
Salesbury Press Ltd., Llandybie,
Dyfed.*

Contents

PART ONE

The Understanding of Natural Laws

PART TWO
Natural Laws in Practice

PART THREE
Maintaining Peace

Acknowledgements

The Editor wishes to record his heartfelt thanks to all contributors, to those whose names are below, especially to David Britton for compiling the Index, to his wife and family, to all who have helped financially, and those who have helped with secretarial work.

Without the generous help and encouragement of these and other friends, this book could not have been contemplated or completed.

Sponsors:

Dame Kathleen Lonsdale, F.R.S.;* Lord Boyd Orr, F.R.S.;* Lionel Penrose, F.R.S.;* Kenneth Lee; Hugh Brock; Leslie Aldous.

Editorial Advisory Group:

James L. Henderson; Donald Groom;* Eric Baker; Margaret Tims; Geoffrey Carnall; Anthony Weaver.

Local Supporting Group:

Howard Diamond;* Mary Mann; Michael Hennings; Brian Dawes; David Britton.

* Since this book was conceived in 1969 these loved and valued friends have unfortunately died.

Foreword

I am daunted by the task of writing a foreword for a book so varied, so searching, so authoritative. What contribution can I make to so grand a theme and to such impressive and comprehensive comment?

I take refuge in my own limited experience and my own strong conviction.

First, I hate violence.

Within the first few days after my arrival in my first overseas post many years ago I saw there the mob had gone the whole length of the long street in Hebron (in what was then Palestine) killing man, woman and child as it went. As a very young magistrate I had to witness a hanging in Acre jail. In the early days of the last world war I saw a boy looter shot dead in the main street of Deraa. Many years later—and I witnessed much violence in the meantime—I saw where villagers in Cyprus had been murdered as they fled in a cornfield on a beautiful sun-lit afternoon, murdered one by one by complete strangers in cold blood.

I learnt early on to hate violence in its many manifestations. All kinds of violence. Violence arising from panic, hate or fear. Or the systematic and efficient destruction of life and mutilation of bodies by military bombing. Or the violence of oppression, the despotism of force. I think I hate most of all the violence of torture, the horror of the secret destruction of the solitary individual by all the inhuman technical paraphernalia of terror in power.

It is well to remember that there is also the violence in extreme resort of honourable resistance to intolerable oppression.

Many years ago when I went back to deal with violence in Cyprus I said:

"Violence is evil but one of the main lessons I have learned is that a worse evil, is fear of violence. If there is fear of violence then the effect of violence is multiplied. It is a positive duty to us all to do what we think is right and not to allow violence—so often mean and cruel—to dictate what we should do".

Brave words, at least they demonstrate the dilemma of anyone who hates both violence and tyrrany.

This brings me to my second proposition: that if violence is to be overcome there must be an alternative. We cannot just hate violence and hope that it will go away. In Indo-China, in the Middle East, in southern Africa, in Northern Ireland, wherever there is violent conflict, we must either accept and condone violence or put forward and advocate and work out practical constructive policies for peace. The more we hate violence the more we must have the will to work for conciliation, for settlement, for agreement.

Obvious enough, you may say, violence is evil: it can be avoided or overcome only by conciliation, by justice in action.

My next and consequent proposition is perhaps less obvious. We do not lack the instrument to keep the peace, and equally important, to make the peace tolerable. What we lack is the will. I do not tire from repeating that there is nothing wrong with the United Nations except the Members. The instrument, the Charter forged in San Francisco in 1945, is available, effective, sharp. All that is necessary for the Council to act and to succeed is to win agrreement, and agreement comes only from hard work, from the will to find a way, and then the determination to follow it through.

Here is a fourth proposition—not so self-evident. Nationalism is the enemy of the individual: internationalism is the champion, the defender, the hope of the individual. When mankind escapes from the narrow confines and constraints and controls of national enclosures into the wider open field of internationalism the individual comes into his own. National governments, even the best of them, dislike the individual. He is a nuisance, an irritant, an impediment to national interest and national security. But in the emerging new world of internationalism and individual matters, he is welcome, he is free. Time and again I have seen the action, the inspiration, of one leader, one man, change the course of world events.

This is the hope of the world. The hope is that national division and discrimination and separatism and suppression and selfishness and subordination will give way to international unity and equality and freedom and compassion and fulfilment. God willing, we shall encourage that tremendous transition on its way. And I trust that this book will help us to do so.

HUGH CARADON

Introduction

War is not inevitable but should be regarded as a disease which arises because we do not understand the natural laws governing human relationships. This book, therefore, is a search for these laws, and a knowledge of their application in today's world in the belief that obedience to them will lead to the rule of law based on justice and right reason.

To many of the younger generation, however, the words "law and order" raise visions of repression, violence and loss of freedom, while to many of the older generation law and order is seen to be sustained by these same coercive forces. Both these attitudes are based on false premises because without law and order freedom cannot survive, while if based on coercive forces, the peace they seek to preserve is undermined. The law we seek, if it is to be of lasting value, must, in the last resort, be grounded on the moral conscience of the community. Conditions which help to create trust and confidence, and which speaks to man's inner being strengthens the foundations of law and order, while conditions which tend to destroy them, destroy foundations of peace. Law and order must be seen to be founded on natural laws, laws which hold the allegiance of man's heart and mind. The following chapters provide illustrations of this understanding and its application.

The editor makes no apology for the first chapter[1] being a long, and perhaps difficult one, but it is included because the old but honourable concept of Natural Law is so misunderstood, and because it also helps to provide the vital link between the academic worlds of philosophy and science and the reality of practical politics.

To deal adequately with the many studies involved, which could be related to our central theme demands resources far beyond those available to the Editor, but this attempt must be made because of the urgency of the task. The aim of this book therefore is to attempt to include the main strands of those important aspects of peacemaking and peacekeeping within the contents of one volume in the belief that the interested, but non-specialist reader wants a book within his means, and not too long to read, but which at the same time gives a comprehensive survey of the understanding of natural laws and the opportunities before us. It is suggested that those who can study this subject further use the suggested reading matter at the end of each chapter, and if possible search for, and relate other subjects, to this same central purpose.

The word *ECOLOGY,* included on the sub-title of this book is defined in the Shorter Oxford English Dictionary as "the branch of biology which deals with mutual relationship between organisms and their environment", also as "the study of spatial[2] distribution of a population in reference to natural[1] and social causes". These definitions are included here because it will be seen from them that ecology must involve more than the pollution of the land, air and water. For instance, we all have longings, fears and appetites which often drive us in opposite directions but which, if harmonized, provide us with the richness of life. Our need is for individuality, for self-expression and even, for many of us, quiet and solitude, while on the other hand we desperately need to be wanted by others, and to be part of the community. It is urgent for us to harmonize these apparent opposite needs within a structure of world organization and these needs can be satisfied through international co-operation and the decentralization of power to create what one contributor[3] calls the "fellowship of life", not, as he carefully points out, "fellowship for power". The foundations of peace can be further strengthened in many other practical ways touched on later in this introduction and outlined more fully in the chapters which follow. If we can identify and obey natural laws our hope must be that we will find new forces arising which remove the causes of conflict, and control it by generating respect for law.

Ecology should concern itself, not only with the pollution of rivers but with the pollution of man's mind, yet the neglect of right values in our educational system and in society generally, makes it ever more difficult to make true judgements, a subject touched on by many contributors. The recent awakening to the importance of ecology has illustrated the inter-dependence of all living matter, and that there are no short cuts where nature is concerned. This is particularly true in world affairs and the reason for this form of book.

The underlying theme, therefore, is that there are natural laws governing human behaviour, which, if understood, could ensure peace and freedom without reliance on violence. Further, that obedience to these natural laws creates a healthy environment in which good law gradually grows and becomes respected.

The importance of this approach to the peace issue first became apparent during the days of popular support for the Campaign for Nuclear Disarmament. The negative "Ban the Bomb" approach adopted by the movement was clearly inadequate, and in an attempt to remedy this, several of us in the Colchester Branch initiated a series of conferences dealing with the possibility of a realistic alternative to war as a means of resisting aggression. The success of these conferences encouraged us to go forward with the production of "ALTERNATIVES TO WAR AND VIOLENCE,[4] a book of 24 essays which the late Sir Stephen King Hall described as "of first-class importance" about a problem "upon whose solution depends the future of the human race". This book was supplemented by s STUDY OUTLINE,[5] sponsored by the Friends' Peace Committee and written by Eric Baker. Later, in response to an American film competition, an amateur film (16mm.) called PEACE THROUGH LAW[6] was made.

Having been so immersed in the search for the alternative to war, the many complex and confusing ideas encountered gradually began to form a coherent shape. War is seen as a malfunctioning of the international body politic, and, as with any disease, expert knowledge and understanding is called for. No expert is needed, however, to tell us that, if we eat an unbalanced diet, ignore hygiene, live in a poisoned environment, and so on, disease will take a foothold. An agriculturalist also knows instinctively that he must obey nature's laws of cultivation, watering, feeding, etc., if he is to create a healthy plant. This principle applies to all living matter and particularly to animals. Nature is seen to be something to live in harmony with, not something to be ignored or fought against.[7]

Obedience to natural laws requires an ecological approach.[8] All life is interdependent, and it is because of the wide range of subjects involved that it has been found necessary to draw so many studies and sciences together in this volume.

How, then, can these natural laws be understood in relation to international affairs, and in particular to creating the foundations of peace and freedom?

Three major ideas are seen to be of most importance, namely, *structure,*[9] *co-operation*[10] and *truth.*[11] So far as the *individual* is concerned, this means respecting man's personality by providing an environment which generates meaning and purpose for his spiritual being. These needs can be met largely by the above three ideas and once they are met, not only are the causes of conflict removed but new forces are set in motion which generate the basis of order based on justice.

Unfortunately, one major difficulty impedes our willingness to understand, namely our impatience for quick results. Obedience to natural laws must always mean a willingness to commit ourselves to long term solutions. There is no other way and the sooner if we do act on a correct understanding of natural laws, our long-term future is assured. Short cuts, attractive though they often appear, almost always lead to disaster. Even if they do not, they delay us in reaching our goal.[12]

Fortunately the U.N. has already travelled further, and made more progress than is generally realised. Much of the machinery has been created; what is now needed is the will to use it. This, in turn, demands a deeper appreciation of values[13]—a constantly recurring idea in many of the chapters that follow. Unfortunately the United Nations[14] is also hovering between disaster and success, uncertain whether to rely on the old paths of violence to maintain order, or to venture forth in a new direction and "ritualize" conflict as outlined in the chapter by Ruth Finnegan.[15]

Before discussing the U.N., however, a few more words are needed about the individual. Accepting that peace begins here, our next step is to understand his needs, both as a member of the community and as an individual. His individuality demands a structure of society, local, national and international, which respects his personality, and this in turn means that power be decentralized to small units. Only then may his inner being find self-expression.

Small units unfortunately, if isolated, are uneconomic, and psychologically the need is to feel wanted and be part of a wider community. By themselves small units will not create peaceful conditions. "No man is an island". He must, therefore, co-operate, and in co-operating learn to accept certain laws for the well-being of all, which, if seen to be based on common sense, soon become accepted. International lawyers recognise that good law is based on "Right reason". Law flows partly from the right form of structure, the importance of which has been insufficiently appreciated. The impact it has indirectly on our environment and subsequently on man's feelings is profound.

Of even greater importance than our environment, however, is the fact that man is gifted with the power of reason, and the wisdom of responding to truth. For example, if poison is offered us to drink, our reason will tell us to refuse , especially if the label states what the bottle has inside it. If facts indicate that a certain course is right, then sooner or later, if only for reasons of self-interest, behaviour patterns are changed. Truth has many sides: it embraces research, communications, education, love, as well as our concept of God. Gandhi made truth the basis of his belief, and taught the concept of Satyagraha: namely, that truth has a creative force of its own.

Truth understood and applied in its many forms dictates all forms of action; indeed it dictates whether we accept the preceding ideas about co-operation and the importance of structure. Truth may sometimes make little impact on immediate problems, because our feelings, caused by our environment,[16] dictate our immediate instinctive response, but truth if sought after a long period must prevail.[17]

The above, far too briefly, provides us with a glimpse of the understanding. What about its application?

The first need is for a new look at our educational establishments. The learning of true values and more about natural laws (and the concept of Natural Law[18]) is of prime importance. We have much to learn from educationalists such as Grundvic,[19] philosophers such as Herbert Read and religious leaders such as Gandhi and Teilhard de Chardin.[20] UNESCO has an important role here,[21] by providing good material, establishing international universities, adequate information and communication services. Peace research also needs to be encouraged.[22]

Little is said in this volume about the political day to day hurly-burly, even though it is on those activities that our attention is frequently focussed by the mass media. No doubt improvements within the political sphere can and should be made, but those will probably only *follow* the application of the above understanding. For example, if the nations of the world co-operate, an environment favourable to political solutions arises naturally.[23] If they do not, division and conflict will grow.

Our understanding of natural laws concerning the individual and his relationship to the state brings us to perhaps the most important and helpful development in the history of mankind. For the first time ever, the world now has a Charter of Human Rights. The implications of this Charter are such that if present thinking, as outlined in Sean Macbride's and Mulford Sibley's chapters, were fully implemented (and again more progress has been made than is generally realised) then most wars could be made impossible almost overnight.[24]

Lastly we are left with the question of enforcement in time of conflict, and the role of a peace-keeping and peace-making force. Such a force would need to be seen as one gaining its authority, not from violence, which tends to destroy authority, but from the training of its members, and by the moral authority it earns, and is given by acting as the conscience of a world public opinion.[25]

Given the will to implement all these aspects of human behaviour and relationships, it will be found that each supports and strengthens the other. All life must be seen as one whole, and as a living being having its source of inspiration in a Supreme Spirit.

As the health of the world community improves, to that extent will the need for armaments be found to be a waste of resources and a cause of conflict. No attention is given to disarmament in this book, because the belief is held that once the realization sinks into people's minds that peace *IS* within our grasp and *action* is taken to achieve this peace, then, perhaps only then, will people feel free to remove the nightmare of war and the burden of armaments.

1 "Natural Law and Natural Justice" by Dennis V. Cowen. (Page 22).
2 "Spatial", defined as "having extension in space".
3 See "True Nationalism leads to True Internationalism" by Peter Manniche. (Page 174).
4 Published by James Clarke Ltd., Cambridge. 1963.
5 Friends' House, Euston Road, London, N.W.1.
6 Concord Film Ltd., Nacton, Ipswich.
7 "Man and the Balance of Nature". (Page 116).
8 See "Natural Theology". (Page 48).
9 See "The Physics of Politics". (Page 197).
See "The Economic Viability of Small Nations". (Page 205).
See "Organization for Peace in the Graeco-Roman World". (Page 217).
10 See "Towards a World Community". (Page 227).
See "Trade and Development". (Page 238).
11 See "Education and Peace". (Page 125).
See "Freedom and Conscience". (Page 137).
See "Straight Thinking as a Factor in Peacemaking". (Page 146).
See "Love and Authority". (Page 155).
See "Authority and Law". (Page 166).
12 See "The Economics of Permanence (Page 93).
13 See "Universal Values". (Page 71).
14 See "World Order—Towards a World Community". (Page 227).
15 See "Peace and Conflict in Non-Industrial Societies". (Page 83).
16 See "Environmental Laws". (Page 107).
See "Planning for Harmony". (Page 186).
17 See "Spiritual Laws". (Page 60).
See "Love and Authority". (Page 155).
18 See "Natural Law and Natural Justice". (Page 22).
19 See "True Nationalism leads to True Internationalism". (Page 174).
20 See "Spiritual Laws". (Page 60).
21 See "Education and Peace—The Potentialities of UNESCO". (Page 125).
22 See "Universal Values". (Page 71).

[23] See "Towards a World Community". (Page 227).
[24] See "Human Rights and the Rule of Law". (Page 296).
See "Coecion of States and World Peace". (Page 315).
[25] See "United Nations Peace-Keeping". (Page 325).
See "Authority and the Law". (Page 166).
See "Non-Violence in U.N. Peace-Keeping Operations". (Page 270).
See "Freedom and Conscience". (Page 137).

PART ONE

THE UNDERSTANDING OF NATURAL LAWS

The assumption underlying all these chapters is that there are natural laws vitally affecting human relationships which must be observed if we are to learn how to regulate and limit violence. Spiritual, economic and environmental laws are all examined.

NATURAL LAW AND NATURAL JUSTICE

DENIS V. COWEN

Advocate of the Supreme Court of South Africa. Of the Inner Temple, Barrister-at-Law. Professor of Comparative and Commercial Law in the University of Cape Town, 1946-61. Professor of Law in the University of Chicago, 1962-65. For many years Special Adviser to the Governments of Basutoland and Lesotho. Currently Chief Law Adviser to the Johannesburg City Council.

Peace and freedom depend on justice and the observance of natural law. The meaning of these old and honourable terms, and their implications for modern society, deserve to be both more widely and more accurately known. In this Chapter Dr. Cowen gives a comprehensive analysis.

Although natural law and natural justice are foundations of peace and freedom, the words themselves are a source of misunderstanding and controversy. Peace, freedom, nature, law and justice are each ambiguous words, designating difficult concepts. In combination the problems which they present are compounded. Let us, therefore, aim at some clarity.

Peace means more than absence of conflict. Peace of that kind is compatible with the inertness of a bomb-flattened city or the docility of a prison. Very different is the peace which consists in a just ordering of human relations designed to promote joy and fulness of life for free human beings. Again, no meaningful claim to human freedom can envisage the lack of restraint by others; nor the absence of self-restraint, for such is licence.

The word "nature" in this context is particularly confusing. The principles of natural law are said to be implicit in the nature of man as a social being. But what is man's nature? In all men we find two opposing tendencies—that toward peace, order and rationality and that toward aggressive self-assertion and the will to dominate. Corresponding to these two tendencies are divergent social ideals, the *eirenic* and the *agonistic*. The eirenic conceives of the good society as a peaceful, predictable and rational ordering of human relations based on justice for each individual human being. The agonistic ideal rejects the eirenic as cowardly and decadent—the ignoble aim of the pimp and the pedlar—and proclaims instead the glad acceptance of dangerous living in a world of inevitable conflict in which the race is to the swift, the strong, and the cunning.

Plainly each of these divergent tendencies and ideals is part of "nature", if we use that word in a broad sense to mean all that actually exists. However it is exclusively the eirenic tendency in man and the eirenic social ideal, which are considered by supporters of what is the oldest—and still perhaps the most influential—tradition of natural law, to be compatible with man's "nature" in the narrower sense of term.

According to this view—the view of the Aristotelian-Thomistic tradition of natural law—the nature of anything is the perfection or completion of its distinguishing or essential characteristics. And man's nature, characteristically and distinctively, is considered to be a life in peaceful and rational association with his fellows. On this view irrational and anti-social acts are interpreted as morbid deviations from normal human nature, just as the instinct of self-preservation may in some people under certain circumstances be blotted out by an urge to destroy their own lives.

There are, however, many other systems and traditions of natural law thinking. To mention a few of the older ones—those of Grotius, Pufendorf, Hobbes, Spinoza, Locke, Montesquieu, Burlamaqui and Wolf. And several new systems have been expounded in the twentieth century. Some of these many systems, for example that of Hobbes and his followers, make assumptions about human "nature" which are quite different from those made by Aristotle or St. Thomas. Hobbes, as we all know, postulated that man is by nature selfish, aggressive and malicious—each man being a wolf to every other. Nevertheless, he too proceeded in a rational way to devise certain "articles of peace" which he called "natural law" or "laws of nature".

Now, it would be unfair to deny that several of the non-Thomistic theories of natural law, including that of Hobbes, have made valuable contributions to the promotion and maintenance of the ideals of peace and freedom. But be that as it may, the term natural law has plainly come to mean a perplexing variety of things—some, if not all, of which are anathema to large groups of people. For example, Locke's preoccupation with the importance of private property, and the attempts made in the United States, at a certain period of that country's history, to elevate the right of private property to the status of the natural right par excellence, have led many critics to associate natural law with reactionary conservatism among the propertied class, and blind obstruction of social reform. Again, the theological implications of Thomistic natural law, at a certain level, may be unacceptable to those whose theology is different or non-existent.

For these reasons it has been suggested that a new term should be found for the hard-core of meaning common to natural law thinking in general; as distinct from the tenets of any particular system of natural law. But though several terms have been mooted, none has yet found wide acceptance; and so in this chapter we shall adhere to the traditional terminology.

Histories of the growth and influence of the various systems of natural law have often been written, and the details of individual systems have also been expounded at length. But the essential character of natural law thinking—the methodology, so to speak, of the various systems—has been far less frequently discussed. Moreover, it is the methodology of natural law which remains the most frequently misunderstood aspect of the whole subject. Accordingly some attempt at clarification will be made here. Reference will also be made to the standing of natural law thinking in the contemporary world—including its status before the tribunal of science, to use the phrase of one of natural law's most distinguished opponents, Hans Kelsen.

If natural law thinking is to continue to play a seminal role in the just ordering of human relations, it is essential that it be protected against over-enthusiastic friends; and especially against those who regard natural law as a sort of moral ready-reckoner, extravagantly claiming to find in it ready-made solutions for the general run of practical problems which confront man in society at all periods of history. Dr. Chroust has very pertinently observed that "the gravest and most deeply rooted misconception of the true nature of natural law is to be found in the assumption that it has a specific concrete content that is both absolute and self-evident".[1]

When, therefore, Kelsen proceeds to refute "the assumption (of natural law) that it is possible to deduce from the nature of society the just solution of our social problems and an altogether adequate prescription for human behaviour"[2] he sets himself the comparatively trivial task of refuting an inflated claim. In the hands of its most influential exponents, the enduring contributions of natural law have been due to reliance upon very broadly stated principles and standards of conduct in deliberate preference to any attempted elaboration of a detailed and "altogether adequate" code of rules.[3] This was characteristic of the approach of Aquinas;[4] it is still the course of wisdom.

The charge that natural law thinking is a prop of sterile conservatism is also based on a misunderstanding. The vitality of the concept has stemmed precisely from its dynamism; its recognition that man's knowledge of human nature is not static but may change and be refined and improved with growing insight.

The validity of natural law thinking would seem to depend on the firm recognition of a truth, much emphasized by Newman[5] and in more recent times by Paul Tillich, that rules for human conduct have always to be applied to infinitely variable factual situations, so that no amount of rule-making, and no amount of rule-study, can relieve men of the agony of personal decision in specific cases. Indeed, precisely because human conduct is necessarily concerned with concrete factual situations—that is, with the historical and the contingent—one "might almost say that rules for just or wise action are, in a sense, a contradiction in terms since rules are general and abstract whereas action is concrete and existential".[6]

And as it is with human conduct in general, so it is with human judgment in particular. Difficulties in adjudication often stem from the need to accommodate and harmonize conflicting interests, each of which may have elements of legitimacy. Right is seldom all on one side. However, there is no known technique, and certainly no natural law theory, which will provide men with a slot-machine facility for evaluating conflicting interests—a sort of open sesame or ready-reckoner which gives patently correct and quick answers to actual problems. Nor is the explanation far to seek. The process of evaluation or judgment involves an act of human prudence; it demands an act—often several acts—of choice and these are always uniquely personal experiences. It cannot be otherwise; for principles and rules, though they may help in shaping the act of decision, are themselves neither self-interpreting nor self-executing. They always have to be consciously applied by fallible human beings to concrete and gritty factual situations.

The Essentials of Natural Law Thinking

Though in the course of a long and chequered history natural law has assumed many forms, and though many different systems have used the name of natural law, basically natural law thinking has always been concerned with two central questions.

First, what are the relations or connections between law and morality, and more particularly that branch of morality which men call justice? As Rommen puts it, "the proper function of natural law doctrine is precisely to show the connection between law and morality".[7] Questions such as "is it essential to refer to morality, in any of its aspects, in deciding whether a particular rule of law exists" or, again, "is law open to moral criticism" are the very marrow of natural law thinking. To both of these latter questions natural lawyers give an affirmative answer.

Secondly, are there any principles of law and justice rooted in the very nature of being, and more particularly in the nature of man's being as a social animal? Are such principles discoverable by human reason and experience? Do they have universal and permanent validity independent of the majority will of any given society at any given time, and independent too of the aspirations of any particular culture as these have developed in historical fact. And here again, an affirmative answer is invariably given by natural lawyers.[8]

It is this latter characteristic of natural law thinking—a characteristic which repudiates any rigid separation between "the is" and "the ought" and appeals to "nature" in support of its oughts—which constitutes the essential methodology of natural law thinking.[9] And, by the same token, it is this characteristic which provokes the charge that supporters of natural law are fatally addicted to the naturalistic fallacy. For although Kelsen seriously overstates the case which he sets out to demolish, he is correct in his main contentions that "the natural law doctrine undertakes to supply a definitive solution to the eternal problem of justice", and that "the answer is based on the assumption that it is possible to distinguish between human behaviour which is natural and human behaviour which is unnatural".[10]

But although this claim of natural law doctrine tends to provoke the charge of logical fallacy, it can be shown, I believe, that the charge itself is unfounded. It is probable, in other words, that a cautious and modestly affirmative answer can be given by natural law doctrine to what Kelsen calls the eternal problem of justice. The emphasis, however, is very much on caution and modesty; for the operative principles are few and elusive, though they are as priceless as they are rare. Nor, I repeat, should we be disappointed if they turn out to be very broad and abstract guidelines—often, what is more, anguishingly hard to apply, rather than instant and easy solution-yielding formulas.

However, before attempting to demonstrate that the charge of logical fallacy is unfounded, it is necessary to particularise in somewhat greater detail the actual claims made by natural law doctrine.

The Moralities of the Law

If one were asked to identify the single most important reason why contemporary discussion of the relations between law and morality continue to be so inconclusive, and sometimes—let it be admitted—unnourishing, it would not be wide of the mark to suggest that insufficient attention is given to distinguishing between the many different moralities which are of legal relevance. As Professor Fuller has observed, "when law is compared with morality, it seems to be assumed that everyone knows what the second term of the comparison embraces. The legal mind generally exhausts itself in thinking about law, and is content to leave unexamined the things to which law is related and from which it is being distinguished".[11]

It will be recalled that Kant in his day was fond of chiding lawyers for the heavy weather which they have always made in defining "law". Yet moral philosophers have not, on the whole, been much more successful in defining the various moralities (in the *plural,* be it emphasized) which cluster together under the name of "morality".[12]

Without here attempting a morphology of morals, it suffices to remark that the term morality may embrace such widely different concepts as the shared social morality obtaining in a given community at a given time, as well as literally scores of moralities of individual conscience—ranging, for example, from the Kantian imperative to Benthamite utilitarianism; from intuitionism to what is empirically measurable. What is more, within each category one could and often should distinguish, further, between a morality of minimum duty and a morality of aspiration.

The merest sciolist would have no difficulty in citing at least two different species of morality which are relevant in discussing the various relations between law and "morality" namely: (a) justice, and (b) the shared social morality. Thus, the well-known rule—obtaining in most modern legal systems—that in construing an ambiguous statute the court will prefer a construction that achieves justice rather than one that leads to injustice, and the equally well-known rule obtaining in most modern legal systems, that transactions *contra bonos mores* are void, are examples respectively of the influence of each of the two specified moralities on the actual content of legal rules.

But while these two particular kinds of morality are no doubt of special importance in discussing the relations between law and morality, it is quite certain that many other moralities would also require attention and analysis in any really comprehensive analysis. In English law, for example, one would have to be very blind or perverse to be unaware of the influence, at various periods, of Christian ethics and—during the nineteenth century—of the impact of Benthamite utilitarianism.

It would, of course, require a substantial book and possibly several books, rather than a short chapter, to trace the relations between all the relevant moralities and the rules of even one great legal system; and in the hands of any single living man the task would be daunting if not presumptuous.[13] However, one of the moralities that has been relevant in most if not all legal systems—namely the idea of "justice"—is so central to natural law thinking in all its aspects, that we cannot escape the duty of trying to clarify its meaning, difficult as the task may be.

In making the attempt, it is convenient to begin with a question which may be phrased as follows. What, if any, are the requirements which make possible the very idea of law as a system of binding and effective rules for human conduct? Are these requirements properly described as requirements of morality, and more particularly, of justice? This is the question posed and most ably discussed by Professor Fuller in his book *The Morality of Law*.[14]

The "Morality" That Makes Law Possible

Professor Fuller's main purpose is to stress the importance of certain requirements which make law possible, or even conceivable, as a successful purposive activity, and more particularly as an effectively operative system of rules.[15] He calls these requirements "the inner morality of law". They are, he claims, a species of natural law.[16] Thus, he argues that if legal rules are to function successfully or effectively they must, affirmatively, be (1) general; (2) promulgated, that is made known to the persons affected; (3) prospective not retroactive; (4) clear and understandable; (5) free from contradictions; and negatively, they must not (6) require what is impossible; nor (7) be too frequently changed; and, finally, (8) there should be congruence between the law and official action.[17]

Professor Hart, in an astringent review, has criticised Fuller for equating the term "morality" with "the requirements for successful purposive activity". An efficient poisoner, he points out, should avoid poisons which cause his victims to vomit, so that if one were to accept Fuller's terminology, one might find oneself speaking of the "inner morality of poisoning"; but this, says Hart, is not only linguistically bizzarre; it also blurs the distinction between purposive activity and the moral evaluation of such activity.[18] He goes further, however, and contends that Fuller's catalogue of requirements is really jejune, and (what is more damaging) compatible with great iniquity. In short, he concludes, rules of law may satisfy all of Fuller's desiderata and still be morally iniquitous.[19]

Three separate points are here involved. First, the question of linguistic propriety. This should not long detain us. Ordinary linguistic usage, as Professor Paul Freund has observed,[20] may well be a begin-all of meaning but it is hardly a be-all and end-all of either meaning or wisdom. Hart himself is prepared to call Fuller's requirements "a minimum form of justice";[21] and indeed from Roman times many of Fuller's requirements have, in standard practice, been described and analysed as "postulates of justice".[22] Kant no doubt would also have levelled a terminological criticism against Fuller, though a different one; for he insists that rules of skill indicating what action is necessary or adequate to bring about certain results are properly described as mere "technical principles", and not as moral imperatives addressed to the human will.[23] At this point, of course, we are concerned with linguistic preference rather than linguistic usage. It is submitted, however, that terminological issues of both kinds, though important, are by no means conclusive.

The more important question is whether Fuller's requirements are, in fact, *sound* no matter whether one calls them "the inner morality of law" as Fuller chooses, or, as Hart prefers, "the minimum form of justice" or "the principles of legality".[24] And in reply to this question it would be difficult to deny that Fuller's requirements are indeed sound and very far from being trivial.

Consider, for example, the requirement of generality. Through the centuries jurists and philosophers have laid stress upon generality as a postulate for rules of law.[25] Law, it is said, should operate impersonally. Its rules should apply to the community generally, or to whole classes of persons (house-owners, married women, minors, etc.) and should contain no proper names. However, in the absence of a constitutional provision making generality a condition of validity,[26] it is quite clear that generality is not a requirement for the validity of all governmental acts having the force of law. Fuller is well aware of this.[27] Accordingly, when he emphasises the postulate of generality he does not have in mind a requirement under which the validity of rules is to be tested by reference to their actual content. He envisages a wholly different idea which was elucidated in the last century by Sir Henry Maine.

Maine perceived that the requirement of generality is a practical or logical postulate, in the sense that it is difficult to conceive how it would be possible in a large community (where personal contact between the governors and the governed is out of the question) for a legislature *to make its will known at all,* except by addressing itself to large classes of persons and by dealing with large classes of acts.[28] Practically speaking, it is impossible for the law-giver to make separate rules for each and every individual and for each and every conceivable act on the part of each person. Generality, in other words, is part of the inner logic of the very idea of successfully operative rules in a large society.[29]

However, quite apart from the logical or practical consideration stressed by Fuller and Maine, it is also *desirable* that laws be general and applicable to all persons within a given class, because this affords a substantial measure of protection against official partiality and oppression.[30] Indeed, for this reason alone, Fuller would contend that he is justified in referring to generality as a "moral" requirement. An argument along similar lines could be developed—and indeed has been developed by Fuller—in regard to each of the other enumerated aspects of what he calls the law's inner morality. We may, therefore, conclude that Fuller's emphasis upon the requirements that make law possible is certainly not trivial.

But there remains a third point. What about Hart's contention that rules of law may comply with all of Fuller's requirements and still be morally iniquitous in content? That this can happen is only too painfully obvious in the modern world. For example, "All American citizens of Japanese origin, or all Jews, or all negroes, shall be required to . . . etc. etc." (the reader may readily fill in a variety of immoral commands from his knowledge of recent history). And when this sort of thing does happen what are we to say about the rules in question? Let us assume—as is likely to be the case—that in the particular country with which we are dealing there is no specific constitutional requirement that laws be just or moral in content. Are we to say, with Hart, that despite their immoral or unjust content these rules are nevertheless valid law which the courts will enforce?

Hart would answer that it is not necessary, and indeed undesirable, to refer to morality in any ordinary sense of that term in determining whether a valid rule of law exists. Provided that the constitutional requirements for making law in any given country have been observed, he contends that the resulting law should be certified as valid no matter how "unjust" it may be; no matter how contrary it may be to the shared social morality; and no matter how much it may offend against the morality of the individual's personal conscience. If, for example, the Queen in Parliament were to take a leaf out of Herod's book and enact a law that all blue-eyed babies in England be butchered, it would not be for the British Courts to question the *legal* status of such a law, however immoral they may consider it to be. Indeed, the clear separation between law and morality in such a case enables all concerned, says Hart, to distinguish distinguishable issues more clearly and to deal with them more honestly.[31] After all, if a judge is really sincere in his conviction that a law is too immoral for him to enforce, there is nothing to prevent him from saying so and then resign rather than enforce the law.

Now, if we confine our attention solely to the actual conduct of courts in most countries of the contemporary world, it must be conceded that Hart's case is very strong. It cannot be denied, for example, that in recent years courts have brushed aside arguments that laws are void because of alleged injustice, and that they have brushed aside such arguments on the score of total irrelevance.[32] Indeed the proposition that most English courts would in modern times act as Hart suggests seems so indisputable as to preclude further comment. It may be conceded, too, that Hart makes a powerful case when he argues that rather than indulge in a blunt-edged denial that an unjust law can be a law, it is more conducive to moral discrimination and responsibility to separate the issues of legality from the many moral questions that may be involved.[33]

But when all this has been conceded, it is submitted that to focus attention—as some contend one should—exclusively upon what modern courts are likely to say about allegedly unjust laws, though in itself a most important exercise, especially for those immediately concerned, is both historically short-sighted and jurisprudentially incomplete. It is historically short-sighted because there have been periods in history when courts have, in fact, declared laws to be void simply because of conflict with the requirements of justice. And possibly a time may come when courts will do so again. It is jurisprudentially incomplete because it takes insufficient account of the fact—vouched for by all experience—that legal systems are likely to be very unstable and prone to disintegrate if their rules are basically unjust. Let us examine this latter point a little more closely.

In a famous essay in which he addressed himself to the fundamental jurisprudential question why do men *in fact* obey rules of law, Lord Bryce suggested that there are five reasons: indolence, deference, sympathy, fear and reason.[34] Though he was inclined to give a somewhat lowly place to reason, he nevertheless conceded that in the ultimate analysis political society imperatively needs a moral justification, and he went on to emphasize that force and fear are in point of fact the most unstable foundations on which either the state or the law can rest.

If it be the case, as I believe, that political society needs a moral justification; if it be true that in the last analysis men will not obey, or will not long obey, laws unless they feel it morally right to do so;[35] if, more particularly, unjust laws are likely to be unstable, as making no claim, in actual fact, to men's allegiance, then it becomes necessary for the law-giver to take account not only of Fuller's "inner morality", but of the more fundamental requirements (to be discussed presently) that rules of law be formally and materially just, and that the procedures for adjudication be just as well. And it is necessary for the law-giver to take account of these requirements, because if he ignores or flouts them, his authority, will, for that very reason, disintegrate. As Seneca long ago observed in a passage quoted by Spinoza: "No one can long retain a tyrant's sway."[36]

All history bears witness to the facts upon which Seneca's proposition is based—the history of Hitler's Germany being a recent case in point. In other words, one may say that rules of law *ought* to be just if they are, *in fact,* to have men's allegiance and survive, the "ought" here being rooted in the very nature of stable social organisation. The plain facts of the world's experience demonstrates that if rules of law are not just they will *in fact* be unstable. Call this particular "ought", if you will, a mere "if/then" proposition, for that is precisely what it is; nevertheless, it would seem to be difficult to deny its validity or its importance.

One is not here naïvely asserting that because something happens in fact, therefore it ought to happen. One is not, in other words, committing the particular "naturalistic fallacy" which Kelsen charges against natural law doctrine when he says: "The fact that in reality big fish swallow small fish does not imply that the behaviour of the fish is good, nor yet that it is bad."[37] What one is here insisting upon is that ought propositions cannot be rigidly separated from reality if they are to make meaningful sense.[38] This, indeed, is an argument which I tried to develop—however obscurely or maladroitly—in my book "*The Foundations of Freedom*".[39] It was not my meaning that courts of law in South Africa, or for that matter in Great Britain, will refuse to recognise and enforce unjust laws as being legally void.[40] It was my meaning, and it remains my conviction, that injustice is not long compatible with social, and therefore legal, stability. And, let there be no misunderstanding, this holds whether we are dealing with the community of nations or with individual states.

Thus far we have given a good deal of attention to the problem of the legal validity of unjust laws; and it is tempting to discourse at even greater length on the various ways in which the idea of justice has influenced the content of legal rules at literally scores of points, especially in the field of international law; or to show how and why justice is particularly relevant as a criterion for the evaluation or criticism of law. It is time, however, for us to come somewhat more closely to grips with the central question—What is justice?

Formal and Substantive Justice

We are quick in the affairs of daily life to praise or blame on the score of alleged justice or injustice. But apart from the technical requirements for the efficacy of rules of law (as elaborated, for example, by Fuller) what are the characteristics of this concept which men use so freely and often so glibly? Is it possible to say anything more satisfactory about justice than Kelsen's conclusion that justice is merely a high-sounding word which serves to cloak the purely subjective predilections or value preferences of a particular person or of groups of persons.[41] Though it would be an exceptionally brash and shallow man who dared to give a short and confident answer to this age-old and most humbling question, some of the contours of a more acceptable answer may be tentatively suggested.

First, it is essential, as Perelman has so clearly demonstrated, to distinguish between justice as a formal concept, and the actual substantive nature or content of just rules, or of a just act, in specific concrete situations.[42] It would be vain to attempt to lay down in advance what the substantively just solutions are for all the specific concrete problems that may arise in human relations; but the provision of broad and, for the most part, rather formal guide-lines is not only possible but also helpful. Consider, for example, two of the best known postulates of justice; namely (i) justice consists in treating equal cases equally; (ii) justice presupposes rationality or reasonableness. Both are very formal propositions, but a little discussion will show that they are valuable, despite the fact that they are not simple solution-yielding formulas, and notwithstanding the further fact that each presents difficulties.

(i) *Equality*

Ever since the appearance of Aristotle's treatises on ethics men have insisted that the idea of justice is closely connected with equality.[43] The realisation of justice, it is said, demands that situations in which the relevant circumstances are the same should be treated in the same way. This requirement of equality is admittedly not free from difficulties which stem precisely from its formal nature; its lack of substantive content.[44] For example, it would not be just to *mistreat* people equally, as would be the case if death sentences were invariably and uniformly imposed for trivial offences. Again, the requirement of equality does not necessarily mean identity or uniformity of treatment; for that would involve treating cases equally when they are in fact unequal.

But if equality does not always mean uniformity, then by reference to what substantive standards are we to weigh the equality of men and their conduct? By what criteria do we justify those differences in treatment which are in truth compatible with—indeed, required by—equality? Many standards are, of course, theoretically conceivable, for example: to each according to his merit; to each according to his worth; to each according to his aptitudes; to each according to his needs; to each according to his physical beauty, and so on. No doubt, too, the choice of specific standards will vary according to the actual needs of communities from time to time. Moreover, even when a measure of content has been put into the formal precept that we are to treat equal cases equally—for example, if the rule is to read "to each according to his needs"—one is still left with the problem of assessing individual needs.

In the face of all these qualifications what, it is often asked, is left of the abstract requirement of equality? Are we not adrift on an ocean of relativities and subjective preferences? To which the short but, perhaps, sufficient answer is that the requirement of equality helps to exclude arbitrariness and caprice. And it does so, because though equal treatment does not necessarily mean identical treatment, the rule does require that differences be rationally justified by reference to openly declared standards. In short, reasons must be given for treating men differently.

What, however, do we mean by giving reasons? This brings us to the further requirement of rationality as a postulate of justice.

(ii) *Rationality*

At one extreme, rationality is set off against non-rational modes or procedures, such as having no reasons for one's conduct. At the other extreme, it is set off against irrational modes, in which reasons are proffered but they are bad reasons.[45] When, however, are reasons bad? At this point the two key notions are said to be (a) the logical relevance of the means used in order to achieve a specific end, and (b) the idea of proportion. To attempt to swim the English Channel by emigrating permanently to the moon would, for example, be irrational, because the means chosen have no relevance to the achievement of the end. Again, to burn one's house, as a standard practice, in order to roast pork would also be irrational, because although the means used are no doubt relevant for achieving the particular objective (if sufficient care is used!) they are wholly disproportionate means.

It will, however, be objected that we are still in the realms of abstraction and formality—no nearer to the provision of substantive criteria of justice. This is perfectly true. Formal requirements of the kind we have been discussing (the relevance of means to ends, and due proportion) give no concrete and specific guidance as to what objectives should be chosen; nor do they help in determining the relative or proportionate value which should be attached to various objectives. The answer very often is just *not* provided by an appeal to the formal principles of rationality.

All this may be conceded; but it would nevertheless be a grave mistake to discount the value of rationality. To insist upon logical relevance and due proportion is to insist upon ideas that are admittedly formal and abstract but by no means trivial. On the contrary, they too, like the formal idea of equality, are an indispensable safeguard against arbitrariness and caprice. There is, for example, a whole world of difference between requiring a ruler to justify his conduct by adducing reasons (whose adequacy may then be judged) and totally exempting him from the requirements of rationality.[46] This cannot be emphasized too strongly.

As we are expressly seeking for criteria of justice which are rooted in the very nature of man as a social being, and which, by definition, do not depend upon convention or *social mores,* we are not—for the purposes of the present discussion—concerned with one extremely useful way in which in practice specific content is given to the idea of rationality or reasonableness. In practice most legal systems employ the concept of "the reasonable man" in a flexible and elastic way so as to bring to bear upon the ordering of human conduct the standards of the conventional or shared social morality actually prevailing at a given time in a given community, whether it be local, national, or international. The practical importance of this technique can hardly be over-estimated; but, to repeat, it does not solve our immediate problem; for we are endeavouring to define natural justice, as distinct from identifying the standards of any particular shared or conventional social morality.

Quite understandably, however, men have wished to infuse greater specificity into the concept of justice; and they have done so by supplementing the two formal aspects which we have discussed above with two other ideas; namely, (a) the idea that justice consists in the fulfilment or satisfaction of reasonable expectations—which, following Bentham, we might call the "expectation-fulfilling principle"; and (b) the idea contained in Ulpian's famous definition that "justice is the constant will (settled disposition) to give to each his due"—conveniently called the *"suum cuique principle"*.

(iii) *The Expectation-Fulfilling Principle*

In a recent essay, Professor Freund has suggested that the most vital concept of justice—the concept which gives it most content in "an operational sense"—is that which regards justice as the fulfilment of reasonable or legitimate expectations.[47] Though the idea is operative in all branches of the law, Freund suggests that the paradigm example is a contract. He argues that a person who has placed his faith (trust or reliance) on another's promise may reasonably expect that the promise will be implemented; and that this is the underlying moral reason why promises should be performed. To illustrate his contention, he cites the problem which may arise where A advertises a reward for information leading to the return of his stolen ring. If B, in ignorance of the advertisement, tracks down the thief, reports the matter to the police, and ensures the return of the ring, may A justly refuse to pay B the reward? To which Freund replies: "Many courts would say so, and it is hard to disagree. That element is lacking which makes a promise binding: another's legitimate expectation that the promise will be performed, an expectation usually evidenced by reliance on the promise".[48]

Freund readily admits that the actual content of people's reasonable expectations depends on, and varies with, the circumstances of time and place. He is well aware, too, that specific legal systems at various periods of their development, may prescribe additional requirements for the enforceability of promises—requirements which vary according to the felt necessities of the time. But the basic requirement that reasonable expectations be fulfilled remains constant. What is more, the quite specific injunction to keep faith where one has given one's word, to be trustworthy where one has been trusted, is also a constant.

It is submitted that there is a great deal of sense in Professor Freund's approach. This is not the place for a lengthy digression into Roman legal antiquities; but it is perhaps pertinent to recall the Roman cult of *Fides*. Good faith—that is to say, keeping faith when one had plighted one's troth—was in fact the special name for justice in all cases where others had been led to place reliance on performance; or, as it was sometimes expressed, where others had credited the promissor with making performance.[49] Savigny, in commenting on the famous trilogy of injunctions in Justinian's Institutes—to live honourably, not to injure another, and to give to each his due—rightly stressed the centrality of the first in-*junction—honeste vivere,* namely, to live honourably, or to show good faith. It was broad and embracing enough, he felt, to include the other two.[50] Good faith *(Treu and Glauben)* is, again, by far the most dynamic principle in one of the most influential of all modern legal codes—the German Civil Code.[51]

It has been suggested that in some at least of its applications, the idea of fulfilling reasonable expectations has a basis in the psychological law of association. Thus, the experience of a thing having been done by others will, on a renewal of the same circumstances, give rise to an expectation of its being done again.[52] Maybe this is, in part, the explanation of the doctrine of judicial precedent; namely, that previous decisions in similar cases should normally be followed.[53] However, it is plain that the "expectation-fulfilling principle" has much wider implications, and is much more deeply rooted.

Sir Ernest Barker cleaved nearer to the heart of the matter when he described "expectability" as being "the foundation of foundations". "Where you have the rule of law," he said, "the individual knows where he is; he knows where he is today and where he will be tomorrow; he lives a life, if a word may be used which is not in the Oxford English Dictionary, of expectability."[54] Unless this is ensured, organised social life would be quite impossible. Indeed, the very idea of stable human relations presupposes trust and trustworthiness. Certainly no mature economic system could be maintained without "credit". Admittedly, "the expectation-fulfilling principle" does not enable one to deduce from it a complete code of rules. It may not provide a ready solution of the general run of specific concrete problems. But it is nevertheless a vitally suggestive point of departure for fair dealing, a principle or guide-line for just action.

(iv) *The suum cuique principle*

Before attempting to analyse the even more famous injunction, "to each his due", it is desirable to dwell for a moment on the earlier part of Ulpian's definition. Justice, he there emphasizes, is a settled will, or *disposition* or habit on the part of individual men. In other words, on this view justice is an attribute of a just man.[55] It may well be that inasmuch as law is concerned primarily with external conduct, and not normally with states of mind which do not manifest themselves in conduct, the just act is legally a more relevant concept than the just man. Nevertheless, it would be wholly unsound to underestimate the importance which should be attached to individual character or disposition in all serious attempts to realize the eirenic ideal.

Justice does not simply happen; it does not materialize out of the air in the shape of concrete acts. Nor is it exclusively, or even primarily, the concern of large collectivities, like governments and international organizations. Its source and life-spring is in the character and hard endeavour of individual men and women. This we dare not forget; for even in international relations the unofficial conduct and example of individual men of good will (including the humble and the obscure) may well count, in the aggregate, for more than the official policy or conduct of the governments of their countries. Few individuals can shape history but each can influence a small part of affairs. It has been well said that each time any person strikes at injustice he sends forth a ripple of hope, and radiating from a million centres of courage these may combine to form a current.

Turning, now, to the second part of Ulpian's definition, namely the injunction "to each his due", the first point to note is that this cannot mean always "to each what is legally his due"; for the laws themselves may be unjust. Again, as Socrates observed in a famous passage in Plato's *Republic,* it would not be acting justly to return to a homicidal lunatic a lethal weapon legally due to him. Nor should the formula be held to mean that it is for the current social mores to define the measure of what is due, for the social mores, too, may be unjust. How, then, are we to give content and meaning to the formula?

One extremely important way of giving specificity, and also—it is submitted—unqualified validity, to the *suum cuique* formula is to add, at the end, the words "as human beings". Justice then becomes respect for the human being as such, or as it is more often said, respect for "human dignity" or "human rights". This approach to the problem of justice has decisively influenced the formulation of "natural human rights"; and is undoubtedly one of the most influential branches of natural law thinking.

The transition or development from natural law to natural rights—from objective rules to the subjective interests protected by such rules—is one of the hard and dark places in the history of jurisprudence. It would take us too far afield to try, here, to elucidate even the main steps in the historical process.[56] It must, therefore, suffice to observe that by the end of the eighteenth century the transition had taken place; and that it had become the practice for jurists to try to spell out whole systems of substantive rights, alleged to belong, or be due, to man by virtue of his very nature.

Some of these attempts may be said to be in the best tradition of natural law thinking, others are calculated to bring it into disrepute.[57] In this regard, if one may venture a generalization it is that the shorter one's list of natural rights, the sounder it is likely to be. Certain it is that the task of suggesting what rights belong to men by virtue of the human quality in them is an extremely hazardous one.[58]

Perhaps the most fundamental thing that one may say about natural human rights is that every person, by virtue of his very existence as a human being, asserts a claim and imposes a corresponding duty on all other persons to recognize that he too is a human being and not a mere thing. And one treats people as human beings precisely by acknowledging their freedom to exercise reason and a comparatively controllable will both in discovering their nature and destiny and in acting in accordance with their convictions.

This, of course, is merely another way of phrasing a famous Kantian proposition. Can its validity be verified rationally? It is submitted that the answer is yes; for if you treat other human beings as mere things—essentially unlike yourself—you are faced, as Kant perceived, with inner contradiction. More specifically, you are opting out of the human kind and out of normal human relations—and acting as if you were either a god or something less than man. You are, as Sir Isaiah Berlin has graphically put it in a recent and most important essay, mad or deranged.[59] The point is that sane people are disposed to recognize that human beings differ, if only in degree, from stones, and even from horses or chimpanzees. The difference between a grain of sand and the Rock of Gibraltar is after all also one of degree. But it is striking and important. Similarly the difference between men and chimpanzees is striking and important; nor does one have to repudiate Darwin to recognize this.

Why, it may be asked, all this emphasis on the difference between human beings and the rest of creation? The reason is that experience shows that man does not simply accept his position in space and time like a stone or a chimpanzee. Unlike things and the rest of the animal creation, man may form and hold many different views about his own nature and destiny; and it is an awesome truth that these views decisively influence what he is and the way in which he acts. In Newman's words, it is man's peculiar gift to be emphatically self-made. Now this capacity of a human being to determine what he is and to shape his life in accordance with his convictions, is what is meant by human freedom. It is an essentially human trait differing starkly from undisciplined licence; and the most basic and characteristic natural human right is to have this freedom respected.

No doubt not one of the human rights which it may be possible to enumerate—not even the right not to be deprived of life without adequate reasons—is absolute. Each, for example, has to be balanced against, and reconciled with, the exigencies of government. On what principles, then, should this "balancing" proceed?

No facile solution-yielding formula can be given to this crucial question; though, here again, a number of guide-lines of a purely formal nature have proved to be helpful. Such, for example, is the principle which aims at maximizing each individual's freedom where the only competing interests are seen to be individual interests.[60] Or again, where the State seeks to qualify such rights by interposing its authority on behalf of the general public, there is the principle that the State should affirmatively show that some duly specified overriding interest of the public actually requires such interference; and, furthermore, that the means used are necessary for the accomplishment of the purpose and not disproportionately oppressive upon individuals. This, in a nutshell, is the basic idea of "due process" as evolved in the course of time by American and other courts.[61]

That all that has been said above is extremely general, admitting of great flexibility in application, and admitting, too, of the intrusion of a wide range of value judgements, can hardly be denied. Are we then to conclude that these broad generalizations of natural law are worthless? It is submitted that the answer is emphatically no; for, however general and abstract the guide-lines may perforce have to be, they do have, *at least,* two great merits. In the first place there is the merit to which I have referred more than once in this chapter. They help to ensure rationality in the ordering of human relations by outlawing arbitrariness and caprice. In addition it is submitted that they have another merit, a supreme merit of a less formal and more substantial nature, which I would like to touch upon at the end of this chapter. But first a few words about procedural justice.

Procedural Justice or Natural Justice in Adjudication

The idea of procedural justice is possibly the greatest single contribution to the overall concept of justice which Anglo-American lawyers have made. A distinguished American judge, Mr. Justice Jackson, once expressed this fact dramatically, if somewhat offensively to Russia, when he said: "If put to the choice, one might well prefer to live under Soviet substantive law applied in good faith by our common law procedures, rather than under our substantive law enforced by Soviet procedural practices."[62]

Briefly—almost inexcusably briefly when one realizes what is at stake—we may state the requirements of procedural justice under five headings. They are by no means all of equal importance. Indeed, possibly only the last is an irreducible minimum of procedural justice. But all, in the present state of man's knowledge and experience, are normally regarded as important postulates of justice in modern societies. They are:

(i) Litigants should have ready access to independent and properly qualified tribunals for adjudication.[63]

(ii) Adjudication should be expeditious; for justice delayed is justice denied.

(iii) An accused person and each of the parties to a civil suit should have an opportunity to state his case. The operative maxim is *audi alteram partem*—hear both sides, and judge no one unheard.[64]

(iv) No one should be judge in his own cause or in cases where his own interests are at stake. *Nemo sibi esse judex vel suis jus dicere debet* is the operative maxim.[65]

(v) Last, but perhaps first in importance, is the requirement of principled adjudication. As Mr. Justice Holmes warned long ago, you can give almost any conclusion a logical form, while behind the conclusion there may lurk, or even be consciously hidden an inarticulate major premise, a judgment of the relative worth and importance of competing analogies and values.[66] If, however, justice is to be done, and be manifestly seen to be done, the process of adjudication must be *honest;* that is, frankly articulated and, as far as possible, free from self-deception. Only in this way may human decisions, and indeed the entire legal process, be subjected to the cleansing and invigorating winds of rational criticism. To give no reasons for judgment, or to conceal or dissemble one's real reasons, is treason to the idea of Justice.

Conclusion

A very distinguished contemporary lawyer, Professor Max Rheinstein, has expressed the view that although reason can help us in determining the relevance and adequacy of the means by which we seek to achieve our ends, it cannot aid us in the choice of the ends themselves.[67] More specifically, given the choice between the eirenic and the agonistic social ideals (objectives), he contends that there is no process of reasoning by which the one may be shown or established or proved to be more worthy of acceptance than the other. If we are materialistically inclined, he argues, we may say that the choice depends upon such factors as ancestry, environment, internal secretions and metabolism. If we are religious we may find our choice determined by faith which, in Christian belief, has its basis in Grace.

One should be slow indeed to question this conclusion, supported as it is by many of the acutest minds from Hume onwards. But is it really beyond question that reason cannot assist in the choice between the eirenic and the agonistic ideals? Much, one supposes, might depend on what one means by reason. Rheinstein himself, defines it as "dispassionate reflection about experience."[68] Admittedly there are philosophers who maintain that empirical verification by means of the traditional five senses, coupled with logical self-evidence (for example, the proposition that two and two are four is implicit in the definition of each term) are the only methods of valid proof—the only rational procedures for verification. But as we learn more about man and his insights this concept of rationality seems increasingly limited.

In addition to a calculus of empirical verification, in addition to a rhetoric of logical persuasion, might there not be room for a more subtle grammar of assent? Are empirical evidence and logical tautology, in fact, the only "rational" (or should we say, sound) procedures for verification? Does the talent for "reasoning", what

Newman called "the illative sense", work more subtly?

But perhaps we do not have to stay too long for the answer to these deep questions: for stripped of non-essentials what, after all, are the ultimate claims of natural law thinking in support of the eirenic ideal? They are (i) that there is a significant difference between human beings and all other objects of creation; and (ii) that the major significance of the difference lies in this, that its recognition carries with it the simultaneous recognition of a duty on the part of men not to treat other men as things or chimpanzees. In other words, there is the controversial mental leap from the is to the ought.

Now, the first of these propositions would seem to be verifiable even at the empirical level. Moreover, it does not involve anthropocentric arrogance but rather the humility which accepts the fact that men find themselves in, and seek to understand, a universe which they did not entirely create. Nor does it involve any insensitiveness to the wonders of social organisation in, for example, the insect world. Nor is it incompatible with reverence for all life. It involves only recognition of the observable fact that the many views which man may form of his own nature and destiny decisively influence what he is. And the second proposition, it is submitted, should not lightly be put aside by calling it an example of the naturalistic "fallacy", because, as I have tried to argue in this chapter, its denial involves self-contradiction. The essential propositions, in short, would appear to be within the range of reason as men ordinarily understand it.

But what if they are, in truth, beyond the range of reason? This would not absolve us of responsibility for choice. The eirenic and the agonistic ways of life would still be there for our choosing. And the consequence of the choice would still be momentous. Nor would there be anything wrong or foolish in resting one's preference on some simple confession, beyond conventional reason, such as Luther's "because I can do no other". As Pascal observed, "there are two extravagances: to exclude reason, to admit only reason". It is perhaps the supreme merit of natural law thinking that it recognizes the centrality of these great issues.

1 "On the Nature of Natural Law" in *Interpretations of Modern Legal Philosophies*, ed. Sayre, New York, 1947, p.83.

2 "The Natural Law Doctrine before the Tribunal of Science" in *Natural Law and World Law*, Yukikaku, 1954, at p.63.

3 In speaking of principles, standards and rules, I have in mind Roscoe Pound's useful distinctions. *Rules*, in the strict sense, are precepts attaching detailed legal consequences to definite and detailed facts (if a freemen strikes a freemen he shall pay 10 shekels of silver); *principles* are authoritative starting points of legal reasoning (if

one person negligently causes injury to another he shall make reparation unless he can justify his conduct); *standards* are measures of conduct (we must observe the care of a reasonable man not to subject others to the risk of injury). See Pound, *Justice According to Law,* Yale, 1951, pp. 56-8.

4 A point stressed by Bodenheimer, *Jurisprudence,* Harvard, 1962, p.134.

5 See, especially, Newman's *Grammar of Assent,* ed. Etienne Gilson, Image Books, 1955, pp.277-278.

6 M. Versfeld. "On Justice and Human Rights", in *Acta Juridica,* Cape Town, 1960, p.6.

7 *Natural Law,* p.267.

8 For a lucid non-technical exposition of this central aspect, see A. H. Chroust, "On the Nature of Natural Law" in *Interpretations of Modern Legal Philosophies,* 1947, p.70. Also, Jacques Maritain, "The Philosophical Foundations of Natural Law", in *Natural Law and World Law,* pp. 133 sq; and, especially, John Wild, *Plato's Modern Enemies and the Theory of Natural Law,* 1953.

9 Fuller, *The Law in Quest of itself,* p.5.

10 "The Natural Law Doctrine before the Tribunal of Science" in *Natural Law and World Law,* at p.63.

11 *The Morality of Law,* Yale, 1964, p.4.

12 On the difficulties of the task, see C. H. Whitley, "On Defining 'moral'," *Analysis,* vol. 20, 141 sqc (1960); D. A. Lloyd-Thomas, "Some Remarks on the Use of the Word 'Moral'," *Journal of Philosophy,* vol. 62, pp.281-93 (1962); P. R. Foot and J. Harrison, "When is a Principle a Moral Principle", *Proceedings of the Aristotelian Society,* supp. vol. 28, pp.95-134 (1954); W. H. Frankena, "Recent Conceptions of Morality" in *"Morality and The Language of Conduct",* ed. Castaneda and Nakhikian, 1963, pp.1-24; A. MacIntyre, "What Morality is Not", *Philosophy* vol. 32, pp.325 sqc; W. K. Frankena, "MacIntyre on Defining Morality", *Philosophy,* vol. 33, pp.158 scq.

13 Biondo Biondi's three volumes, entitled *Diritto Romano Cristiano,* give some indication of the magnitude of the problems involved in tracing the influence of Christian ideas in one legal system; namely Roman Law.

14 Yale, 1964.

15 The idea of law as a "purposive activity" was central to the thinking of the great German jurist, Rudolf von Ihering; it has been enormously influential.

16 *op. cit* at p.96.

17 *op. cit* chapter 2.

18 *Harvard Law Review* vol. 78, pp.1281-88.

19 See, particularly, *The Concept of Law,* p.202.

20 *Social Justice* ed. R. B. Brandt, 1962, p.93.

21 The Concept of Law, p.202.

22 For a recent account, see Hahlo and Kahn, *The South African Legal System,* 1968, pp.31 sqq.

23 *Critique of Practical Reason,* Beck's translation, Liberal Arts Press, p.25, note 1.

24 *The Concept of Law* p.202.

25 For early examples, see Ulpian in *Digest,* 1.3.8; Capito in Aulus Gellius' *Attic Nights,* 10.20.2; and Aristotle, *Nicomachean Ethics,* 5.10.4.

26 For examples of such provisions, see Fuller, *The Morality of Law,* p.47, note 4.

27 *op. cit.* p.49.

28 *The Early History of Institutions,* 4th ed., 1885, p.393.

29 Fuller, *op. cit.* p.48.

30 Patterson, *Jurisprudence,* 1953, p.102.

31 *The Concept of Law,* pp.203-7.

32 Injustice as a criterion of invalidity has been rejected more than once in recent years by South African courts in regard to apartheid legislation, the issue of justice or injustice simply not being considered *relevant* where a sovereign legislature has clearly expressed its will. Courts in many other parts of the world have acted in a similar way in regard to other laws impugned on the score of immortality.

33 For Radbruch's contrary contention that in an extreme case an unjust law should not be enforced as law, see the references in Bodenheimer, *op. cit.,* p.134, note 36.

34 *Studies in History and Jurisprudence,* vol. 2, p.1.

35 Pascal, *Pensees,* 326, makes some penetrating observations on this truth.

[36] *Tractatus Theologico-Politicus,* chapter XVI.

[37] "The Natural Law Doctrine before the Tribunal of Justice" in *Natural Law and World Law,* p.66.

[38] This is what I understand to be the hard core of common sense in Fuller's remarks on the difficulty of rigidly separating the ought and the is—as opposed to distinguishing between them. See *The Law in Quest of Itself,* p.77 seq. For criticism of Fuller, see Morris Cohen, *Reason and Law,* Collier Books, 1961, chapter 8; also F. Nagel, *"On the Fusion of Fact and Value",* vol. 3, *Natural Law Forum,* (1958) 77.

[39] Oxford Press, 1961.

[40] However, I must have been very maladroit; for my book is sometimes quoted, even by professionally qualified critics, as a paradigm case illustrating the heretical view that laws of the apartheid variety are legally void. See Dennis Lloyd, *The Idea of Law,* p.334, note 3. Ironically enough, I am also alleged by Lloyd to place excessive faith in the efficacy of paper barriers against injustice, which may be contained in constitutional guarantees, although my whole professional experience—and indeed everything I have written on the subject—is directly and painfully to the contrary. What is more, I would certainly *not* contend that all the apartheid laws are unjust; some of them benefit the blacks as well as the whites. Indeed the whole pattern of race relations in South Africa is currently very complex. fluid and constantly evolving. See *The Foundations of Freedom,* pp. 80-81. 114.

[41] "The Pure Theory of Law", vol. 50, *Quarterly Review* (1934) at p.482.

[42] *The idea of Justice and the Problem of Argument,* Petrie's translation, London, 1963, pp.15 sqq.

[43] *Politics,* Book III 1282b, p.129, Barker's translation, Oxford, 1946; *Nichomachean Ethics,* Book V, iii, Everyman's ed., pp.107, sqq.

[44] For a concise discussion of the main difficulties see W. K. Frankena, "The Concept of Social Justice" in *Social Justice,* ed. Brandt, Prentice-Hall, 1962, pp.1, sqq.

[45] Recent instructive analyses of the idea of rationality are to be found in *Nomos,* vol. VII, "Rationality in Decision", ed. Carl Friedrich, New York, 1964.

[46] A. E. Taylor in his introduction to Plato's *Laws,* pp. xvii-xviii, discussed the great value of giving reasons for legislation in preambles—a practice, unhappily, falling into desusetude.

[47] P. A. Freund, "Social Justice and the Law" in *Social Justice,* ed. Brandt, pp.93 sqq.

[48] op. cit. at p.95. For a discussion in depth of the foundations of contractual liability, see M. R. Cohen, "The Basis of Contract", vol. 46 *Harvard Law Review,* 533 (1933).

[49] Pollock and Maitland make this very plain in their *History of English Law,* 1911, vol. 2, p.188, note 4, where they refer to some of the sources, including *Dig.* 12.1.1.

[50] *System des heutigen romischen Rechts* (1840) vol. 1, para. 59. Savigny's own words are that *honeste vivere* "bears in itself the germ of the other two precepts".

[51] Art. 242 of the BGB. For discussion, see Weber in vol. 2, Staudinger's *Kommentar,* 11th ed., pp.1-1388. For comparable provisions in the United States, see E. A. Farnsworth, "Good Faith Performance and Commercial Reasonableness", vol. 30, *University of Chicago Law Review,* 1963, pp.666 sqq; E. W. Patterson, Report of the *New York Law Revision Commission on the U.C.C.,* 1955, vol. 1, pp.310 sqq.

[52] Pollock, *Essays in Jurisprudence and Ethics,* p.54.

[53] *loc. cit.*

[54] *The Western Tradition,* 1949, p.30.

[55] Allen, *Aspects of Justice,* p.5, stresses this aspect of Ulpian's definition. Compare Hobbes' statement that a just man "does not lose that title by one or a few unjust acts"; *Leviathan* (in *Works,* Molesworth's ed., vol. 3, p.136).

[56] On this, see, Michel Villey, *Lecons d'Histoire de la Philosophie du Droit,* Paris, 1957.

[57] See my *Foundations of Freedom,* pp.218-220, for discussion.

[58] See H. L. A. Hart, "Are there any Natural Rights", vol. 44, *Philosophical Review,* (1955).

[59] "The Rationality of Value Judgments" in *Nomos VII, Rational Decision,* pp.221 sqq.

[60] This, too, is a Kantian principle whose validity is not yet spent, despite the obvious importance of qualifying it by reference to conflicting *social* interests. Cf. Pound, *Interpretations of Legal History,* pp.28 sqq.

[61] See *Lawton v. Steele,* (1893) 152 U.S.; *NAACP v. Alabama* (1963) 377 U.S. 308-8.

[62] Mr. Justice Jackson in *Shaughnessy v. Mezei* 345 U.S. at 244. cf. Mr. Justice Frankfurter in *McNabb v. United States* 318 U.S. 332 and Dr. A. L. Goodhart in 1964 *Cambridge Law Journal,* 51.

[63] This is, perhaps, the most debatable of all the requirements. The extent to which poverty precludes ready access to the courts, the question of appropriate judicial qualifications and the various methods of ensuring judicial independence, are all obviously important but very controversial issues.

[64] An early formulation of the principle is to be found in Seneca's *Medea,* 195.

[65] See Code 3.5.1. As Coke put it, "it hath been said, *iniquum est aliquem suae rei esse judicem", Dr. Bonham's Case,* 4 Coke's Reports, Thomas and Fraser's ed., 1826, p.375.

[66] "The Path of the Law", *Collected Legal Papers,* 167 sqq.

[67] "Standards of Justice" in *Natural Law and World Law,* p.213.

[68] *op. cit.* at pp.211, 213.

AN ECOLOGICAL NATURAL THEOLOGY
SIR ALISTER HARDY, F.R.S.

Emeritus Professor of Zoology and Hon. Fellow of Merton College and Exeter College, Oxford: Gifford Lecturer in the University of Aberdeen 1963-65; now Director of the Religious Experience Research Unit, Manchester College, Oxford.

It is urgent for our civilization that we should satisfy the unappeased and frustrated desires for spiritual experience, with a philosophy that can be seen to be in harmony with the modern scientific outlook.

Quite apart from all those who, in this scientific age, have dismissed religion altogether from their minds as wishful thinking, there are those to whom it still means something vital but who nevertheless—and these include many theologians—look askance at the concept of natural theology. There are perhaps two main reasons for this.

In the minds of some the term is still associated with the obsolete ideas of William Paley who, in his famous book *Natural Theology or Evidences of the Existence and Attributes of the Deity* (1802), put forward the thesis that the wonderful adaptations of living things pointed to the existence of God as their creator and designer just as surely as the mechanism of a watch signified that there must be a watchmaker. Such ideas were, of course, discarded on the coming of Darwinian evolution which explained nature's adaptations in terms of natural selection. Others have thought that the very idea of a natural theology in the sense of it being a scientific study must be an impossible one in that they have held, erroneously as I hope to show, that it implies a contradiction in terms. Karl Barth opened his celebrated Gifford Lectures at Aberdeen in 1937 by referring to Lord Gifford's idea of a science of Natural Theology by saying "I do not see how it is possible for it to exist."

I want in this brief essay to explain just why I believe that a theology for today must be a natural one—in the sense of being in harmony with the scientific outlook—and that its recognition as a reality is of prime importance as one of the foundations of peace and freedom.

I was particularly pleased that the editor, in his instructions to contributors, stressed the ecological approach to the whole subject of the volume, because I believe that the ecological method must be used in laying the foundations for our new natural theology.

Apart, however, from applying the ecological method to the building of a new theology—and I shall presently explain how I think it will be done—I wish first to point out that this very approach sweeps away the imagined contradiction of terms which, it was thought, made a scientific theology impossible. It was thought impossible because it was supposed that a true science must always, by its very nature, reduce everything in its domain to physical and chemical terms. This widely held view I believe to be sheer dogma. It is true, of course, that we can describe all the activities within the living bodies of plants and animals, including ourselves, in physical and chemical terms; it is, however, but a fashionable falsity to assume that the whole of biology can be reduced to biophysics and biochemistry. Physics and Chemistry are sciences just because they are based upon statistical laws concerning the behaviour of particles, electrons, atoms and molecules. The new branch which we call ecology is, in just the same way, a true science *in its own right* based upon the statistical treatment of the inter-relations of complete living animals and plants as units, and the interactions between themselves and their environment; it is scientifically studying their behaviour as living wholes. There is no need for ecology, as a true science, to be wedded to the unproven hypothesis of materialism; animal bodies may be completely described in physico-chemical statements, but it is as yet merely a pretence, a dogma, to suggest that we understand their mental side in similar terms. I believe, with Sherrington, Eccles and others, that mental events may belong to a different order of nature, but are, in a way we do not yet understand, linked with the physical order through the organic nervous systems. The mystery of the mind-body relationship is still unsolved. Sherrington in his Gifford Lectures *Man on his Nature* said "We have it seems to me to admit that energy and mind are phenomena of two categories."

It is not remarkable that so many scientists today either regard consciousness as a pleasant illusion or completely ignore it. I was delighted when the late Sir Cyril Hinshelwood gave such prominence to the problem in his Presidential Address to the Royal Society in 1959 as follows:

"It is surprising that biological discussions often underestimate human consciousness as a fundamental experimental datum. In science we attach no value to unverifiable deductions, or to empty qualitative statements, but nobody defends the neglect of experimental data. Among these we cannot validly disregard those of our own consciousness except by a deliberate abstraction for which we must assume responsibility, and which we should not forget having made . . . There is at present no obvious answer to the question of what kind of advance can possibly be hoped for in the problem of psycho-physical concomitance. This, however, is no reason for giving up thought which at least helps to avoid the kind of errors so easily made both about physics and about biology when the problem is ignored."

On account of the dogma of materialism an increasing number of people today regard the idea of a spiritual or transcendental side of the universe as a pleasant illusion, a myth remaining from a pre-scientific age which civilization must grow out of. I believe, on the contrary, that a systematic ecological study of man's behaviour will show that religion is just as much a vital part of man's natural history as is sex, but one much less understood. By religion here I do not mean dogmatic doctrines, but a sense of some power beyond the self. It is this ecological approach that I believe will give us the new natural theology for the modern scientific age.

Many people today are still inclined to regard the term ecology as nothing more than a more modern new-fangled name for natural history; there is, however, a real difference. Natural history is the qualitative description of nature, whereas ecology is a quantitative science. Let me illustrate the difference. When we record that a particular kind of fish is confined to warm oceanic water and feeds upon various kinds of shrimps, that is simply natural history. When we can determine the actual ranges of temperature and degrees of saltness of the water which limit its distribution, and when, by the post-mortem examination of the stomach contents of a vast number of freshly caught specimens, we can work out the average percentage proportions of the different species making up its food at different times of the year and for fish of different ages, we are beginning to know a little of its ecology. We are beginning to express the inter-relationships of animals one to another, and to their environment, in numerical terms. From such a quantitative analysis we hope in time, step by step, to discover more of the laws operating in the world of living things.

I have spent the greater part of my life, when not teaching as a professor, researching into marine ecology, particularly into the relations between the plankton (the small life of the sea) and the larger forms of life, the fish and whales that are dependent upon it. Now I seek to apply my experience of these ecological methods to the affairs of man and particularly to making a contribution however small, to the building of a new natural theology. Some may think that this development is just a senile whim. To show that this is not so, I will here quote from the inaugural lecture I gave when taking up my duties as Regius Professor of Natural History in the University of Aberdeen more than thirty years ago:

"I have worked hard at marine ecology, but I have done so only partly because I have had a desire to benefit the fishing industry; I have the desire most sincerely, but also I have felt that I have been working towards a better understanding of animal relationships and making contributions to the development of general principles in ecology . . . I will go further—I will confess that perhaps my main interest in ecology is the conviction that this science of inter-relationships of animals and their environment will eventually have a reaction for the benefit of mankind quite apart from any immediate economic one. I believe that one of the great contributions of biology in this century, to the welfare of the race, will be working out of ecological principles that can be applied to human affairs: the etablishment of an ecological outlook. I believe the only true science of politics is that of human ecology—a quantitative science which will take in not only the economic and nutritional needs of man, but one which will include his emotional side as well, including the recognition of his spiritual as well as his physical behaviour . . ."

Then, after saying more about ecology being a true science of life without being reduced to the terms of physics and chemistry, I go on as follows:

"There is, of course, no doubt that the laws of physics and chemistry hold good within the animal body as outside it—as we take it to pieces in our analysis we find more and more remarkable mechanisms—more fascinating chemical interactions than we find outside it. No wonder that those who spend more time on analysis in the laboratory than in the study of living animals in nature are apt to come to the conclusion that in their physical and chemical discoveries they are explaining life . . .

"I cannot help feeling that much of man's unrest today is due to the widespread intellectual acceptance of this mechanistic superstition when the common sense of his intuition cries out that it is false. I believe that the dogmatic assertions of the mechanistic biologists, put forward with such confidence as if they were the voice of true science, when they are in reality the blind acceptance of an unproven hypothesis, are as damaging to the peace of mind of humanity as was the belief in everyday miracles in the middle ages. I believe what Professor Joad said the other day (that was in 1942) to be profoundly true: that the unconsciously frustrated desire for spiritual experience is no less important than the unconsciously frustrated sex upon which the psycho-analysts have laid so much stress."

That last sentence brings us back to the urgency of the new ecological approach to man's spiritual side. When I gave this lecture, I had, I'm afraid, forgotten that Aldous Huxley had much earlier (in his *Proper Studies* of 1927) said much the same thing:

"Much of the restlessness and uncertainty so characteristic of our time is probably due to the chronic sense of unappeased desires from which men naturally religious, but condemned by circumstances to have no religion, are bound to suffer."

I believe it is indeed urgent for our civilization that we should satisfy these unappeased and frustrated desires with a spiritual philosophy that can be seen to be in harmony with the modern scientific outlook.

The reader may well wonder, if I felt this to be so more than thirty years ago, why was it that I postponed my active attack upon this problem for so long. I feel I should, in passing, answer this reasonable charge. The fact is that, whilst I felt this urgency, I was also convinced Darwinian; it took me all that time, with hard thinking and a searching of the literature, before I was really satisfied that the spiritual side of man could be reconciled with the Darwinian doctrine of natural selction (and more recently with that of the DNA genetic code). It had seemed that the firm establishment of neo-Darwinism in the world of science of today could only point to a doctrine of materialism. This had been another powerful reason for the abandonment of religion by so many in the intellectual world. I eventually became convinced that the two could be reconciled, but only fully worked out the thesis by the time I was invited to give the Gifford Lectures in 1963; I devoted the first series, published as *The Living Stream* in 1965, to the development of this theme.

I must not, however, go into this in a brief chapter on Theology save to say that within the higher ranges of evolution new patterns of behaviour can spread through populations of animals by being copied: once established, such a new habit can exert a powerful selective force within the Darwinism system. Thus, I think it likely that *conscious behaviour* plays an increasing rôle in true Darwinian evolution as we come to the higher forms of life. This makes the crucial difference. Darwinism need not be considered an essentially materialistic doctrine.

We can come with an unbiassed mind to investigate the claims of those who state that religious feelings are a very real part of their conscious life whatever their psychological causes may be. When I speak of a more natural theology you may well ask what kind of theism it would embrace. By theism I do not mean belief in a deity with an anthropomorphic image, but I mean at least a belief in an "extra-sensory" contact with a Power which is *greater than,* and in part lies *beyond the individual self.* Towards this element, whatever it may be, those who are conscious of it may have a feeling—no doubt for good biological, psychological, reasons linked with the emotions of an early child-parent affection, (but none the worse for that)—a feeling of *personal* relationship, and they call it God. Whilst Freud has taught us much about this personification, I do not believe that his super-ego gives us the complete explanation of this feeling and the results it gives rise to.

Science of course cannot be concerned with the inner essence of religion any more than it can be concerned with the nature of art or the poetry of human love. I would maintain, however, that eventually we could build up an organized scientific knowledge—indeed one closely related to psychology—dealing with the records of man's religious experience in its many forms and his feelings of an extra-sensory contact with some Power beyond himself. Such a scientific study need not destroy the elements of religion which are most precious to man—any more than our biological knowledge of sex need diminish the passion and beauty of human love.

The natural theology I envisage could not come about without at first building up a much more extensive natural history of religion than we have at present, to provide the facts for a more systematic study. Through the work of the social anthropologists, we now know a great deal about the religious attitudes and ideas of the more primitive peoples. The work I would like to see developed would be an extension of the methods of social anthropology to the study of the experiences of more sophisticated man. The two great pioneers in this field of empirical theology were both Americans who wrote at the turn of the century; Edwin Starbuck with his *Psychology of Religion* of 1899 and William James, building upon Starbuck's work, in his classical study *The Varieties of Religious Experience* (his Gifford Lectures) of 1902. The whole tenor of William James's massive study points to the reality of man's contact with a Power beyond the conscious self which affects his actions and of which he gives innumerable examples. In his final philosophical postscript to the volume he says:

"I am so impressed by the importance of these phenomena that I adopt the hypothesis which they so naturally suggest. At these places at least, I say, it would seem as though transmundane energies, God, if you will, produced immediate effects within the natural world to which the rest of our experience belongs."

Compare this with a statement by another psychologist, the late Professor Sir Fredric Bartlett, who was giving the Riddell Memorial Lectures in 1950, nearly half a century after James's Gifford Lectures. He writes as follows:

"I confess that I cannot see how anybody who looks fairly at a reasonable sample of actions claiming a religious sanction can honestly refuse to admit that many of them could not occur, or at least that it is highly improbable that they would occur in the forms in which they do, if they were simply the terminal points of a psychological sequence, every item in which belonged to our own human, day-to-day world. I am thinking not of the dramatic and extraordinary actions which people who write books about religion mostly seem to like to bring forward. They are rare anyway. I remember the ways of life of many unknown and humble people whom I have met and respected. It seems to me that these people have done, effectively and consistently, many things which all ordinary sources of evidence seem to set outside the range of unassisted humanity. When they say 'It is God working through me,' I cannot see that I have either the right or the knowledge to reject their testimony."

Next let me take a quotation from that most liberal of theologians, Dr. L. P. Jacks, who in *Religious Perplexities,* his Hibbert Lectures of 1922 says:

"All religious testimony, so far as I can interpret its meaning, converges towards a single point, namely this. There is that in the world, call it what you will, which responds to the confidence of those who trust it, declaring itself, to them, as a fellow-worker in the pursuit of the Eternal Values, meeting their loyalty to them, and coming in at critical moments when the need of its sympathy is greatest; the conclusion being that wherever there is a soul in darkness, obstruction or misery, there also is a Power which can help, deliver, illuminate and gladden the soul. This is the Helper of men, sharing their business as Creators of Value, nearest at hand when the worst has to be encountered: the companion of the brave, the upholder of the loyal, the friend of the lover, the healer of the broken, the joy of the victorious—the God who is spirit, the God who is love."

Now let me turn back for a moment to the writings of a pioneer social anthropologist Dr. R. R. Marett who was Reader in Social Anthropology at Oxford before he became Rector of Exeter College; he was the first to break with the ideas that had been current in anthropology before him—those of Sir Edward Tylor deriving primitive religion from animism and those of Sir James Frazer deriving it from magic. Marett points to a more general and earlier feeling experienced by man in primitive religion all over the world; a feeling of his being in contact with a 'power' that helps him in his life. In his *Psychology and Folk-lore* (1920) he writes:

"Put very shortly, the moral of the history of primitive religion would seem to be this—that religion is all along vital to a man as a striving and progressive being . . . Enough has been said to show that, corresponding to the anthropologist's wide use of the term 'religion', there is a real sameness, felt all along, if expressed with no great clearness at first, in the characteristic manifestations of the religious consciousness at all times and in all places. It is the common experience of man that he can draw on a power that makes for, and in its most typical form wills, righteousness, the sole condition being that a certain fear, a certain shyness and humility, accompany the effort so to do. That such a universal belief exists amongst all mankind, and that it is no less universally helpful in the highest degree, is the abiding impression left on my mind by the study of religion in its historico-scientific aspect."

Does it not seem to us that there is an extraordinary similarity in the nature of religion in its simplest form among whatever people—primitive or sophisticated—it may be found? Here is some factor in human life, whatever its cause, that appears to have a profound effect. Something which, if he responds to it, provides man with a power over his difficulties that he might not otherwise have; it gives him a feeling of confidence and it generates courage in the face of adversity. It helps him to lead the good life.

It is the systematic study of such experiences which I believe must form the basis of our natural theology of the future. We are now making a start in this with the Religious Experience Research Unit which I have recently set up at Manchester College, Oxford; very humbly we are trying to follow in the footsteps of William James whose work of over seventy years ago was never followed up as I feel it should have been. "Religion" said Dean Inge "is concerned with that which is and not with that which was". If religion is to survive in the modern age it must be seen to be firmly based upon present-day experiences. A full account of the ideas underlying this venture will be found in my new book *The Biology of God.*

We are beginning by asking the readers of many different journals to send in records of their own experience. At first we had said that we were not at once going to be concerned with the more ecstatic or mystical states, important, as these are, but for sometime we would be collecting and studying records of a more general experience which, it is thought, may be felt by many people. Now, however, we are pleased to receive records of religious experiences of any kind. In addition to the quotations already given I would like to conclude with another example of the more general type of experience; it is taken from an address which Baroness Mary Stocks gave to the World Congress of Faiths entitled "The Religion of a Heretic". She says:

". . . Is there something that comes to meet us? Beatrice Webb's answers as recorded in her autobiography carries straight into the realm of religious faith. 'For my part', she writes 'I find it best to live as if the soul of man were in communion with a superhuman force which makes for righteousness' . . . Beatrice Webb was conscious of experiencing a sense of reverence or awe—an apprehension of a power and purpose outside herself—which she called 'feeling' and which was sometimes induced by appreciation of great music or corporate worship. But her experience went further than this nebulous fleeting 'feeling'—because as a result of it she achieved a religious interpretation of the universe which satisfied and upheld her and enabled her to seek continuous guidance in prayer—and this without compromising her intellectual integrity . . . Now that is a big step forward from rationalism, and once it is taken (as I take it in company with Beatrice Webb) it opens up a great expanse of undiscovered country—the territory that lies beyond reason—and includes what those who have explored it have discovered, or thought they had discovered, by extra-sensory perception."

In our survey we have already received over 4,000 records of such experiences and we expect to receive many more. The research is a long term project; whilst preliminary reports may be issued, the full results and the discussion of them will be published in a series of volumes the first of which should appear before long. When they are available, it is hoped that many who are at present sceptical may come to realise that these experiences are something very potent and valuable in the lives of those concerned. People, who would not otherwise have done so, may be induced to try the experiment of approaching this Power in a particular way, not by prayer for the alteration of physical events or for personal safety or material ends, but for spiritual strength and guidance for a better way of life or perhaps, more specifically, how best to deal with some difficulty or to achieve some worthwhile purpose. I believe they would find that it gave results: "ask and ye shall receive". Religion could become animated by a more vital and dynamic faith than one which rests mainly upon the acceptance of dogmas from the past. It would become truly an experimental faith.

The new natural theology which I believe will emerge may well turn out to be even more exciting to the younger generations of tomorrow than are the findings of molecular biology to those of today.

But exactly why, may be asked, did I say at the beginning that the recognition of such a natural theology would be of prime importance as one of the foundations of peace and freedom? I gave a partial answer (on p.6) in recalling the remarks of Aldous Huxley and Professor Joad that much of the unrest and uncertainty so charateristic of our time is to be explained by frustrated desires for spiritual experience. An equally important reason is that if such experience is to be a force for the moral good of the community—and it is surely upon the moral behaviour of man that both peace and freedom will ultimately depend—then religion must, in this scientific age, be seen to fit into the framework of our modern culture. It is only through a truly natural theology that this link can be made.

For further reading:

Argyle, Mitchell, 1958. *Religious Behaviour*. London. Routledge and Kegan Paul.

Evans-Pritchard, E. E. 1956. Chapter on Religion in *The Institutions of Primitive Society*. Oxford: Blackwell.

Hardy, Alister, 1965. *The Living Stream*. London. Collins.

Hardy, Alister, 1966. *The Divine Flame*. London. Collins.

Hardy, Alister, 1975, *The Biology of God*, London, Jonathan Cape.

Huxley, Aldous, 1947. *The Perennial Philosophy*. London. Chatto and Windus.

James, William, 1902. *The Varieties of Religious Experience*. New York and London: Longman, Green & Co.

Maret, R. R., 1932. *Faith, Hope and Charity in Primitive Religion* Oxford. Clarendon Press.

Miclem, Nathaniel, 1948. *Religion:* Home University Library. Oxford. University Press.

Starbuck, E. D. 1899. *The Psychology of Religion* London. Walter Scott.

SPIRITUAL LAW
ERIC DOYLE, O.F.M.

Priest of the Franciscan Order. Member of the Faculty of the Franciscan Study Centre, University of Kent, Canterbury.

Inner peace and freedom are indispensable conditions for world peace and freedom. As we look to the future there are grounds for hope. Following the world view of Teilhard de Chardin, there is no reason to suppose that evolution stopped with the advent of man. It continues in the sphere of mind conscious of belonging to a totality and is dependent on the free giving of love over the whole world.

To speak of spiritual law introduces a dimension of existence which we cannot ignore in our efforts for the peace and freedom of mankind. It brings us to the reality of self-awareness in the universe. Man belongs to the earth. He is made up of different combinations of the same chemical elements as the food he eats, the air he breathes and the ground he walks on. But he is also something more. He is spirit. In him the evolving earth reached the point of self-consciousness, in him the earth became *spiritualized.*

When we have said this, however, the question arises: Does development continue in the sphere of spirit? On the answer to that depends the ultimate significance of knowledge, being and death. For if there is no spiritual development then man has nothing more to know for, nothing more to be for and, what is worst of all, nothing more to die for.

The "Within" of Man

Spiritual law concerns the "within" of man. It turns our attention to the interiority of the pentadactyl plantigrade who discovers reality in the inner depths of his own being. It is about that fine point at the core of his existence which compels a man to cry out in anguish and joy: "I am"; the point where he finds himself plunged into the flow of existence winding its way inexorably to a term, an end, that will be a beginning; a beginning that will last forever; a beginning that will transform death into the supreme moment of living. It dwells upon that aspect of human life which convinces a man that it is against the truth to say: "You don't miss what you've never had". It focuses attention on the power in man, as Teilhard de Chardin says, to centre all reality on himself partially.[1]

Spiritual law touches upon that area wherein a man finds himself the product now of everything he has achieved, experienced, suffered, omitted and longed for in life; that area wherein he realizes he is not an isolated monad but a being-in-the-world, a being-with-others, a being-for-others. In a word, it is about the self-awareness of the human spirit which has in its very structure an openness to others, to the world and to Mystery and Transcendence, the Mystery of ultimate meaning and the Transcendence of greater than self that we call God: the incomprehensible, all-holy, all-embracing, ever-present, adorable Someone Who is the Primal Origin of all that is.

Inner Freedom and Peace

The question of spiritual development (increase in consciousness), cannot be ignored because it is dependent on inner freedom and peace. There will be no lasting peace and no true freedom on a planetary scale unless individuals acquire that inner peace which surpasses all understanding, and that inner freedom which, while allowing a man to remain himself, takes him out of himself towards the other. Inner peace comes from self-knowledge (and *all* knowledge is at the service of being—we know more to be more), which recognizes self as it is. Self-knowledge must not be confused with morbid introspection; it is knowledge of *this* self situated in the world, *this* self in its relationships. Thus, through humility and truth comes inner peace bringing self-possession in self-realization. Inner freedom is the power of self-determination in the face of the good. It drives a person to seek out the other for the other's sake, destroying egoism which is ultimately self-destructive. It is therefore an error to imagine that world freedom and peace lie exclusively in the hands of governments and in the decisions of heads of state. They lie in the hands and decisions of all of us together, as our consciousness of belonging to an ever-greater unifying whole increases. The more we are at peace with ourselves, just so much more is the world at peace; the more we are united with others in the freedom of love, just so much more is it a world freedom.

A World of Science and Technology

When we speak of man's self-awareness through inner freedom and peace as being-in-the-world, we do not understand "world" in some abstract sense. We mean it as in this world as it is now,developing from its past into the future.

The lunar landing in July 1969 is perhaps the best evidence that we belong to a world of science and technology. To achieve what at first had seemed incredible, we assembled bits of earth and hurled them at the moon as Apolo 11. The moon used to be called the mother of lunatics and to them all she had given her name. Now she has become the symbol of the most breath-taking achievements of *homo sapiens,* and she has given us a new name: luneraut. It is said that soon we will be able to take a holiday on the moon. Accommodation will be provided in an enormous plastic bag filled with fresh air—a lunar hotel. And all this, journey and holiday, for the price of a transatlantic air ticket. There is talk of space stations, hydroponic farms, hibernation in space, of leaving the solar system and of reaching Proxima Centauri. Meanwhile, here on earth, machines and computers do the work of hundreds of pairs of hands. Through science leisure is increasing; and leisure will be a problem in the future. The day is fast approaching when salaries will be earned for going down twice-a-week to the local museum to dust a Greco-Roman vase or the skeleton of a dinosaur. We'll come home for our tablets and glass of air (that will be lunch), then float off to the next room to chat with relatives in Brisbane about topics of purely local interest, like what's happening in the Galaxy of Andromeda.

Despite the advances that have brought us more comfort, speedier travel and longer lives, we still live in a world of political, social and religious unrest. It is a world sick for peace. The last twenty years have been years of hot wars, cold wars and rumours of wars. There is widespread pessimism about the powers in the hands of *homo sapiens* as a result of his exploitation of nature. Some would argue that the very word *sapiens* has been proved a misnomer. Others are extremely doubtful whether we will have enough time to lay even the foundations of a Planetary Economic Community.

Grounds for Hope

Whatever may be felt about the achievements of science and technology, the undeniable fact is that they have unified the globe. The media of communication have brought a knowledge and information explosion through which we can be actively and passively present on the furthest continents and even in outer space. It is as though a vast brain had been constructed around the earth. Man's selfawareness is of belonging, not merely to a family, a class, a nation, or a continent, but to the world: Planet Earth, and to the entire universe. His environment is no longer circumscribed by the boundaries of nations, but only by the outer reaches of space.

To dismiss as groundless the pessimism mentioned earlier would be, of course, to play the ostrich. Future development lies in the hands of men and so depends on the right use of freedom. Moreover, the paradox is that though science has unified the globe, there is by no means universal awareness or recognition of the intrinsic unity of mankind. Yet there are grounds for hope based on a significant development in the sphere of spirit on the earth. These may be listed as follows: increasing awareness of the unity of mankind: searching questions about man and his future; widespread interest in meditation.

1. *Increasing awareness of the unity of mankind*

Over the past twenty years or so there has grown up imperceptibly a greater awareness of the intrinsic unity of mankind. More and more people have come to see the simple truth, which no distinction of race, colour, creed or culture can possibly alter, that to be man is to be brother. This is not at all as extensive as it ought to be. But the fact is that it exists and is increasing. Qualitatively speaking it gives reason for hope. Its chief cause is undoubtedly the scientific and technological advances that have unified the earth. The scientific revolution contained from the beginning the seeds of a deeper humanization. This has manifested itself during recent decades. Almost two hundred years have passed since the French Revolution proclaimed the principles of freedom, equality and brotherhood. But it is only over the span of the last generation that there has been any appreciable awareness of the responsibility of establishing those principles on a universal scale.

Against this background the *Universal Declaration of Human Rights* adopted and proclaimed by the General Assembly of the United Nations in 1948, marks a turning point in history. There has been much criticism of the United Nations, and no doubt the last twenty years provide ready material for the cynic, and are more than enough to temper even the most moderate of optimists. However, the *Declaration* stands and no one can claim inculpable ignorance of its articles. Whatever open contradictions of world unity exist, whatever crises man may still have to encounter, the plain and irreversible truth is that there is an increasing awareness that mankind is one.

It should be noted in this context that the Christian Unity Movement cannot be understood as an isolated event. It is bound up with the present movements of world history towards unity.

2. *Searching questions about man and his future*

These are inseparably linked to the growing awareness of human unity. They take a variety of forms which may be reduced to the following: Where are we going? What does it all mean? Can we look forward to the future? Are we really any better off for all our scientific discoveries? To ask questions means problems have been recognized which opens the way to solutions. Now, these questions show a concern about man and his future which has led to *dialogue* among individuals and groups of the most varying beliefs and divergent ideologies. Here we may note particularly the Christian Marxist Dialogue and the study groups of the Teilhard de Chardin Association. The Teilhard de Chardin Association has as its object to make people increasingly aware of their responsibility for directing the future.[2] Dialogue at every level, which is crucial for the future, proves that passive resignation, pessimism, despair and cynicism are not the only reactions possible to the state of the world and the future of mankind.

Science was once believed to have the key to the riddle of existence and the meaning of life. This, however, proved to be a chimera. Science *in itself* does not bring satisfaction to the mind and heart. As a source of knowledge, it is subservient to being. Questions about the value of scientific advances indicate that there is a growing realization of this. Scientific advances are gains in so far as they contribute to the convergent tendencies of evolution in the sphere of spirit. However, we must be on our guard not to allow the misuse of science to lead us into condemning science itself. That would be like condemning the washing machine because it can provide opportunities for laziness. Where science is misused we can condemn only ourselves.

3. *Widespread interest in meditation*

This, in the present writer's opinion, is one of the most important phenomena of recent years. Only those who are unacquainted with its results can dismiss it as an esoteric pusuit of a few cranks. Meditation heightens self-awareness, increases inner freedom and peace and discloses to the mind the truth of human unity. One of its most important aspects is the effect it has on the individual's time outside the periods of formal meditation. It gives an all-embracing calm and deepens the sense of responsibility for others.

The *International Spiritual Regeneration Movement* has established centres in every country of the world. The purpose of the *Movement* is to teach a method of transcendental meditation in order to conquer the world with love. It is a direct way of reaching the peace in all men.[3] Equally important here at home is *The Fellowship of*

Meditation which has its headquarters in Guildford. More and more people are drawing spiritual comfort and inner peace from the simple method explained in the pamphlet published by the *Fellowship* under the title: *Inner Peace*.[4]

The *sine qua non* condition for meditation is, of course, silence (and goodness knows we need it!). It is a reason for the greatest joy that we have begun once more to discover the positive value of silence in a world where noise breaks in on us from all sides

Teilhard de Chardin and Spiritual Development

We began these reflections on spiritual law by noticing that the evolving earth reached the point of self-consciousness in man. We then submitted that, as a result of the humanizing influence of science there is some evidence of spiritual development in the increase of self-awareness of belonging to a unified and unifying whole. To draw together all that has been said thus far, we turn now to Teilhard de Chardin's phenomenology of evolution which, based on a scientific examination of the *whole* phenomenon of man, establishes that evolution continues in the sphere of spirit and that man's total environment leads in fact to the reality of love in the universe.

1. *Scientific Phenomenology*

Teilhard develops a scientific phenomenology of the universe in which the whole phenomenon of man (the "within" as well as the "without") is central. Scientific phenomenology or hyperphysics is "a branch of science which reflects on its own results in order to find their true import—a science which learns the total lesson of its discoveries".[5] In his explanation of evolution Teilhard made one his love of God and his love of the world by relating the discoveries of science to man's spiritual and religious experiences. He has shown that religion (and specifically, the Christian religion) does not alienate man from the world, but gives a greater love-energy in the sphere of spirit, impelling towards human unity. Thus, Teilhard crossed the no-man's-land between science and religion which have gone their respective ways for centuries in mutual distrust and isolation. It was his strongest conviction that all truth is one and that light from one source cannot extinguish light from another.

2. *Complexity-Consciousness*

For Teilhard de Chardin the universe is an essentially dynamic, organic, evolving reality. He speaks always, not of cosmos, but of *cosmogenesis:* a universe in process. Over the millions of years of cosmic evolution he saw operative a process of complexification extending from the subatomic particles of hydrogen to the neuro-cerebral system of man. Along with the increasing complexity of anatomical structure there has gone a corresponding increase in consciousness, unity, interiority. Consciousness is understood as a vast spectrum stretching from the most primitive power of matter to unite to the unifying self-consciousness in *homo sapiens.*

With the appearance of man millions of years of dynamic development reached their purpose. Thought had come and evolution attained its most important stage. Teilhard now draws our attention to the fact that man, confronted with space-time, experiences a certain anxiety: "After the long series of transformations leading to man, has the world stopped?"[6] He cannot accept that it has. Meditating on the total past it would be irrational and to render the whole process absurd to imagine that the operation of the Law of Complexity-Consciousness suddenly ceased. His scientific phenomenology will not permit so unscientific a conclusion! Not only are there not reasons to say it has ceased, there are positive indications it is actually continuing. Some of these, we would submit, are the growth in awareness of human unity, the desire to create a United States of the World, questions about the future of man and interest in meditation.

3. *Creative Evolution*

The evolution of man is unique in showing the dominance of convergence over divergence. The sphere of mind (noosphere) is progressing to higher levels of hominization: it is a *noogenesis.* The future of the noosphere lies in the development of persons through inter-personal relationships. Thus, with the appearance of man, evolution becomes the growth of humanity as a whole. The individual is becoming more conscious of his belonging to a whole, and this because of the threefold property possessed by every conscious being:

1 "of centering *everything* partially upon itself;
2 of being able to centre itself upon itself *constantly;*
3 of being brought *more* by this very super-centration into association with *all the other centres* surrounding it."[7]

Socialization depends on the free giving of love over the whole earth. Thus, the process of continuing evolution is one of *amorization.* That is to say, everything now depends on love: the reaching out towards the other for the other's sake, in order to discover oneself. Love means communicating to the other what is deepest and most interior in oneself. It means unity and consistence which belongs to its very dynamism.

4. *Omega Point*

Creative evolution in the noosphere is tending towards a centre which Teilhard calls *Omega Point.* The individual centres of consciousness are not destroyed because Omega is a point of convergence, not of submergence. Spiritual synthesis, or the union of persons can only be achieved on the basis of enduring personal identity and uniqueness. Union does not mean being dissolved into the 'All'. Here the principle is:

> "In any domain—whether it be the cells of a body, the members of a society or the elements of a spiritual synthesis—union differentiates. In every organized whole the parts perfect and fulfil themselves."[8]

Teilhard goes on to identify Omega Point, which is loving and loveable at this moment, with the Risen Christ. I am not directly concerned here with this aspect of his teaching since my terms of reference are natural spiritual law. It may be noted, however, that the identity is made because of the central Christian truth that God is Love.

5. *Love on the Earth*

What is clear from Teilhard's teaching is that there can be no heightening of self-awareness in isolation, there can be no increase in spiritualization without love. In a pluralistic world, unity will be achieved only through the love and good will of all men. Love alone will break down the centrifugal forces of individualism, nationalism, racialism, collectivism and class consciousness; love alone will convince us that war is not necessary; love alone will show us that we are Earthmen and that our task is to build the Earth. As Teilhard says: "Love is a sacred reserve of energy, and the very blood stream of spiritual evolution; that is the first discovery we make from the Sense of Earth."[9]

Knowledge and the Future of the World

There is no doubt that the future development of freedom and peace in the world and increase in self-awareness of belonging to the Earth are inextricably linked with progress in knowledge in every sphere. Self-knowledge, knowledge of mankind and of the world will being us to a greater degree of being. Knowledge destroys fear because it dispels ignorance. With fear removed man becomes free to love.

To conclude these reflections on spiritual law I want to give some practical suggestions in the spirit of Article 26,§2 on Education of the *Universal Declaration of Human Rights.*

I would suggest that it ought to be considered basic to education and formation at every stage:

1. To inculcate an ever deeper appreciation of the uniqueness and dignity of every person. Each individual person has an originality, an incommunicability (what the medieval philosopher John Duns Scotus called *haecceitas,* "thisness") which is the source of his irreplaceable value in the world. Literature, art, science, theology, philosophy, offer ample opportunities for this.
2. To show that no individual can be fully a person without others. Man is by definition a being-with-others. The only true foundation of interpersonal relationships is love which takes a person out of himself to the other for the other's sake.
3. To communicate that man belongs to the human family and that his home, in the first place, is the Earth.
4. To demonstrate the intrinsic meaning of history and to introduce as early as possible the study of Universal History. Nothing is intelligible without its history, least of all man and the world. From a knowledge of the past man understands himself in the present, and prepares himself for the future. As the *magistra vitae,* history teaches us that we have a duty to the past, a task in the present and a responsibility for the future.
5. To teach by shared experience that unity is not uniformity, diversity is not division.
6. To instruct the students in the history and methods of meditation of the East and West. This would include a thorough knowledge of the great mystics of East and West. Methods and techniques found suitable and attractive would be taught to those wishing to learn them.
7. To instil an awareness of the constructive value of silence. Could not the possibility and advisability be investigated of introducing periods of silence into school curriculax?
8. To teach respect for the sacredness of matter and of life in all its forms. This could be done in the most graphic way, for example, by familiarizing the students with the mysticism of St. Francis of

Assisi who called the sun, the moon, the stars, water, fire, the birds, the wolf,—his brothers and sisters; or with the teachings and practices of the Jains; or with the life and writings of Mahatma Gandhi. This would be a most positive way of teaching the horrors of violence in all its forms.

1 Pierre Teilhard de Chardin, *The Phenomenon of Man*. With an Introduction by Sir Julian Huxley, Collins, Fontana Books, 1966, 284.
2 Membership of the Association is open to anyone. Further details may be obtained from the Honorary Secretary at the Association's office at 3, Cromwell Place, London, S.W. 7.
3 Further information may be obtained from Spiritual Regeneration Movement Foundation of Great Britain, 20, Grosvenor Place, London, S.W. 1.
4 *Inner Page*, obtainable from *The Fellowship of Meditation* 3, Longdown, Guildford.
5 Oliver Rabut, *Dialogue with Teilhard de Chardin*, Sheed and Ward, London and Sydney 1961.
6 Teilhard de Chardin, *The Phenomenon*, 256.
7 *Ibid.*, 284.
8 *Ibid.*, 288.
9 Pierre Teilhard de Chardin, *Building the Earth*, Geoffrey Chapman, London-Dublin 1965, 40.

UNIVERSAL VALUES
J. W. BURTON

Director of the Centre for the Analysis of Conflict, London.

Research into the nature of values is fundamental to international peacemaking.

A contemporary need is to look behind structures, systems and institutions to discover the drives, fears, anxieties, aspirations or other motivations that create them. Only thus will we understand Biafra, Vietnam, Ireland, the Middle East, China, Rhodesia, South Africa and other problem areas. This seems to require a consideration of human values.

There has always been a wide interest in values among philosophers and political scientists. Probably no single topic has been more discussed. However, it has never been clear what precisely was being discussed. "Values" has been used to describe the long-term aspirations of states, such as peace and prosperity; the national interest of states as perceived by authorities; immediate policy objectives; the strategies by which goals are sought; and ethnic, religious and ideological norms that are associated with different cultures and traditions. It has also been employed as a generic term to cover all the above:that is anything which is held to be valuable, the test being a willingness to expend resources in its defence or attainment. A recent usage relates to conditions necessary for the preservation of social systems, for example, the value attached to preserving rates of change that are within the capabilities of systems to absorb. General Systems Theory and the use of Systems Analysis have drawn attention to values of this type.[1] These are now being incorporated into political theory.[2]

These are all institutional values, that is values that relate directly to the survival of institutions, or to the cultural goals of separately organised societies. Contemporary problems involve social-psychological values. Thought is now being given to them, probably stimulated by political experience, such as student behaviour and struggles for independence by national groups within states, and by experience in the handling of social problems, such as that of social caseworkers and probation officers.[3] These values held at individual and small group levels include priorities and preference such as the attainment of certain conditions of freedom, self-determination even at the expense of life itself, group integrity, equality of opportunities in education and employment, the preservation of cultures, and those values described by creative writers who endeavour to depict the lives and drives of peoples and social groups living within their institutional frameworks. They are the preferences of people, the drives that finally underpin or destroy institutions.

Social-biological Values

In examining social-psychological values from the point of view of political science, and especially political science concerned with world society, one is not concerned only or even mainly with individually held values that are acquired and subject to change. Interest is in those that are fundamental in human behaviour, and for this reason presumably universal. There is a distinction to be made between, on the one hand, values that people of one culture or ideology believe others should share, for example, values associated with parliamentary institutions, laissez-faire trading and the religion of particular sects, and, on the other values that are held by people within all cultures and ideological systems. This latter type of social-pschyological values can be described as social-biological values, because they are closely related to, if not direct expressions of, biological drives and motivations.

What precisely are the social-biological values postulated is an emprical question. As in so many cases in the natural sciences, elements are discovered only after they are hypothesised, and when the observer knows what he is looking for. Techniques can then be developed to find them, if they exist. We are familiar with 'participation', 'justice', 'equality of opportunity', identification', 'certainty', 'reciprocity', even though we cannot be precise about any one of these. The reason why we cannot be precise is that we have never examined them as fundamental values worthy of detailed biological and sociological research. Whatever they are, they must form part of an analysis of any aspect of world society. They are fundamental particles of human behaviour. They are connected with survival, personality development and self-maintenance within any social environment. They are not unique to men: conformity, participation, social exchange and such social phenomena can be observed in more primitive organisms. Social-biological values, like more basic reflex behaviour, are probably more the outcome of the information content of human organisation than they are of cultural, educational and other such influences that affect adult human behaviour. They are probably an example of homeostasis, that is a property that remains constant despite external forces.

Failure to distinguish between social-psychological values and social biological ones has led us to regard social behaviour as something different in kind from physical and biological behaviour. There has been an ill-defined hypothesis that human behaviour is controlled by 'will' or some such influence that does not occur in other biological behaviour. Certainly social-psychological values change with altering conditions and different environments; cultural, religious and ideological values are evidence of this. Social-biological values have the same appearance of alteration or emergence, but this is probably due to altering environmental conditions that allow them to find expression. It may be that we have mistakenly regarded these values as evolving or altering overtime, instead of merely coming into evidence as social and political changes have taken place.

We have had difficulty in explaining the widespread and apparently spontaneous nature of independence movements, political revolutions and social rebellions that have been recorded in history. A hypothesis that there are social-biological values that are fundamental particles, parts of the information content of biological organisation, serves to explain the historically evident phenomenon of continuity of social and political changes in certain directions, as for example, the continuing struggle for participation and freedom to develop personality within a social environment. Aggressive and power drives cannot be regarded as having this same fundamental quality. They are less universal, and may be no more than a manifestation of frustrated values and evidence of the existence of more basic drives. At a political level, such a hypothesis serves to explain the persistent demand for independence of nations, and for identification of groups within states. These manifestations of nationalism have clear biological origins and protective functions.

There is a supposition here that in the course of social evolution, basic drives and motivations have been suppressed by institutional restraints of a purely social or community character, and later by those resulting from economic specialisation and organisation. In accordance with this supposition, the overt expression of values that characterises every level of contemporary municipal and world society is a reaction against this institutional overlay. In other words, there is a supposition that social-institutional development includes an interaction between the expression of values and their control, and that either one can be the dominant influence in some localities, and in some periods of time.

In a relatively stable and satisfied political community, the process of political socialisation effectively channels and controls social-biological drives. Where, however, there are ethnic communities that feel threatened, economic groups that feel prejudiced, or minorities that have no means of effective participation in political decisions, there is reduced political socialisation. This applies as much, if not more, to highly developed industrial societies as to under-developed ones where the problem of alienation is becoming acute.

Nor is social-biological behaviour an attribute of less educated peoples. There is a qualitative difference between reflex or instinctive behaviour—used in the common sense of basic drives—and social-biological value behaviour. Instinctive behaviour is regulated by cortical dominance as required by the social environment. A good deal of it is irrelevant to survival in a civilised social setting. For example, there are social responses to threat that do not necessarily require violence, as for example, calling for police help. Value behaviour, on the other hand, is more and not less relevant to survival and personality development as the social environment becomes more highly organised. It is not subject to the same cortical control. On the contrary, cortical dominance helps to stimulate and to direct it sometimes into aggressive and even destructive activity.

One of the normative corollaries of the hypothesis that some types of values are incorporated in the information content of organisms, and have this special qualitative feature, is that suppression of social groups, denial of political participation and of equality of opportunity, are possible only in the short-term, and in particular circumstances. Institutions that prevent the expression of value behaviour are under constant threat. The legitimised status and authority of institutions is finally derived from value behaviour at this socialogical-biological level.

On this reasoning, observation of situations, and the making of policy, could be subjected to rules based on homeo-stasis. Prediction of behaviour, in given circumstances and over periods of time, could come within statistical probability. Indeed, intuitively we are coming to this view by reason of experiences such as in Vietnam, where expectations of behaviour based on power theories with little reference to values have been shown to be false. Eastern European history in the last decade has also stimulated thought about the nature and persistence of social-psychological and social-biological values in particular.

Images of World Society

On this reasoning it is possible to interpret more satisfactorily the history of thought in politics and international politics. Waltz postulated three images: man, the state and the international system.[4] In each of these are origins of conflict, and each diagnosis suggests a remedy. Man has been assumed to be aggressive, and the remedy is his conversion to a set of norms, or his control. The state was thought to be an origin of conflict; by some, because it intervened and endeavoured to control; by others, because it did not control enough. The inter-state system was merely an extension of the institutions of state defence, through which powerful states could control the behaiour of other peoples. Other images have emerged since Waltz wrote in the 'fifties. One is the decision-making image, which recognises the need to take into account the response of the environment, and other cybernetic processes of decision-making. It is an image that departs from the three previous ones in that decision-making is no longer seen as a simple power input and distribution: decision-making within a power framework can be more successful if account is taken of feedback from the environment. The values of others, even though they are values at an institutional level, are seen to be relevant. Associated with this image is a change in the model employed, from the billiard-ball model of the previous images, to a systems one based on cross-national transactions. Another recent image is the social change and spillover image, which attributes conflict to struggles within states that spill over into international conflict. This directs attention to the conflict within political structures between institutional and social psychological values. What is suggested here is a sixth image, one that substitutes fundamental and perhaps universal values as explanations of behaviour at the individual and state levels, and thus even further breaks down any distinction between political behaviour within and among states.

One of the curious and politically important aspects of values that are widely held, if not universal, is that they are not treated as such. Even where it is generally accepted that the right of participation in decision-making, or the right of association, is a widely held value and a human 'right', the exercise of this right by others is nonetheless often resisted within and between groups. Other 'values' or institutional norms of behaviour are invoked, such as values associated with particular forms of law and order, and they are held to be overriding and to justify the suppression of these social-psychological values. The drives and motivations of people are thus suppressed by institutional and cultural 'values'. The reason for this conflict between human values and institutional norms is not hard to find. Specialisation in social exchange leads to loss of independence and to relations based on bargaining and power.[5]

Institutionalised norms then serve to legitimise and preserve the resultant social structures. Normative sanctions emerge as the means of controlling power relationships. In these circumstances the motivations and responses of others—even though they are identical with one's own—come to be regarded as a threat to existing institutions and positions of privilege. Indeed they are: there is a latent conflict between changing values and state institutional norms. The pursuit of their values by some actors is interpreted by others as ideology and even irrationality. In historical and political writings, values are sometimes treated as being among influences in world society that should be curbed, and against which institutions of restraint should be directed. Nationalism, which is a universal and integrative force in social organisation, has accordingly been perceived as though it were a malign influence in world society.

The Emergence of Social-psychological Values

It is not relevant here to describe in any detail changes in the environment and in thought in various areas that have brought social-psychological values to attention. Broadly, municipal and world society have both been regarded—and are still widely viewed—by men of affairs and by many scholars, as comprising institutions within which members are required to conform to traditional patterns of behaviour. The institution of feudalism, and the institutions of capitalism and socialism, required—and still require—a high degree of conformity, and human values were—and still are—submerged and even sacrificed to institutional values. Education. communications, rising expectations of participation in decision making and the welfare state are among influences that have helped to bring individual and group values to the surface. Acceptance by people of existing circumstances has diminished with knowledge of what is possible. What was once thought by the individual to be a natural order is now seen to be subject to change by human protest and political organisation. Independence movements, student protest and the growing North-South confrontation, are particular symptoms of the emergence of an expression of values at levels lower than institutions. The development of social studies, especially those dealing with individual and group response to environmental conditions, such as neuroses, delinquencies, learning and adjustment, have helped further to focus attention on behavioural values rather than institutional ones.

Not only have societies been preoccupied by institutional values; world society comprised state units that paid high regard to institutional values, and was structured in ways that submerged all other outlooks and objectives.

Until a few decades ago world society effectively comprised a relatively small number of states each dominated by one of a few greater ones. States could then reasonably be considered as the main actors, and, as such, entities. Sovereignty, rules of war and neutrality, protection of nations of great powers, treaty rights and privileges of great powers, were the main subjects of discussion, negotiation and study. The human interests and values of peoples in smaller states and colonies were not politically important. World politics could then reasonably be described and explained in the simple terms of the interests of powerful and hegemonial states to which smaller states and subject peoples had to accommodate themselves. In municipal and in world society, values were relevant only to the extent that they were a by-product of power.

Understandably, theories of political behaviour were based upon an acceptance of human struggles as being related to some natural and inevitable aggressiveness. Even today little attention is paid in foreign policy making to the values of others. We are content to refer to the pursuit of others of their values as a form of aggressiveness or anti-social behaviour to be curbed by national and international restraints. It is only in academic political analysis, and not always there, that it is acknowledged that individual and group behaviour of a type that does not conform with normative patterns is sometimes explicable in terms of values that are as strongly held, and as important to those holding them, as the values which our own society has traditionally accepted. The emergence of new nations, and the surfacing of cultures and behavioural patterns previously submerged by European and indigenous overlordship, are causing scholars to entertain the idea that the responses that politically have been regarded as 'aggressive' for example, nationalist movements, revolts against feudal systems and resistance to racial discrimination, may be to those concerned their inevitable responses to the perceived and environmental conditions in the light of the knowledge available. Perhaps they are sometimes the only politically practicable responses to a set of intolerable options that have been imposed by the environment - that is, by other groups, nations and states. We are just beginning, intellectually, to understand the significance of values in a world structure which contains no in-built processes of gradual change for the satisfaction of values, except those that involve violence. There has been an important shift in the study of world society in the last few decades from a normative approach to one that analyses and endeavours to understand political response, violent or non-violent, as a reaction to an environment, a major part of which is the behaviour of other actors. The values of the units being observed are beginning to be the subject of analysis, even though as yet they are still grossly described, and usually at an institutional level. It is this which has made Political Science both more realistic and more complex. The study of politics is no longer history or the study of organisation; it is the study of behaviour in all its human aspects.

Behaviour at an institutional level is an end result; its study is a descriptive one and adds little to an understanding of its origins and drives. It cannot explain behaviour, which ultimately must be traced to political motivations and responses at all political levels. The motivations and responses of the individual Vietnamese agricultural worker after World War II were affected by the knowledge that feudal systems of land tenure were not the only possible ones. The fears of individual Biafrans for their lives and futures, the threats perceived by individual Arabs and Israelis, the felt resentments of individual Africans against Europeans and Asians, are the influences ultimately to be included in any explanation of international society and its altering structures. Values at these levels are specific and can be examined by social-science techniques.

The next step in political analysis is to acertain which values are common in world society. If not power, which is a means to an end, is it participation in decision-making, certainty, reciprocity, or are there other values along the means-end spectrum? Do social-psychological values have an absolute quality not conspicuous in institutional values: what leads men to burn themselves and to fight losing battles? Are some social-psychological values universal? Is there some connexion between student demands for participation and the Biafran defiance of the Federal Government? What are the circumstances in which participants are prepared to give support to, or alternatively to destroy, institutions in which they hold minority opinions? Why do parliamentary systems survive in some circumstances and not in others? There are no philosophical answers to these questions: they are empirical questions, and furthermore, they are questions that must be asked and answered at a social psychological or a social-biological level. There is no substitute for finding out what the values are that exist in particular situations by asking relevant people relevant questions. The relevant people are those who make up communities and help to create institutions that wholly reflect their values—legitimised institutions—and not authorities that sometimes lack legitimised status and must in due course either give place to others or alter their value systems. It would clear a great deal of philosophical argument and give us knowledge of municipal and world society if we were to get down to the job of finding whether this is so, and what the common values are. The philosophical questions will then be answered. Do East and West Germans, and North and South Koreans have different values, and if so, why should peoples of the same culture have different values under different administrations? How long will these differences persist? Did the different institutions create different political and social values or merely submerge some, as colonialism submerged values? Did conflict in Cyprus and Nigeria occur because of fears within the communities, or because of fears promoted by ambitious leadership? These are empirical questions that cannot be answered in the comfort of a philosopher's study, or probably, by reference to the contemporary records of the past.

If theories concerning the making of policy and the behaviour of systems generally take into account only institutional attributes, such as system values, decision-making processes, the status of authorities, roles and other aspects of society, neglecting the motivations and responses of its members, then they are likely to have very little, if any, predictive value. The theory of the balance of power was an explanation of world society at a particular time and also a policy orientation. It depended, in theory, on states having no cultural or traditional values or links that would inhibit them from supporting one power today and another tomorrow in order to maintain a balance. For this reason alone it could not succeed. The theory of collective security, under which existing structures were to be maintained and the behaviour of smaller states controlled, took no account of changing political and social values and espectations. From time to time the system broke down, and wars occurred, under the built-up pressures of frustrated change. So today, theories and domestic policies that rest on the institutional, structural and decision-making aspects of society but which neglect the influences that were responsible for this apparatus, must likewise fail.

The Practical Importance of a Value Approach

There are some practical reasons for stressing a value approach to politics. Social-psychological values are essentially subjective phenomena: it is their existence that gives to politics whatever flexibility or non-deterministic features it has. They are subjective in the sense that they are arrived at within a framework of perceived opportunities, whether or not the opportunities in some realistic sense occur. They are also subjective in the sense that these values are themselves given relative values, thus forming a value system or set of priorities. Because they are subjective, they are also subject to change and manipulation. By working on values, institutions and relationships can be altered; but values cannot as readily be changed by working on institutions and relationships. An institutional approach to society leads to structures designed to ensure conformity with some preconceived norms of behaviour, and threat, coercion and deterrence are the instruments. They can do no more than suppress or frustrate value systems. A value approach opens up quite different ways of handling conflict and relationships generally. The objective comes to be not restraint and deterrence, but ways by which actors can be helped to reassess relative values in the light of increased knowledge of the environment, the values of others, and the cost of pursuing immediate ones in terms of loss of other values that are likely to be incurred. A value approach takes us away from judicial and coercive settlements to the type of adjustments that are made out of court by social caseworkers, psychiatrists, industrial mediators, and others who have found that adjustment to an environment and the avoidance of conflict are most directly and permanently affected by adjustments within the actors themselves. The extension of a value approach to international conflict along the lines of the contemporary approach to small group conflict is one that is only now being explored.[6]

Social-biological values are universal, and provide a basis on which parties in conflict can identify with each other, and begin to understand the notion of mirror images. Parties in a conflict struggle to attain the same values—security and certainty. But these are not scarce products. Their availability is increased by functional co-operation in securing them.

Conclusion

One of the responses of political scientists to the circumstances in which they work is to indulge in discussions on methodology. While an awareness of methodological problems and dangers is important, getting on with the job is more important. It is only by working on the subject matter that the methodological problems will be resolved. Those who are by temperament or training measurers, modellers, thinkers, or field workers all have plenty of useful scope within their own areas of interest. Consideration of methodological problems is useful in that it points to the need for teaching and research to encourage the combining of all these approaches within the one individual, to the extent that this is possible, and within teaching and research groups of scholars working together. It points to the need for everyone, especially students, to be aware of these problems and to take advantage of whatever opportunities exist for direct observation of political situations, interdisciplinary discussion and other means of coming into close personal contact with the phenomena being observed. In this way theory will ultimately encompass values.

1 See D. Easton: *A Framework for Political Analysis*, Prentice-Hall, 1965, and—J. N. Rosenau *Linkage Politics*, Free Press, 1969.
2 See J. W. Burton *Systems, States, Diplomacy and Rules*, Cambridge, 1968.
3 See J. W. Burton *Conflict and Communication*, Macmillan, 1969.
4 K. N. Waltz: *Man, the State and War*, Columbia, 1959.
5 P. M. Blau: *Exchange and Power in Social Life*, Wiley, 1964.
6 See J. W. Burton: *Conflict and Communication*, Macmillan, 1969.

PEACE AND CONFLICT IN NON-INDUSTRIAL COMMUNITIES

RUTH FINNEGAN

Dr. Ruth Finnegan (Mrs. Murray) is Senior Lecturer in Comparative Social Institutions at the Open University. She has spent seven years in Africa engaged in university teaching and research. Her books include *Survey of the Limba People of Northern Sierra Leone* (H.M.S.O. 1965), *Oral Literature in Africa* (Clarendon Press 1970), *Modes of Thought* (ed; with Robin Horton, Faber, 1973).

It is often assumed that "primitive societies" are either totally free from all conflict or, (the opposite view), so naturally violent that only a strong super-power can keep them in check. Neither extreme view is true. In fact, conflict is inherent in non-industrial (as in other) communities. But the conflicts are regulated and limited. The ways which are adopted for this are of interest for anyone concerned with regulating conflict in the contemporary Western World. In particular we can note the regulation and limitation of conflict through the use of mediators, through inter-community ties and through the existence of shared values between communities.

There are certain ideas about the nature of "primitive" man and "primitive" communities which tend, often unconsciously, to influence discussions about peace and conflict. It is easy to move from assumptions about so-called "primitive men" to inferences about human nature in general, and for this in turn to influence discussions about the mechanisms of peace-keeping. But if these assumptions themselves are dubious, then we shall necessarily fall short of the truth in such arguments about peace. It is, therefore, worth examining some of these ideas about "primitive communities" to see how far they accord with the contemporary state of knowledge on the subject of non-industrial societies.[1]

Among a number of different assumptions on this subject I will pick on two. Both may seem far-fetched when stated in a crude form, but nevertheless in one form or another they tend to underline the thinking of many people on this subject and are prevalent enough to deserve direct consideration. As will emerge later, both are particularly relevant for the main topic of this book.

First of all, there is the assumption that "primitive man" is violent, self-seeking and anarchic, and that it is only through the use of superior violence that he can be kept under control and that law and order of any kind can be brought about. This view of man "in the state of nature" was perhaps most forcibly stated by Hobbes when he spoke of the war "of every man against every man—continual fear and danger of violent death" and the consequent need for a sovereign force to curb this. It is still a very common idea. People tend to have this kind of model in mind when they suggest that without the use of superior force human society would disintegrate, and violence and disorder between communities and nations would reign uncontrolled. The implication that follows from this is often that the most powerful mode for maintaining peace and order is soveriegn force and, in particular, the modern nation state.

The second model of "primitive man" is the exact opposite. This pictures him as peace-loving, non-individualistic, living in a state of harmony and the absence of all conflict—the Noble Savage in short. Following on from this it is easy to assume that if only we could remove the artificial bonds and frictions of modern society and return to this idyllic natural state, there would no longer be problems about peace-keeping—peace would become the natural situation in which people and communities would live.

In fact, as I hope to show in this essay, neither of these assumptions fits the facts about non-industrial communities as we now know them. If these two models of "primitive man" are tested against modern knowledge on the subject it is clear that they are mistaken—together with the implications that follow from them for the question of peace-keeping.

I will take the second assumption first. All the evidence we have suggests that conflict, far from being merely a recent or unnatural phenomenon, is in fact universal in all human society. Recent work by sociologists has emphasised that in every sphere of human life—factory, government administraion, school, church or sports club—there is conflict between individuals, between generations, between groups. Non-industrial societies present no exception to this. As one eminent social anthropologist has put it: "Conflict is just as basic an element as sex in the mammalian and cultural nature of man. We shall never banish conflict."[2] One group of social anthropologists has particularly (some would say exaggeratedly) emphasised the existence of conflict in a number of non-industrial societies.[3] But anyone with first hand experience of non-industrial societies or expert knowledge of the literature concerning them would now admit that the evidence lends no support to the view that such societies are free from conflict.

The conflicts in non-industrial communities are of many kinds. They can be between individuals, between families or between groups. They range from verbal abuse to physical violence. There are conflicts between individuals about who will be village headman, between co-wives of one man about the treatment of their children, between hostile bands about rights to water or to pasture, between village communities about boundaries, or between opposing rulers about the allegiance of a particular group of subjects. There are vendettas and feuds between families, hit and run raids on neighbouring villages, expeditions for booty, actual military campaigns and outright war by organised armies.

When one looks at these societies, it becomes clear that there is no clear cut distinction between war and conflict generally. Internal and external conflicts shade into each other. Where societies do not have strict territorial or political boundaries, it is really not possible to differentiate between an (internal) feud and an international war, or between a feud among family groups and a conflict between smaller groups or even individuals. In all these kinds of conflict violence may be used. But there may, at the same time be no complete severing of the ties so that the state of war is only a relative one, far more limited than what we describe as the "total" war of the modern world.[4] War can therefore be treated in these societies at least as merely one type of conflict and will be approached in this way in the rest of this essay.

These conflicts and hostilities, then, exist even in societies which we would like to picture as harmonious and free from all passions and disturbances. These conflicts furthermore play a part in the social processes of the societies. It is relevant here to say something about the kinds of effects and functions which these conflicts achieve. For clearly if one wants to regulate or remove such conflicts, it is necessary to gain an understanding of their functions and, therefore, of the area in which one needs to look for alternatives.[5]

First, there is the function of external conflict in uniting groups internally. This is familiar from our own experience, but can perhaps be seen particularly clearly in some non-industrial societies. There is the famous case of the Nuer, cattle-herders of the Southern Sudan, who have no formalised state or central rulers, but whose various family groups are internally united through their hostility to other such units. At other times they may join together into larger groups—in the face of conflict with yet another external force.[6] Similarly a whole kingdom—of which a number exist even in non-industrial societies—can be given greater unity precisely through its potential or actual conflict with a neighbouring kingdom. Conflict can thus help to maintain unity and cement interpersonal relationships. Another function that has been suggested for conflict is the psychological one of keeping tension and aggressiveness under control by allowing it expression through certain regulated channels. There are various "safety valve" mechanisms of this kind in non-industrial societies—the Eskimo song duels and ritualised buffetting matches, for instance, the various ball games among the American Indians (the "Red Indians"), or the great interest in football among many contemporary African peoples. Again conflict (including its extreme form of outright war) is used to settle questions of power and authority. This may involve competition between a number of sons or grandsons of a late ruler about who should succeed him and about the exact balance of power between ruler and subjects. Here rebellions by various groups or subjects are not uncommon and have been much discussed in the context of traditional African kingdoms.[7] Economic functions are also achieved through conflict in the sense of the distribution of desired goods. Conflict (including war) may lead to the transfer of various goods: perhaps cattle taken in raids by pastoral people like the Nuer and others, or territorial expansion and the economic exploitation of the conquered peoples as in the states of ancient Peru or Mexico.[8] Finally, conflict, often in the form of potential and actual violence, may have the function of regulating relations between different groups. When there is no central authority, dealing with offences by members of an outside group may take the form of killing one of its members for revenge or of taking back by force articles considered to have been stolen from them—both actions which take place among the Nuer and very many others.[9]

Conflict then (including its extreme form of war) can be found in non-industrial as well as in industrial societies. The idea of the Noble Savage living in constant peace and harmony is at variance with the known facts.

This leads us on to a discussion of the second assumption. Is it really true that communities in the non-industrial parts of the world are inherently violent and uncontrolled and that it is, therefore, only through the use of superior force (in particular the modern nation state) that peace and order can be imposed?

The answer to this is twofold. First, while it is true that there are conflicts in non-industrial communities, nevertheless there are many ways in which these conflicts are also regulated and controlled. Second, the means of controlling them are not by any means always through force or through the imposition of the rule of a centralised state. I will discuss these two aspects in turn.

If we look at non-industrial societies we can see a multiplicity of interesting ways in which conflicts are dealt with. Some of these have already been mentioned. Among the Eskimos, people can work off grudges and disputes of all kinds through a conventional system of song duels. The result of these is to bring the quarrel into the open, air it and, through this process, settle the dispute and restore normal relations. Another way of achieving the same results is through a kind of ceremonial combat in which the two individuals concerned try to vanquish the other in front of a crowd of onlookers either by a series of blows to the side of the head or butting with the forehead. The occasion is a festive one, and the conflicts are dealt with in a way that leads the contestants to retire satisfied.[10] Similar types of ceremonial combat are to be widely found. The point in each case is that the conflict is expressed and dealt with in a *regulated* way. There are limits beyond which the combat must not go and rules which the contestants and the audience agree to accept. The conventions and values, in other words, are shared by both sides. Other regulated ways of dealing with conflicts are largely by verbal means. For example, among the West African Limba villages of northern Sierra Leone, disputes are settled by lengthy speeches by the disputants so that the anger in men's hearts can be "spoken out" and removed. The disputants are reconciled after long soothing speeches by a group of counsellors, all taking place according to strict rules of procedure and ceremonial. This kind of approach is very widespread in non-industrial societies. Again there is the common system referred to as the "joking relationship". This is a special relationship between two individuals who might otherwise be likely to be in frequent conflict. The potential conflict is regulated through an accepted system of ceremonial joking and mock abuse between the two—the mock abuse keeping in control the open conflict that might otherwise break out. There are also a number of other more familiar and straightforward ways of regulating disputes and conflicts. The two sides (or their representatives) may meet together in a village court to state their cases and have the dispute jointly discussed and settled according to the local values. Or there may—as in some non-industrial kingdoms—be organised courts over which the king or his representative presides and delivers the ultimate verdict. The Lozi people of Zambia are a well-known example here. They have a highly organised tradition of judicial procedure, carried out according to a complex system of rules and ceremonies which include the hearing of witnesses, cross-examination, and a series of successive verdicts (sounding rather like sermons) which are delivered by a large number of councillors in turn, ending up with the king's final verdict.[11]

But what happens when there is no formal state power or ruler and thus no formalised courts? Must there then necessarily be a breakdown in law and order? This brings us to the second point to notice here. This is that the regulation of conflict does not necessarily depend on the *enforcement* of order by a superior power in the form of a sovereign ruler or state.

Now it must be admitted that in societies without formalised rulers or courts, a direct recourse to force by an individual or group which considers itself aggrieved is more likely than in societies in which people can appeal to the law via the police or constituted courts. Among the state-less Eskimo or Nuer, for instance, a man is liable to take the law into his own hands since there is no-one else to take responsibility for his rights. He may thus take revenge by murdering his opponent or go and take back something by force which he considers was stolen from him. But there are two points to notice here—first, that even such activities may be strictly regulated by public opinion or explicit rules so that there are limits beyond which such action is unlikely to go; and secondly that even in such contexts there are also peaceful mechanisms for settling disputes. Among the Nuer, for instance, the killing of a relative may result in a return murder by the dead man's group. But a more frequent pattern is for the families of the killer and the killed to be reconciled through the mediation of a priest. This priest has no power to *force* the contestants to remain at peace, but by mediating between them and trying to induce them to end their anger he finally persuades the dead man's family to accept compensation in the form of cattle rather than another death.[12] In spite of their anger, the two opposing families may secretly want to be reconciled: they probably have economic and friendship ties with each other, they share certain common values, and quite likely women from one family are married to men of the other. The same sort of situation applies even to conflict between wider groups; the ties may be rather more tenuous, but there are usually some, and it is often to the long term interest of all of the parties to avoid outright conflict, provided some mediator can be found as a kind of face-saving device to persuade them to become reconciled. Another way in which disputes can be settled and culprits punished without recourse to centralised force or formal courts is through satirical songs or verbal abuse. Among the Chopi people of Portuguese East Africa, for example, someone who is guilty of some offence finds abusive and satirical songs being sung about him—to such good effect that the victim (and his potential imitators) is deterred from further offences.[13]

The detailed ways in which conflict is dealt with naturally vary according to the kind of values and type of upbringing of each society. Thus—to take one example—among two neighbouring peoples in Sierra Leone, the individuals in one (the Temne) are taught from childhood to stand up for their rights, physically if need be; there is frequent recourse to violence, with the result that strong courts are necessary to control the resultant conflicts. Among the Limba, on the other hand, people grow up knowing that speeches are to be preferred to physical action and, though there are, of course, occasional fights, most conflicts are resolved through measured oratory rather than physical violence. But the point is that, with all these differences, there are always *some* means, more, or less, effective according to the context, in which the conflicts inherent in human society are regulated in non-industrial communities.

Thus, even without the Western system of "courts, codes and constabulary" and without the powers of the modern centralised state, there are ways in which conflicts can be minimised, regulated and settled.

What are the implications of this discussion for the topic of the present volume? There are two main points I would like to make in conclusion.

First, the romantic idea of a Golden Age of primitive man, of peace and harmony to which we would return if only we could strip off the frictions of modern industrial life, is a myth. We are merely deluding ourselves if we think it is possible to arrange life or society so that no conflicts exists. As Weber put it "conflict cannot be excluded from social life . . . 'peace' is nothing more than a change in the form of conflict or in the antagonists or in the objects of the conflict" . . .[14]

But if conflict exists, there are also many ways in which it can be regulated. This is the second point on which I want to insist (and, of course, the practical problem to which we must address ourselves). We need, in the first place, to understand what are the functions of conflict and, if they are necessary ones, to consider alternative means of attaining them. This may involve looking for alternative non-violent ways of expressing inner group solidarity or external aggressiveness, or alternative means of settling disputes about the distribution of power or economic goods. Obviously a state organisation and legal system is one way of dealing with some of these problems, but, as we have seen, conflict can also be regulated even without the state. This is a hopeful point when we look at the sphere of international relations in which no one state can take responsibility, but in which the United Nations, say, may be able to play the role of creating an inter-state system.

In addition we can also learn something from seeing the many ways in which non-industrial societies go about regulating their conflicts. Here it is worth recalling some of the more important and widespread ways in which this can be achieved. First there is the use of mediators when no formalised authority is accepted by both sides. This is something which can be helpful not only among peoples like the Nuer but in modern international conflicts. The use of mediators in recent conflicts—whether under the auspices of church bodies, the Red Cross or international political organisations like the United Nations or the Organisation of African Unity—is something which the social anthropologist would recognise, and that we can welcome as one well-tried way of alleviating conflict. Second, there is the creation and extension of inter-community ties which can help to limit and mitigate even violent conflict. In industrial as well as non-industrial societies one can encourage links of friendship, trade, or common interest which can cut across the other, conflicting, interests and help to bind together people and communities which are otherwise in conflict. This is something which may be significant even in a violent and apparently "total" war situation. Finally conflict, as we have seen, tends to be in some respects limited by the existence of at least some shared values (religious and otherwise) between conflicting communities. This is something which the modern width and speed of communications in the contemporary world is making increasingly feasible.

All in all, this kind of approach gives us both a more realistic and a more hopeful view of the nature of the problem than if we continue to be influenced by outdated models of "primitive man". Conflict, in short, is inherent in all human society, industrial and non-industrial. But conflict can be regulated. It is for us to consider and exploit the various ways in which human societies everywhere have developed for so regulating it. To quote Paul Bohannan again "We shall never banish conflict. Indeed it is wrongheaded and blind of us to think that we should. Rather, conflict must be controlled and must be utilised profitably in order to create more and better cultural means of living and working together".[15]

[1] Since the word "primitive" is both emotive and potentially misleading I prefer to use "non-industrial" in most of the description here.
[2] P. Bohannan (ed), *Law and Warfare,* New York, 1967, p.xi.

[3] Especially the group of social anthropologists associated with Manchester. See e.g. M. Gluckman, *Custom and Conflict in Africa,* Oxford, 1963.

[4] Even in this case the severance of all relationships is not, of course, total. Quite apart from the fact that many sociologists would consider the hostilities themselves as one form of relationship, many other links (both personal and organisational) continue in spite of the war—a relevant point which will be taken up later.

[5] On the effects of conflict, see in particular L. A. Coser, *The Function of Social Conflict,* London, 1956.

[6] For a brief account of this kind of situation see the chapter entitled "The peace in the fued" in M. Gluckman, *Custom and Conflict in Africa,* Oxford, 1963.

[7] See Gluckman op. cit. especially chapter 2; and M. Gluckman, *Order and rebellion in tribal Africa,* London, 1963.

[8] But even outright war in these communities often does not lead to the actual transfer of land, and it has been suggested that the economic functions of war are possibly less striking in non-industrial than they are in industrial societies.

[9] For further comments on the possible functions of conflict (especially war) see the useful general discussion on Primitive Warfare by A. P. Vayda, in the *International Encyclopedia of the Social Sciences,* New York, 1968, Vol. 16, pp.468-72.

[10] For further details on Eskimo mechanisms for settling disputes see E. A. Hoebel, *The Law of Primitive Man,* Cambridge, Mass., 1954, a book well worth consulting on this topic in general.

[11] For details see M. Gluckman, *The judicial process among the Barotse,* Manchester, 1955.

[12] This process is described in E. E. Evans-Pritchard, *The Nuer,* Oxford, 1940.

[13] For examples see H. T. Tracey, *Chopi Musicians,* London, 1948.

[14] M. Weber, *The methodology of the social sciences,* Glencoe, 1949, pp.26-7 (quoted in Coser op. cit. p.21).

[15] P. Bohannan (ed), *Law and Warfare,* New York, 1967, p.xi.

THE ECONOMICS OF PERMANENCE
E. F. SCHUMACHER

Dr. E. F. Schumacher, born in Germany in 1911 and resident in England since 1937, is best known as Economic Adviser of the National Coal Board from 1950 to 1970 and as the originator of the concept of Intermediate Technology for developing countries. He is Chairman of the Intermediate Technology Development Group, Ltd.; President of the Soil Association, concerned with the development of organic systems of agriculture and horticulture; and a director of the Scott Bader Organization, based on new methods of common ownership in industry.

This essay, originally prepared for the Gandhi Centenary in 1969, has been published in various journals here and abroad. An extended version appears in Dr. Schumacher's book *"Small is Beautiful*—a study of economics as if people mattered", published by Blond & Briggs, London, 1973.

Science and technology must plan for Permanence, not just for the immediate future.

The dominant modern belief is that the soundest foundation of peace would be universal prosperity. One may look in vain for historical evidence that the rich have regularly been more peaceful than the poor, but then it can be argued that they have never felt secure against the poor; that their aggressiveness stemmed from fear; and that the situation would be quite different if everybody were rich. Why should a rich man go to war? He has nothing to gain. Are not the poor, the exploited, the oppressed most likely to do so, as they have nothing to lose but their chains? The road to peace, it is argued, is to follow the road to riches.

This dominant modern belief has an almost irresistable attraction as it suggests that the faster you get one desirable thing the more securely do you attain another. It is doubly attractive because it completely by-passes the whole question of ethics; there is no need for renunciation or sacrifice; on the contrary! We have science and technology to help us along the road to peace and plenty, and all that is needed is that we should not behave stupidly, irrationally, cutting into our own flesh. The message to the poor and discontented is that they must not impatiently upset or kill the goose that will assuredly, in due course, lay golden eggs also for them. And the message to the rich is that they must be intelligent enough from time to time to help the poor, because this is the way by which they will become richer still.

Gandhi used to talk disparagingly of "dreaming of systems so perfect that no one will need to be good". But is it not precisely this dream which we can now implement in reality with our marvellous powers of science and technology? Why ask for virtues, which man may never acquire, when scientific rationality and technical competence are all that is needed?

Instead of listening to Gandhi, are we not more inclined to listen to one of the most influential economists of our century, the great Lord Keynes? In 1930, during the world-wide economic depression, he felt moved to speculate on the "economic possibilities for our grandchildren" and concluded that the day might not be all that far off when everybody would be rich. We shall then, he said, "once more value ends above means and prefer the good to the useful".

"But beware!", he continued, *"The time for all this is not yet. For at least another hundred years we must pretend to ourselves and to every one that fair is foul and foul is fair; for foul is useful and fair is* not.

This was written forty years ago and since then, of course, things have speeded up considerably. Maybe we do not even have to wait for another sixty years until universal plenty will be attained. In any case, the Keynesian message is clear enough: Beware! Ethical considerations are not merely irrelevant, they are an actual hindrance, "for foul is useful and fair is not". The time for fairness is not yet. The road to heaven is paved with bad intentions.

WHAT IS ENOUGH?

I propose now to consider this proposition. It can be divided into three parts:

First, that universal prosperity is possible;

Second, that its attainment is possible on the basis of the materialist philosophy: "enrich yourselves";

Third, that this is the road to peace.

The question with which to start my investigation is obviously this: Is there enough to go round? Immediately we encounter a serious difficulty: What is 'enough'? Who can tell us? Certainly not the economist who pursues "economic growth" as the highest of all values, and therefore has no concept of 'enough'. There are poor societies which have too little; but where is the rich society that says: "Halt! We have enough"? There is none.

Perhaps we can forget about 'enough' and content ourselves with exploring the growth of demand upon the world's resources which arises when everybody simply strives hard to have 'more'. As we cannot study all resources, I propose to focus attention on one type of resource which is in a somewhat central position—fuel. More prosperity means a greater use of fuel—there can be no doubt about that. At present, the prosperity gap between the poor of this world and the rich is very wide indeed, and this is clearly shown in their respective fuel consumption. Let us define as 'rich' all populations in countries with an average fuel consumption—in 1966—of more than one metric ton of coal equivalent (abbreviated: c.e.) per head, and as 'poor' all those below this level. On these definitions we can draw up the following table (using United Nations figures throughout):

TABLE I (1966)

	Rich	(%)	Poor	(%)	World	(%)
Population (millions)	1,060	(31)	2,284	(69)	3,344	(100)
Fuel Consumption (million tons c.e.)	4,788	(87)	721	(13)	5,509	(100)
Fuel Consumption per head (tons c.e.)	4.52		0.32		1.65	

The average fuel consumption per head of the 'poor' is only 0.32 tons—roughly one-fourteenth of that of the 'rich', and there are very many 'poor' people in the world—on these definitions nearly seven-tenths of the world population. If the 'poor' suddenly used as much fuel as the 'rich', world fuel consumption would treble right away.

But this cannot happen as everything takes time. And in time both the 'rich' and the 'poor' are growing in desires and in numbers. So let us make an exploratory calculation. If the 'rich' populations grow at the rate of 1¼% and the 'poor' at the rate of 2½% a year, world population will grow to about 6,900 million by 2000 A.D.—a figure not very different from the most authorative current forecasts. If at the same time the fuel consumption *per head* of the 'rich' population grows by 2¼%, while that of the 'poor' grows by 4½% a year, the following figures will emerge for the year 2000 A.D.:

TABLE II (2,000 A.D.)

	Rich	(%)	Poor	(%)	World	(%)
Population (millions)	1,617	(23)	5,292	(77)	6,909	(100)
Fuel Consumption (million tons c.e.)	15,588	(67)	7,568	(33)	23,156	(100)
Fuel Consumption per head (tons c.e.)	9.64		1.43		3.35	

These exploratory calculations give rise to a number of comments: Even after more than 30 years of rapid growth, the fuel consumption of the 'poor' would still be at poverty level.

Of the total *increase* of 17,600 million tons c.e. in world fuel consumption (an increase from 5,509 million tons in 1966 to 23,156 million tons in 2000), the 'rich' would take 10,800 million tons and the 'poor' only 6,800 million tons, although the 'poor' would be over three times as numerous as the 'rich'.

The most important comment, however, is a question: Is it plausible to assume that world fuel consumption *could* grow to anything like 23,000 million tons c.e. a year by the year 2000? If this growth took place during the 34 years in question* about £425,000 million tons of c.e. would be used. In the light of our present knowledge of fossil fuel reserves this is an implausible figure, even if we assume that one quarter or one third of the world total would come from nuclear fission.

It is clear that the 'rich' are in the process of stripping the world of its once-for-all endowment of relatively cheap and simple fuels. It is their continuing economic growth which produces ever more exorbitant demands, with the result that the world's cheap and simple fuels could easily become dear and scarce long before the poor countries had acquired the wealth, education, industrial sophistication, and power of capital accumulation needed for the application of nuclear energy on any significant scale.

Exploratory calculations, of course, do not *prove* anything. A *proof* about the future is in any case impossible, and it has been sagely remarked that all predictions are unreliable, particularly those about the future. What is required is judgment, and exploratory calculations can at least help to inform our judgment. In any case, our calculations in a most important respect *understate* the magnitude of the problem. It is not realistic to treat the world as a unit. Fuel resources are very unevenly distributed, and any shortage of supplies, no matter how slight, would immediately divide the world into 'haves' and 'have-nots' along novel lines. The specially favoured areas, such as the Middle East and North Africa, would attract envious attention on a scale scarcely imaginable today, while some high consumption areas, such as Western Europe and Japan, would move into the unenviable position of residual legatees. Here is a source of conflict if ever there was one.

PROBLEM OF POLLUTION

As nothing can be *proved* about the future—not even about the relatively short-term future of the next thirty years—it is always possible to dismiss even the most threatening problems with the suggestion that something will turn up. There could be simply enormous reserves of oil, natural gas, or even coal. And why should nuclear energy be confined to supplying one-quarter or one-third of total requirements? The problem can thus be shifted to another plane, but it refuses to go away. For the consumption of fuel on the indicated scale—assuming no insurmountable difficulties of fuel supply—would produce environmental hazards of an unpre-

* i.e. 1966 (Table I) to 2000 (Table II).

cedented kind.

Take nuclear energy. Some people say that the world's resources of relatively concentrated uranium are insufficient to sustain a really large nuclear programme—large enough to have a significant impact on the world fuel situation, where we have to reckon with thousands of millions, not simply with millions, of tons of coal equivalent. But, assume that these people are wrong. Enough uranium will be found; it will be gathered together from the remotest corners of the earth, brought into the main centres of population, and made highly radioactive. It is hard to imagine a greater biological threat, not to mention the political danger that someone might use a tiny bit of this terrible substance for purposes not altogether peaceful.

On the other hand, if fantastic new discoveries of fossil fuels should make it unnecessary to force the pace of nuclear energy, there would be a problem of pollution on quite a different scale from anything encountered hitherto.

Whatever the fuel, increases in fuel consumption by a factor of four and then five and then six . . . there is no plausible answer to the problem of pollution.

I have taken fuel merely as an example to illustrate a very simple thesis: that economic growth, which viewed from the point of view of economics; physics, chemistry and technology, has no discernible limit, must necessarily run into decisive bottlenecks when viewed from the point of view of the environmental sciences. An attitude to life which seeks fulfilment in the single-minded pursuit of wealth—in short, materialism—does not fit into this world, because it contains within itself no limiting principle, while the environment in which it is placed is strictly limited. Already, the environment is trying to tell us that certain stresses are becoming excessive. As one problem is being 'solved', ten new problems arise as a result of the first 'solution'. As Professor Barry Commoner emphasises, the new problems are not the consequences of incidental failure but of technological success.

Here again, however, many people will insist on discussing these matters solely in terms of optimism and pessimism, taking pride in their own optimism that 'science will find a way out'. They could be right only, I suggest, if there were a conscious and fundamental change in the *direction* of scientific effort. The developments of science and technology over the last hundred years have been such that the dangers have grown even faster than the opportunities. About this, I shall have more to say later.

Already, there is overwhelming evidence that the great self-balancing system of Nature is becoming increasingly unbalanced in particular respects and at specific points. It would take us too far if I attempted to assemble the evidence here. The condition of Lake Erie, to which Professor Barry Commoner, among others, has drawn attention should serve as sufficient warning. Another decade or two, and all the inland water systems of the United States may be in a similar condition. In other words, the condition of unbalance may then no longer apply to specific points but have become generalised. The further this process is allowed to go, the more difficult it will be to reverse it, if indeed the point of no return has not been passed already.

We find, therefore, that the idea of unlimited economic growth, more and more until everybody is saturated with wealth, needs to be seriously questioned on at least two counts: the availability of basic resources and, alternatively or additionally, the capacity of the environment to cope with the degree of interference implied. So much about the physical-material aspect, of the matter. Let us now turn to certain non-material aspects.

There can be no doubt that the idea of personal enrichment has a very strong appeal to human nature. Keynes, in the essay from which I quoted already, advised that the time was not yet for a *"return to some of the most sure and certain principles of religion and traditional virtue—that avarice is a vice, that the exaction of usury is a misdemeanour, and the love of money is detestable"*.

Economic progress, he counselled, is obtainable only if we employ those powerful human drives of selfishness, which religion and traditional wisdom universally call upon us to resist. The modern economy is propelled by a frenzy of greed and indulges in an orgy of envy, and these are not accidental features but the very causes of its expansionist success. The question is whether such causes can be effective for long or whether they carry within themselves the seeds of destruction. If Keynes says that "foul is useful and fair is not", he propounds a statement of fact which may be true or false; or it may look true in the short run and turn out to be false in the longer run. Which is it?

I should think that there is now enough evidence to demonstrate that the statement is false in a very direct, practical sense. If human vices such as greed and envy are systematically cultivated, the inevitable result is nothing less than a collapse of intelligence. A man driven by greed or envy loses the power of seeing things as they really are, of seeing things in their roundness and wholeness, and his very successes become failures. If whole societies become infected by these vices, they may indeed achieve astonishing things but they become increasingly incapable of solving the most elementary problems of everyday existence. The Gross National Product may rise rapidly: as measured by statisticians but not as experienced by actual people, who find themselves oppressed by increasing frustration, alienation, insecurity, and so forth. After a while, even the Gross National Product refuses to rise any further, because of a creeping paralysis of non-co-operation, as expressed in various types of escapism, such as soaring crime, alcoholism, drug addiction, mental breakdown, and open rebellion on the part, not only of the oppressed and exploited, but even of highly privileged groups.

One can go on for a long time deploring the irrationality and stupidity of men and women in high positions or low, "if only people would realise where their real interests lie!" But why do they not realise this? Either because their intelligence has been dimmed by greed and envy, or because in their heart of hearts they understand that their real interests lie somewhere quite different. There is a revolutionary saying that "Man shall not live by bread alone but by every word of God".

Here again, nothing can be 'proved'. But does it still look probable or plausible that the grave social diseases infecting many rich societies today are merely passing phenomena which an able government—if only we could get a really able government!—could eradicate by simply making a better use of science and technology or a more radical use of the penal system?

I suggest that the foundations of peace cannot be laid by universal prosperity, in the modern sense, because such prosperity, if attainable at all, is attainable only by cultivating such drives of human nature as greed and envy, which destroy intelligence, happiness, serenity, and thereby the peacefulness of man. It could well be that rich people treasure peace more highly than poor people, but only if they feel utterly secure—and this is a contradiction in terms. Their wealth depends on making inordinately large demands on limited world resources and thus puts them on an unavoidable collision course—not primarily with the poor (who are weak and defenceless) but with other rich people.

FAR TOO CLEVER

In short, we can say today that man is far too clever to be able to survive without Wisdom. No one is really working for peace unless he is working primarily for the restoration of Wisdom. The assertion that "foul is useful and fair is not" is the antithesis of Wisdom. The hope that the pursuit of goodness and virtue can be postponed until we have attained universal prosperity and that by the single-minded pursuit of wealth, without bothering our heads about spiritual and moral questions, we could establish peace on earth, is an unrealistic, unscientific, and irrational hope. The exclusion of Wisdom from economics, science, and technology was something which we could perhaps get away with for a little while, as long as we were relatively unsuccessful; but now that we have become very successful, the problem of spiritual and moral truth moves into the central position.

From an economic point of view, the central concept of Wisdom is Permanence. We must study the Economics of Permanence. Nothing makes economic sense unless its continuance for a long time can be projected without running into absurdities. There can be 'growth' towards a limited objective, but there cannot be unlimited, generalised growth. It is more than likely, as Gandhi said, that "Earth provides enough to satisfy every man's need, but not for every man's greed". Permanence is incompatible with a predatory attitude which rejoices in the fact that "what were luxuries for our fathers have become necessities for us".

The cultivation and expansion of needs is the antithesis of Wisdom. It is also the antithesis of freedom and peace. Every increase of needs tends to increase one's dependence on outside forces over which one cannot have control, and therefore increases existential fear. Only by a reduction of needs can one promote a genuine reduction in those tensions which are the ultimate causes of strife and war.

The Economics of Permanence implies a profound re-orientation of science and technology, which have to open their doors to Wisdom and, in fact, have to incorporate Wisdom into their very structure. Scientific or technological 'solutions' which poison the environment or degrade the social structure and man himself, are of no benefit, no matter how brilliantly conceived or how great their superficial attraction. Ever bigger machines, entailing ever bigger concentrations of economic power and exerting ever greater violence against the environment do not represent progress: they are a denial of Wisdom. Wisdom demands a new orientation of science and technology towards the organic, the gentle, the non-violent, the elegant and beautiful. Peace, as has often been said, is indivisible—how then could peace be built on a foundation of reckless science and violent technology? We must look for a revolution in technology to give us inventions and machines which reverse the destructive trends now threatening us all.

What is it that we really require from the scientists and technologists? I should answer: We need methods and equipment which are

(a) cheap enough so that they are accessible to virtually everyone;
(b) suitable for small-scale application; and
(c) compatible with man's need for creativity.

Out of these three characteristics is born non-violence and a relationship of man to nature which guarantees permanence. If only one of these three is neglected, things are bound to go wrong. Let us look at them one by one.

Methods and machines cheap enough to be accessible to virtually everyone—why should we assume that our scientists and technologists are unable to develop them? This has been a primary concern of Gandhi's, "I want the dumb millions of our land to be healthy and happy, and I want them to grow spiritually. As yet for this purpose we do not need the machine . . . If we feel the need of machines, we certainly will have them. Every machine that helps every individual has a place," he said, "but there should be no place for machines that concentrate power in a few hands and turn the masses into mere machine minders, if indeed they do not make them unemployed."

Suppose it becomes the acknowledged purpose of inventors and engineers, observed Aldous Huxley, to provide ordinary people with the means of "doing profitable and intrinsically significant work, of helping men and women to achieve independence from bosses, so that they become their own employers, or members of a self-governing, co-operative group working for subsistence and a local market . . . this differently orientated technological progress (would result in) a progressive decentralisation of population, of accessibility of land, of ownership of the means of production, of political and economic power." Other advantages, said Huxley, would be "a more humanly satisfying life for more people, a greater measure of genuine self-governing democracy and a blessed freedom from the silly or pernicious adult education provided by the mass producers of consumer goods through the medium of advertisements."*

SELF-MADE TECHNOLOGY

If methods and machines are to be cheap enough to be generally

* Quoted from *Towards New Horizons* by Pyarelal, a superbly excellent book.

accessible, this means that their cost must stand in some definable relationship to the level of incomes in the society in which they are to be used. I have myself come to the conclusion that the upper limit for the average amount of capital investment *per workplace* is probably given by the annual earnings of an able and ambitious industrial worker. That is to say, if such a man can normally earn, say, £2,000 a year, the average cost of establishing one workplace should on no account be in excess of £2,000. If the cost is significantly higher, the society in question is likely to run into serious troubles, such as an undue concentration of wealth and power among the privileged few; an increasing problem of 'drop-outs' who cannot be integrated into society and constitute an ever-growing threat; 'structural' unemployment; maldistribution of the population due to excessive urbanisation and general frustration and alienation, with soaring crime rates, etc.

To choose the appropriate level of technology is an absolutely vital matter for the (so-called) developing countries. It is in this connection that, some ten years ago, I began to talk of 'intermediate technology', and very energetic work has since been undertaken by the Intermediate Technology Development Group in London, and by others, to identify, develop and apply in developing countries a genuine self-help technology which involves the mass of the people, and not just the privileged few, which promotes the real independence of former colonial territories, and not just political independence nullified by economic subservience, and which thereby attempts to lay at least some of the essential foundations of freedom and peace.

The second requirement is suitability for small-scale application. On the problem of 'scale', Professor Leopold Kohr has written brilliantly and convincingly, and I do not propose to do more than emphasise its relevance to the Economics of Permanence. Small-scale operations, no matter how numerous, are always less likely to be harmful to the natural environment than large-scale ones, simply because their individual force is small in relation to the recuperative forces of nature. There is Wisdom in smallness if only on account of the smallness and patchiness of human knowledge, which relies on experiment far more than on understanding. The greatest danger invariably arises from the ruthless application, on a vast scale, of partial knowledge, such as we are currently witnessing in the application of nuclear energy, of the new chemistry in agriculture, of transportation technology, and countless other things.

Although even small communities are sometimes guilty of causing serious erosion, generally as a result of ignorance, this is trifling in comparison with the devastations caused by large organisations motivated by greed, envy and lust for power. It is moreover obvious that men organised in small units will take better care of *their* bit of land or other natural resources than anonymous companies or megalomanic governments which pretend to themselves that the whole universe is their legitimate quarry.

CREATIVITY

The third requirement is perhaps the most important of all—that methods and equipment should be such as to leave ample room for human creativity. Over the last hundred years no one has spoken more insistently and warningly on this subject than have the Roman pontiffs. What becomes of man if the process of production "takes away from work any hint of humanity, making of it a merely mechanical activity?" The worker himself is turned into a perversion of a free being.

"*And so bodily labour* (said Pius XI) *which even after original sin was decreed by Providence for the good of man's body and soul, is in many instances changed into an instrument of perversion; for from the factory dead matter goes out improved, whereas men there, are corrupted and degraded.*"

Again, the subject is so large that I cannot do more than touch upon it. Above anything else there is need for a proper philosophy of work which understands work not as that which it has indeed become, an inhuman chore as soon as possible to be abolished by automation, but as something "decreed by Providence for the good of man's body and soul". Next to the family, it is work and the relationships established by work that are the true foundations of society. If the foundations are unsound, how could society be sound? And if society is sick, how could it fail to be a danger to peace?

"War is a judgment that overtakes societies when they have been living upon ideas that conflict too violently with the laws governing the universe . . . Never think that wars are irrational catastrophies: they happen when wrong ways of thinking and living bring about intolerable situations." (Dorothy L. Sayers in *Creed or Chaos?*). Economically, our wrong living consists primarily in systematically cultivating greed and envy and thus building up a vast array of totally unwarrantable wants. It is the sin of Greed that has delivered us over into the power of the machine. If Greed were not the master of modern man—ably assisted by envy—how could it be that the frenzy of economism does not abate as higher 'standards of living' are attained, and that it is precisely the richest societies which pursue their economic advantage with the greatest ruthlessness? How could we explain the almost universal refusal on the part of the rulers of the rich societies—whether organised along private enterprise or collectivist enterprise lines—to work towards *the humanisation of work?* It is only necessary to assert that something would reduce the "standard of living", and every debate is instantly closed. That soul-destroying, meaningless, mechanical, monotonous, moronic work is an insult to human nature which must necessarily and inevitably produce either escapism or aggression, and that no amount of "bread and circuses" can compensate for the damage done—these are facts which are neither denied nor acknowledged but are met with an unbreakable conspiracy of silence—because to deny them would be too obviously absurd and to acknowledge them would condemn the central preoccupation of modern society as a crime against humanity.

The neglect, indeed the rejection of Wisdom, has gone so far that most of our intellectuals have not even the faintest idea what the term could mean. As a result, they always tend to try and cure a disease by intensifying its causes. The disease having been caused by allowing cleverness to displace Wisdom, no amount of clever research is likely to produce a cure. But what is Wisdom? Where can it be found? Here we come to the crux of the matter: it can be read about in numerous publications but it can be *found* only inside oneself. To be able to find it, one has first to liberate oneself interiorly from such masters as greed and envy. The stillness following liberation—even if only momentary—produces the insights of Wisdom which are obtainable in no other way.

They enable us to see the hollowness and fundamental unsatisfactoriness of a life devoted primarily to the pursuit of material ends, to the neglect of the spiritual. Such a life necessarily sets man against man and nation against nation, because man's needs are infinite and infinitude can be achieved only in the spiritual realm, never in the material. Man assuredly needs to rise above this humdrum 'world'; Wisdom shows him the way to do it; without Wisdom, he is driven to build up a monster economy, which destroys the world, and to seek fantastic satisfactions, like landing a man on the moon. Instead of over-coming the 'world' by moving towards saintliness, he tries to overcome it by gaining pre-eminence in wealth, power, science or indeed any imaginable 'sport'.

These are the real causes of war, and it is chimerical to try and lay the foundations of peace without removing them first. It is doubly chimerical to build peace on economic foundations which, in turn, rest on the systematic cultivation of greed and envy, the very forces which drive men into conflict.

How could we even begin to disarm greed and envy? Perhaps by being much less greedy and envious ourselves; perhaps by resisting the temptation of letting our luxuries become needs; and perhaps by even scrutinising our needs; to see if they cannot be simplified and reduced. If we do not have the strength to do any of this, could we perhaps stop applauding the type of economic "progress" which palpably lacks the basis of permanence and give what modest support we can to those who, unafraid of being denounced as cranks, work for non-violence: as conservationists, ecologists, protectors of wild life, promoters of organic agriculture, distributists, cottage producers, and so forth? An ounce of practice is generally worth more than a ton of theory.

A LIVING FAITH

It will need many ounces, however, to lay the economic foundations of peace. Where can one find the strength to go on working against such obviously appalling odds? What is more: where can one find the strength to overcome the violence of greed, envy, hate and lust within oneself?

I think Gandhi has given the answer: "There must be recognition of the existence of the soul apart from the body and of its permanent nature, and this recognition must amount to a living faith; and, in the last resort, non-violence does not avail those who do not possess a living faith in the God of Love."

ENVIRONMENTAL LAWS
ROY and JANE DARKE

Jane and Roy Darke both trained in architecture at University College, London. Jane Darke went on to read for a higher degree in Sociology at the University of Essex; Roy Darke to read for a higher degree in Urban and Regional Planning Studies at LSE. They are jointly preparing a review of literature relating to human behaviour and environment, the research being funded by the Centre for Environmental Studies and the Royal Institute of British Architects. Roy Darke is currently a lecturer in the Department of Town and Regional Planning at Sheffield University.

If harmony or conflict largely depends on our environment, are there environmental laws which affect us?

What is the relationship between the environment and human behaviour? How can an understanding of environmental laws be used to improve the environment present and future?

By environment we mean all those factors external to the individual which actually or potentially affect his behaviour. In this essay we are concentrating on the environment at the scale of the home and neighbourhood. Of course, the individual is affected at other levels, for example by environmental pollution, and in other settings, such as the work environment. But the environment of the home and neighbourhood has a particular salience for most people, and the relationship between this environment and individual behaviour is peculiarly complex because of the interplay between *physical, social* and *cultural* components.

Physical and social elements of the environment present no serious definitional problems. The third aspect is more difficult, because cultural environment includes both physical and social components. Culture is generally taken to mean the knowledge, habits, beliefs and laws which a society inherits from past generations. It is transmitted by agents of socialization such as the family, the educational system, and formal or informal groups to which we belong. The cultural environment consists both of objects as symbols, and ideas, ways of behaving, etc.

In searching for environmental laws we are basically looking for the important factors in the individual's environment which affect his behaviour. If he is dissatisfied with his environment in the widest sense, then as scientists we should isolate the specific causes and hence formulate policies to reduce his dissatisfaction. The search for causality between the environment and human behaviour has been the subject of various studies which we have recently attempted to summarise. Different disciplines stress different parts of the environment as the main independent variables which result in certain behaviour. The sociologists have generally stressed the socio-cultural aspects of environment as the main constraints on our lives and have described how we are moulded by and adapt to the social structure and the social system. The disciplines which stress the physical environment have tended to see things in a slightly different way. Architects, physical planners and geographers have considered or assumed that physical factors have a major determining effect on human behaviour and the human condition.

To take an example. British town planning grew out of the social reform movement of the 19th century which was mobilised in response to the rapid urbanisation of an industrialising nation. Urbanisation brought poor housing conditions to the public eye and it was noticed that poor housing was accompanied by poverty, disease, vice and other social ills. The reformists and their followers, the planners, believed that improvement in the physical environment would lead to an improvement in these other social problems. The physical environment was seen as the causal factor in social malaise.

The sociologist, on the other hand, has argued that improving the physical environment will not materially affect the main problems that the poor working-class family is faced with. The causative factors behind the low income, unemployment, poor health and so on among these disadvantaged groups is seen to lie in the social and economic structure of society. If society accepts that some jobs carry low financial rewards, then the result will be that a section of the population has a struggle to make ends meet. According to this argument, the behaviour of individuals and families in slum housing arises, not from the depressant effects of the poor physical environment but mainly as a functional adjustment to a particular set of circumstances and expectations which the social system offers.

This extreme example is often taken to prove the point that the physical element of environment is a very weak or even neutral factor in the total man/environment relationship. However, it is very dangerous to argue general laws from single cases. There are other studies which show that friendship patterns on housing estates can develop in ways which are largely caused by the physical layout of the estate. The way paths run, the position of external door compared to those of neighbours and other design factors all seem to affect social behaviour among the residents, given that they have certain specific social characteristics.

It is important to make the analytical distinction between physical, social and cultural environments. In any real situation, however, the different aspects of environment are all acting simultaneously and may be inextricably mixed in the individual's consciousness. Perhaps we can use a simple example of this. Studies of working class families who have been forced by redevelopment to move from an area in which they have lived for a considerable part of their lives have shown that they experience a great emotional upheaval. Often there is great misgiving and regret at having to leave the home, sometimes even distress and grief, as if the family were losing one of its members. The affective reaction comes not only from the loss of the physical environment or the social environment of neighbours and friends, but rather is an emotional response to the combined loss. It is extremely difficult to separate these aspects of environment from each other. There is other evidence of the overlap between physical and social environments in the way that people are able to describe their local neighbourhood. These descriptions embrace physical and social components.

We are arguing that in some extreme cases it is possible to attribute aspects of human behaviour almost completely to elements in the physical or the social environment. This leaves a great many studies of the Man/environment relationship where the casual relationship is not at all clear. Much seemingly contradictory evidence can be found in this extensive middle area.

Turning to the behaviour side of the relationship, we must distinguish two aspects of behaviour, which Gans has called "behavioural norm" and "situational response". Behavioural norms are desired patterns of behaviour, which the environment may or may not allow the individual to follow. For example, a housewife might want to be friendly with neighbours without appearing socially aggressive, but may be prevented from being so if the layout of her housing estate does not provide for casual contacts on neutral territory. A situational response, on the other hand, is a mode of behaviour which is forced on the individual by the environment but is not desired by the individual. For example, a family may be forced to live a long way outside the city where the breadwinner works, because of lack of suitable housing closer in. A study of the relationship between environment and behaviour is meaningless unless we distinguish which aspects of behaviour are situational responses and which behavioural norms. Having made these distinctions, it is still not a straightforward task to discover the causal relationships between environment and behaviour. One of the fundamental facts of social science is that many forms of causal relationship may be found and not least among these is multi-causality. Nonetheless, this is no reason to abandon the attempt to explain the complex relationships involved. One of the great dangers in this search for explanation is that we may attribute spurious relevance to certain factors. People may be extremely critical of the physical environment when they move into new houses but the underlying deficiency may lie in the social environment. The initial period after moving house is when contacts with neighbours are made. These contacts may be developed or may lapse according to the impressions gained from the first few chance contacts. If the newly arrived family meets hostility from neighbours after being used to a very gregarious social life they may feel very unhappy. This dissatisfaction might be rationalised into complaints against minor deficiencies in the house, but the main cause lies in the unsympathetic social environment. On the other hand, several studies have shown that given a good social environment among neighbours, quite drastic physical deficiencies in the home will be considered largely unimportant. One study of a very socially cohesive neighbourhood found that one family who had to take action stations against roof leaks whenever there was a heavy storm did not feel that this was important, and it did not seem to affect their satisfaction with living in the house. This "halo effect" suggests that advantages or disadvantages in the environment may interact with each other so that we cannot take questionnaire responses at their face value. We need to know a great deal about people's attitudes, past experiences and other background details as well as their aspirations for the future.

It would seem to be a gigantic task to attempt to understand the relationship between human behaviour and the physical, social and cultural environments, but there are some important steps in that direction. We have outlined a few of these above, though inevitably at the present state of knowledge we have done more to show up the problems than to provide the answers.

Some important characteristics of human behaviour deserve underlining. Firstly, the human ability to adjust and adapt to different circumstances means that any environmental laws we might evolve will not be invariant. Apart from this, we all have the capacity to choose among courses of action. This choice will be more or less limited according to the particular activity, by social structure, by norms of behaviour, and so on. Environmental laws involving man will therefore almost without exception be probabilistic.

This fact of human choice is a crucial one in the social sciences. We want to go beyond the scientific objectivity which we have attempted to bring to the discussion so far. There is wide disagreement on the question of whether as scientists, people within the social sciences should make value judgments on society. We can personally see no worth in knowledge if it is not used to some practical purpose. We are all involved in the human condition and should be committed to alleviating the problems of those groups who get a bad deal. We are not advocating change for its own sake, but where change is desired by those groups who are constrained from fulfilling their human potential then we should set about undermining the causes of these constraints and alleviating the problems of the disadvantaged. Here we think the whole question of choice is fundamental to society in the future. The ability of society, as a collectivity, to make decisions about its future seems to be nearer and more feasible than ever before. We agree with scholars like T.S. Simey and Amitai Etzioni who believe that man can begin rewriting social laws. Etzioni refers to the way in which man is no longer a passive observer watching a world beyond his control. The scientific approach to knowledge serves an important role in this active orientation, for it is knowledge that is needed in sharpening society's consciousness, in making objectives clearer and more realistic and in ensuring that the active society does not become another example of the few controlling the many.

We ought to have accepted by now that in a pluralistic society, conflicts will inevitably occur. Perhaps we should try to ensure that these conflicts are overt and not hidden, so that issues get an airing and are not left to ferment. Of course, in such a simplistic exposition we beg too many crucial and fundamental questions, such as who holds the power, and how do we ensure that there is less exploitation and differential access to resources? There are many object lessons to be learned from the way that many issues brought into the public consciousness are only aggravated because the existing social, political and economic structure will not accept the implications of policies aimed to alleviate some of the social problems within society. Recent citizen participation in policy formation and planning in the United States seems mainly to have shown the disadvantaged that their position relative to the rest of American society is very poor. Few actual changes in their social and economic positions have occurred. The power situation was not fully considered from the outset, and the result is mainly increased frustration and disenchantment. We must consider both ends and means in our efforts to improve the environment.

Perhaps there is little hope for consensus about many of the issues that present themselves. Indeed, consensus may not be a desirable goal, but at least we will have to agree to aim for a society which allows for and can contain conflict. In a free society we should try to solve some of the major environmental deficiencies which limit the freedom of others. In the example above, of poor families in slum housing, our main object of concern is the social and economic structure. Physical environmental improvement alone may improve the life-situation of this sort of family very little. Yet slum families are not a homogeneous group. Some families may suffer from chronic unemployment due to ill health or low skills. Their main worries are low wages and/or job permanence. Other families may be suffering some temporary setback. A change of housing environment for these families may mean a great deal in terms of enhanced self-esteem, and help pull them through a rough patch more quickly. For economically safe families, physical environment and immediate social environment may be important factors in their satisfaction with their life-situation. Further up the social scale the immediate environment may be less important because these more affluent families have cars and telephones and so have the means to choose and maintain friendships over long spatial distances. We should not forget, of course, that the home and neighbourhood as pieces of physical environment have prestige value as well as being purely functional. This is the cultural element again.

The person applying environmental knowledge in design and policy making must consider all these aspects simultaneously. Certainly there seems to be very little point in rehousing people in better physical conditions if we cause them distress by destroying meaningful and vital social environments. This sort of thing has happened often, as numerous reports indicate, possibly because a good or bad social environment is less easy to recognise and measure than is physical environment. The converse possibility of providing better social environment with much less good physical conditions is much less common or even likely. People are largely their own agents in arranging their social environments, though they are not all equally skilled at this. Some groups are fairly easily satisfied, while others have more exacting requirements and so are often found to be dissatisfied. Examples are young families or the disabled. Planners and policy makers should be particularly aware of the social as well as the physical needs of such groups.

For all groups, the long term aim must be in overall improvement of both physical and social environments, (improvements of course must be as defined by those affected by that particular environment) with the proviso that the opportunity for choice between alternatives is ensured.

The real task is to use our understanding of environmental laws to set up a situation in which all groups can fulfil their personal potential. Stein has made the assumption "that human groups exist to provide their members with full opportunities for personal development through experimentation. This experimentation presupposes sufficient openness in personal identity so that an expanding range of possibilities is appreciated, sufficient enclosure in personal identity so that an integral personal style gradually evolves and sufficient dramatic perspective so that alien styles espoused by others can be appreciated without weakening ones own commitment." One of the major tasks in changing the environment is to help ensure that inequalities in environmental circumstances are reduced and hopefully eliminated, so that we all have opportunity for such individual development. We should not be concerned that the resulting physical and social environment will be one of monotony and sameness. On the contrary, given equal opportunity it is likely that we shall foster increasing diversity in personal and community styles.

Small intimate fact-to-face groups are an important source of personal satisfaction and identity. If the wider community plays a part in this process of self awareness and tolerance, so does the small group provide a nurturing social environment. We need the opportunity for interpersonal relationships on all scales as well as facilities for privacy and quiet to satisfy our personal and social needs. We think this aim of personal fulfilment implies a partial devolution of power to much smaller units; contrary to the present trend towards aggregation of political and administrative units. Of course, there are some functions best carried out at regional, national or international levels, but individuals and groups should have maximum possible control of their own environment.

The above chapter forms the basis of a larger article to be published later.

Further Reading:

1. Etzioni. A. (1968) *The Active Society* London & New York. Collier-MacMillan Limited.

2. Festinger L. Schachter S. & Back K. (1950) *Social Pressures in Informal Groups* New York. Harper & Bros.
3. Fried M. & Levin J. (1968) Some social functions of the urban slum in Frieden B.J. and Morris R. (eds) (1968) *Urban Planning and Social Policy* New York Basic Books.
4. Gans H.J. (1961) Suburbs and Planners *Landscape* Vol. XI No. 1. pp. 23-24.
5. Gans H.J. (1963) Social and Physical Planning for the Elimination of Urban Poverty. *Washington University Law Quarterly* No. 1. (February) pp. 2-18, and in Frieden B.J. and Morris R. (eds). op. cit.
6. Hall E.T. (1966) *The Hidden Dimension* New York. Doubleday and Co. Inc.
7. Jennings H. (1960) *Societies in the making* London Routledge & Kegan Paul.
8. Kuper L. (1953) Blueprint for living together, in Kuper L. (ed) *Living in Towns* London Cresset Press.
9. Rein M. and Marris P. (1968) Poverty and the Community Planner's Mandate, in Frieden B.J. and Morris R. op. cit.
10. Simey T.S. (1968) *Social Science and Social Purpose* London. Constable & Co.,
11. Stein M. (1960) *The Eclipse of Community,* Princetown University Press.
12. Townsend P. (1957) *The Family Life of Old People* London. Routledge & Kegan Paul.
13. Young M. & Willmott P. (1957) *Family and Kinship in East London* London. Routledge & Kegan Paul.

MAN AND THE BALANCE OF NATURE

ROBERT WALLER

Associate editor of the *Ecologist;* author of *Be Human or Die*--a study of ecological humanism (Charles Knight, 1973).

Attitudes of mind toward nature have determined our treatment of the countryside and how we have farmed. First man thought he was a part of nature and even participated in the revolutions of the sun. Then he thought he stood apart from nature and that nature was simply a mechanical thing. Is nature 'It' or 'Thou'? The problem of today is to strike a balance between the personal and the impersonal attitudes to nature. Our survival may depend upon our understanding nature and ourselves as the creation of mind. This will mean determining in what respects we can treat nature as a mechanism, and in what respects as a living organism or creature. In this article Robert Waller traces the history of our changes of belief about nature.

Primitive people live primarily in the imagination: they project upon the world the image of their own feelings and where we would explain natural events by a chain of causes they explain them by motives, as if everything acted from personal intention. To explain nature in mechanical terms is thus inconceivable, just as it still is to a young child. The sun goes to bed at night and rises in the morning because it reigns over its kingdom or because some greater god has ordered it to give light and warmth to the world. Some primitive people talk to the sun and worry about whether it might not feel too tired to fulfil its duties: they perform magical rites, such as turning cartwheels to remind it of its diurnal course—and to show a sympathetic participation in the cosmic life. Fertility rites, which have no effect whatsoever on the soil and are technically valueless, share in the life and death of the seasons. For primitive man has this curious sense, this intuition, that unless he plays his part in the total personal drama of existence, it may all suddenly stop, almost as if the gods said, "O.K., if you aren't interested, neither are we: we have other concerns: to Hell with you." In such a universe in which everything was addressed as 'Thou', holding the attention of the higher powers was emotionally exhausting: much more exhausting than dealing with the 'It' of an impersonal material universe. Nevertheless as it was dramatic and poetic, even when evil from our point of view, this strange drama was a necessary part of our inner development: it drew out of our depths many latent feelings and imaginative powers now civilised by reflection. When this universe, however, failed to deliver the goods—as it did, for when we pray for rain, rain only comes by coincidence—we were thrown further back into our inner life as it exists wrenched apart from that of the universe as a whole. When we come to the men who wrote the myth of Genesis, self-consciousness was already quite highly developed. We don't always realise that when we become conscious of our own individual existence we are simultaneously aware of everything else as an object as well. The continuation of this kind of thought which discriminates between the thinker and what he is thinking about, leads to an ever greater separation of man, nature and god.

However, this objective-consciousness which has reached its highest development in modern science has always been interfused with older forms of consciousness and we cannot draw any neat historical lines of development.

Around 700 B.C. when Genesis was written and when the myths of the Greeks were coming to birth there was no doubt that the emerging gift of self-conscious thought—which had expelled man from Eden—was making him gloomy about his own condition. The Genesis myth and the myth of the Golden Age both reflect a deep sense of guilt that man had cut himself off from god and nature, and lost, as it were, the spontaneous intercourse with the higher powers and was being punished for it in the worst possible way—by having to think everything out for himself. And then making mistakes and then being punished—usually in what seemed to be a capricious and irrational way, for which there was no explanation, so that all that men could do was to submit and acknowledge that the gods knew best.

Wasn't it perfectly natural that when man first cultivated the soil and the crop yields dropped year by year that he should have thought he had thrown a curse over nature and the gods were angry? There is nothing unreasonable about this, given a lack of technical knowledge and a belief in a personal universe. It is excellent logic.

We must understand two things: first how the primitive Garden of Eden attitude of mind—which treated all events as having a personal or supra-personal motivation—prevented men from thinking about the universe objectively: and secondly what a prodigious effort it was to transcend it. We can oversimplify this very complex development by saying that the dividing line is the difference between pre-technological and technological civilisations.

Plato, the greatest of the early metaphysicians, had already begun to think technologically both about the nature of matter and the soul. In *The Critias* he says that the soils of Attica must once have been much more fertile as they had maintained a greater proportion of citizens, that indeed Athens owed its growth and power to the fertility of its soils. But now these soils were declining in fertility. And the reason for this was, he said, that the forests on the mountain slopes had been cut down without—and I quote—'digging in such a way as to prevent the rain carrying away the soil.' No fertility rites here; instead a straightforward recommendation that there should be research into techniques for preventing soil erosion. Unfortunately the suggestion was not followed up. Perhaps an older way of looking at nature prevented the farmers from understanding what Plato meant. His superiority as a thinker was due to the fact that he was as interested in *how* we think as in *what* we think about. All revolutions in thought have this philosophic foundation. You can go on thinking for ever in an old mode and only ramify old errors: some of us think the pre-ecological residue of scientists do that.

In the classical world there was a great debate as to whether the earth was like an ageing mother who was becoming barren through too much child-bearing, or whether she was potentially fertile for ever. The poet Lucretius took first one side and then the other: which annoyed Columella, the famous agrarian writer of the first century A.D. To rebuke Lucretius he asserted categorically that if the fertility of the earth failed, this could only be because we had done violence to it by our methods of husbandry. What we need to prevent Mother Earth from becoming barren, he asserted, is good husbandry—especially composted manure!

As rural discipline and feeling for the land decayed when the Roman people became more urban, it also became easier for the agroindustrialists of the time to use slaves like machines—without protest from the people and the state. Columella's cry of despair was too late: the soils of the Roman Empire were condemned to a destructive cereal monoculture under the influence of social and economic changes. 'The fertility of Sicily went down the sewers of Rome,' says Victor Hugo—with terrible social consequences to Sicilian society. The knowledge of good husbandry that the Romans had used in the great Republican days when Cincinnatus, the Roman dictator, made a living off 2½ acres, was swept aside.

The interplay of husbandry, philosophy, religion and social change goes on all the time: it is not so easy to separate them as one might suppose. They build up into an attitude of mind. Systems of ownership and communal organisation play as big a part as agricultural knowledge in what happens to the land. The manorial open field system for instance was bound to decline in fertility for open fields prevented intensive grazing and one fallow after two cereal crops was not enough to restore lost nutrients to the land: so the system was bound to run down. Nevertheless, it was part of a communal organisation that given feudalism was just to the cultivator. Unfortunately it was the rapacious sheep farmers who displaced the peasant when the Feudal system crumbled; nevertheless the sheep farmers arrested the decline and restored the fertility of the land by putting it down to grass, though they did not know that they were restoring fertility. In agriculture man as often as not has done the right thing with the meanest intentions and the wrong things with the best of intentions. To reconcile social justice, economic opportunity and good husbandry, we must learn the laws of nature—for they do not change. So that in the long run necessity is not economics but ecology.

What is the basic principle of good husbandry? It is to realise that if a living system such as the earth is to persist and not disintegrate it must replace its losses with something equivalent. Equivalent is the important word here: not something almost equivalent, for in that case it will run down, although it may take a long time. Now we have analysed so much of nature, surely we know how to return as much as we have taken out?

On the contrary I think our system may be running down because analytical logic selects from the whole pattern of nature one or two primary causes to which it attaches excessive significance, such as sex in the personal life, economics in society, and N.P.K. in plant growth. The variety of life is thus over simplified—for example, the fact that chemical fertilizers feed the plant but not the soil is overlooked: yet a good soil structure is necessary to make the best use of fertilizers, otherwise the humus-clay particles will not hold the nutrients in store. Unless we follow nature's example and feed the soil as well as the plant, the system must run down in the long run. I notice that Dr. Jacks in his excellent book on soil says that we must put up with humus until we can discover how to do without it. I submit that we shall never be able to construct a substitute for humus by intellectual analyses because the total process of growth and decomposition is too complex and dynamic to be recorded in exact detail. I believe that the idea that we shall be able to do it marks the extreme limit of the use of our intellect—and is a delusion. The source of this delusion is the assumption that we can take nature to pieces like a machine and then use the parts to reconstruct it in forms more convenient to our economy.

Life is a principle of order that holds together forces which are of themselves unstable: if we change the relationships too radically the order collapses and the organism dies. We can see for ourselves that when life abandons any organism it disintegrates: and when it disintegrates it returns to more stable and simple forms conforming to the laws of chemistry and physics. Only some superimposed order we call LIFE could have prevented this happening before, unless we hold there is no difference between a living organism and a decaying one. As scientists can't account for the extraordinary way Life builds up a new order out of the atoms and molecules, they ignore the fact that there is a problem. Nevertheless, modern ecological thinking is having to abandon the old explanations in terms of a chain of mechanical cause and effect and think instead in terms of living systems; in such systems everything goes-with everything else under the rule of the purpose served by the system—the thinkers of the organic movement have always accepted this purposive logic—the logic of the ORDER imposed by life. Their contention that soil-plant-animal, and man, must be considered as one complex in which everything goes-with everything else conforms to the ecological logic now emerging among advanced thinkers. It is true, of course, that soil, plant, animal and man are not an organism in the same enclosed sense that any one of the chain is an organism in its own right. When we say the earth is a living organism we are thinking metaphorically. Nevertheless the earth in the sense of soil, air, water, sunlight and so on, sustains organic life: it is the home of multitudes of living organisms which not only have their own purpose but which co-operate in larger purposes. Without this larger environment the ORDER OF LIFE could not be maintained in each separate organism. We must, therefore, learn to think what part everything plays, for example in a lake or a river, to keep every organism in it alive— and the same with the soil. The order of life can easily be destroyed and then the organic breaks down into the inorganic— death.

An imaginative grasp of this unity of life explains why the organically minded tend to be tolerant of pre-technological attitudes, sensing in them certain valid intuitions. The idea of Mother Earth is not so embarrassing to an organic thinker as to a mechanistic scientist, because it symbolises the idea of the earth as an organism with a productive function. Obviously this does not mean that we literally speak to the earth as 'Thou' or attribute human feelings to it. But it does mean that we perceive it has a life that is 'in some ways' similar to our own: it is like us in some respects, for instance it breathes and feeds. This unity of all life enables us to draw some general conclusions which are universally valid for all living things. Since all living things must exist as part of the earth's community, they are affected by what happens to other living things. The laws of evolution demonstrate this in a startling way. If, for example, we substitute a chemical poison for a predator—probably because we have already destroyed the predator—we succeed in killing the susceptible individuals which may be the majority, but the few that through genetic peculiarities are not killed survive as the parents of succeeding immune generations. Thus we have neither chemical nor predator to play an essential part in the biological balance and we are left with an uncontrollable pest.

As we cannot hope to discern and record every single instance of immunity to antibiotics or other biocides, it is a proper scientific procedure to respect the general law on the assumption that life is a unified process: that the same thing will always happen sooner or later. If this is the case, then the destruction of pests, weeds and even diseases by chemical means must be looked upon as a temporary measure to be used while we investigate the deeper biological causes, as for instance the manner in which methods of husbandry have departed too far from the natural processes of growth. It is dangerous to ignore all relationships between the chemical and its victim which extend beyond the death of the victim by the chemical. To take account of the many ways in which the chemical and its intended target are both parts of a dynamic, interchanging bio-chemical pattern is not yet fundamental to our scientific tradition. Until it is, man is not playing his proper part in agriculture.

Although it would be absurd to suggest we should return to pre-technological attitudes to nature such as I have described, it is possible that in our effort to transcend them we have allowed feelings and thoughts to drop out of our minds which are essential to understanding nature. Is this a reason why we have been spellbound by the analytic approach and not sufficiently critical of its defects? Why have we found it so easy to forget the unity of life? It is at least worth putting this question to ourselves.

When the Jesuits went to China, the inhabitants were astonished to see some of them jump overboard to rescue a drowning Chinese. To them this was wholly irrational and without any justification. Why save the life of somebody you don't even know? Your duty was only to be responsible for your family and clan. The Jesuit's answer was because all men belong to the same clan under the Fatherhood of God. How you act then depends upon what you believe about the nature of creation. Those who believe that man, animals and the landscape are also part of one total creation sharing in the same intelligence act differently to those who believe that nature is simply a mechanism stuck outside man to serve him like an automatic cafeteria.

One reason why people of good will have been deceived about this is because there *is* part of life that can be explained mechanistically, another which is organic and a third which is intellectual or spiritual. All these fields are complementary and interact: but if we invert their value or eliminate any of them we make machines or monsters of ourselves. Even a purely spiritual world is monstrous. I am sure the more balanced civilisations of the future will consider our attitude to nature as barbarous—anyway as reflected in our management of our environment. We shall be forced into thinking about our planet as one biological organism which is host to man. If he kills his host, he kills himself.

Further Reading:

Prophet of the New Age, biography of Sir George Stapledon—a life of an agrarian philosopher—by Robert Waller (Faber & Faber).

Human Ecology, by Sir George Stapledon, edited by Robert Waller (Charles Knight).

Soil and Civilization, by Edward Hyams (Thames and Hudson).

Science and Survival, by Barry Commoner (Cape).

Ecology, Food and Civilization, by Harry Walters (Charles Knight).

The Eco-Activists, by Michael Allaby (Charles Knight).

Be Human or Die, a study of the impact of ecology on humanism, by Robert Waller. (Charles Knight).

The Closing Circle, by Barry Commoner (Cape).

PART TWO

NATURAL LAWS IN PRACTICE

TRUTH

Truth is probably the most important ingredient in our search for peace. Truth has many, many sides but all penetrate to man's inner conscience and creates the "climate of opinion" which, in turn, dictates the actions of those who hold power.

The following chapters discuss education, man's conscience, straight thinking, the police and the law, and the necessity for beauty.

EDUCATION AND PEACE — THE POTENTIALITIES OF UNESCO

H. L. ELVIN

Head of Education Department UNESCO 1950-56; Director of London Institute of Education since 1958.

Is UNESCO doing as much as it should, more or less directly, for the promotion of peace through the rule of law and for international understanding?

The United Nations Educational, Scientific and Cultural Organisation (UNESCO) exists to promote education, science and culture through international action. But it has an additional obligation which probably seemed even more important to its founders: it is expected to promote peace and international understanding *through* education, science and culture.

Much of the frustration from which UNESCO suffers comes from this complexity of its double task and from the unfavourable atmosphere in which it has to discharge the second.

It is not surprising, given the present state of the world, that the member countries should be thinking more of their defence and of their alliances than of education and science disinterestedly considered or of persuading their young people to form a sentiment of sympathy and solidarity with all mankind.

In this paper I shall note what the Constitution says about the responsibilities of UNESCO in this matter, look at what it has done and is now doing, and then discuss its potentialities in greater detail.

UNESCO was established immediately after the end of the second world war. Its founders were acutely conscious that in Hitler's Germany, Mussolini's Italy and Imperial Japan education had been grossly perverted. It had been used to instil in the minds of the young aggressive nationalism, and a belief in the rightness of authoritarian regimes which ruthlessly crushed the critical conscience of those who protested. Education had been used for war; it must now be used for peace. It had been used for aggressive nationalism; it must now be used to promote the conception of a world-wide community of peoples. Accordingly it is not surprising to find that the first Article of the Constitution of UNESCO runs as follows:—

"The purpose of the Organisation is to contribute to peace and security by promoting collaboration among the nations through education, science and culture in order to further universal respect for justice, for the rule of law and for the human rights and fundamental freedoms which are affirmed for the peoples of the world, without distinction of race, sex, language, or religion, by the Charter of the United Nations."

The second Article goes on to say how this is to be done: by advancing mutual understanding, helping to spread popular education and culture, and maintaining, increasing and diffusing knowledge.

This sounds excellent. But the construction of the long sentence that constitutes the first Article is an odd one. UNESCO is to contribute to peace by promoting collaboration among the nations. This implies that if they collaborate that itself will contribute to peace—a tenable view. But then they are to collaborate not "in" but "through" education, science and culture. And they are to do this "in order to" further justice, the rule of law, etc. In fact, this Article is thoroughly confused. Latent in it are two ideas, which might be thought of as twins or as quite distinct from one another. The first is that UNESCO is to promote education throughout the world and that this in itself, but indirectly, will be its contribution to peace. The other is that the purpose of its work in education must be the promotion of the things for which the UN Charter stands (peace, security, the rule of law, fundamental freedoms and qualities and the like): in other words it is to further all these things directly, not indirectly, through education, science and culture.

If these two purposes are twins, they are not identical twins. The emphasis, in speeches about UNESCO and in defence of its work, was in its early days on the second purpose. All sorts of things it did, had to be defended at its Conferences on the ground that they contributed to peace—even its modest studies in child development, even its more grandiose plans for combating ignorance and low standards of living (then called 'fundamental education'). Yet if you use the real test, the proportion of the budget that has gone to direct educational action to promote peace and international understanding, you find that this has never been its major activity. And it has become less so. More and more it has been agreed that the major task of UNESCO is the advancement of education in the low-income countries. If an innocent enquirer wanted to ascertain what proportion of UNESCO funds went to the direct effort to promote peace and international understanding through the schools, the universities and adult education, he would no doubt look up the appropriate section of the

Education Chapter of the biennial Programme and Budget. This is headed 'Education for International Understanding, Co-operation and Peace'. For the biennium 1969-70 he would find against this entry the figure of $317,225. This is a tiny proportion of the regular budget allocation to Education alone, $16,337,907. At the present time one may say that both in terms of pronouncements as to what UNESCO should be doing, and in terms of hard cash, the direct promotion of peace and international understanding through education would seem to be quite a small part of the Organisation's total effort.

Let me hasten to add that it would not be fair to regard this as the whole of the story. There are many activities that are in pursuance of the purpose described in the first Article of the Constitution and that can properly be held to help to develop the idea of the moral solidarity of mankind. You do not have formally to say the words 'peace' and 'international understanding' to be working for them. The work of UNESCO to diminish improper discrimination in education, especially in terms of sex and in terms of race; the programme of fellowships for study abroad; the publishing of world-wide factual information about education and of the excellent magazine *The Courier* (which does get into many schools and colleges); even the rallying of world opinion and the collection of funds to save the statues at Abu Simbel or help restoration after the floods in Florence;—all these activities, if not quite directly for the promotion of peace and international understanding, are so closely associated with that purpose as to make no matter.

Yet when all such various activities have been taken into account the shift of emphasis to which I have referred remains. With the funds that have become available, outside the regular budget, through the United Nations Development Programme, UNESCO has come to think of itself much more as the 'animateur' and in part adviser and organiser for educational and scientific progress in its member states, not least through work actually conducted in those states. Is this comparative shift of emphasis a matter of regret? It would be a bold man who would say so, and I for one would not. Even if one is thinking of international understanding, is not the best way to promote international co-operation to co-operate internationally? In all the countries where a UNESCO team is at work international solidarity is being demonstrated, both in the sense that aid is visibly being given by the community of nations and to each such country, and in the sense that the teams of workers and advisers are themselves drawn from many countries.

The direct effort to get schools and universities to 'teach about the United Nations' has never had much success. The UN observer at sessions of the General Conference always used to exhort UNESCO to do more about this. It wasn't wrong (there was something in it) but it always sounded a bit unreal to those who knew schools and universities, especially if it argued for formal instruction in the structure of the United Nations. The most successful organisations in this work, like the Council for Education in World Citizenship in the United Kingdom, don't go about it in this way. They start where young people are likely to be interested: in what is being done, and in the problems themselves, and let knowledge of the United Nations come in through getting interested in, and indeed often involved in, these activities themselves. Knowledge of the United Nations does not make a school or university subject of itself: it is part of a larger whole. Once the interest is engaged in world problems, from war and peace to disease and illiteracy, the need for an emerging world order reveals itself. It is in this larger sense that the direct educational responsibility of UNESCO is to be seen.

It must be said also, in common honesty, that to teach young people that the United Nations is a growing organ of world order lacks credibility. One could still reasonably believe this at the time of the Korean War and through the difficulties in Cyprus and the Congo. But an honest discussion of the United Nations as keeper of the peace now could not rest on underpinning a growing institution of world significance with knowledge and appropriate attitudes, but would involve an examination of the causes for its patent inability, thanks to the refusals of its member states, to act as anything of the kind. This, in the sixth forms, might of course be attempted. But it is not what was meant by 'teaching about the United Nations' in its earlier days. Discussion of the problems of a world order, yes; but just teaching about the United Nations, alas no.

Yet when all this has been said there remains a certain doubt. Is UNESCO doing quite as much as it could, more or less directly, for the promotion of peace through the rule of law, and for international understanding? Its first drive seems somewhat to have run down. There was, for instance, a very laudable attempt to persuade member states to consult with each other about national bias in their school textbooks. There was at one time quite a number of UNESCO-inspired bilateral committees looking at such textbooks. Something—a little at least—was accomplished. But complaints continue much as before that there are plain errors of fact, serving a governmental purpose which some governments just will not make a serious and honest effort to correct. Much more important are the distortions of emphasis, through sins of omission as well as of commission, that produce occasional protests but rarely get changed. In a better world there would be an international Commission of scholars that could summon governments, publishers and authors to defend themselves when a charge of factual error or obvious bias was made, even though such a Commission might have no powers of enforcing correction. But at present such a Commission's work, especially if its proceedings were published, would not be likely to add to international amity. If the proceedings were kept private some countries might voluntarily subscribe to such a procedure, but few people would feel that at this moment such a proposal would have much chance of success. In all the circumstances for UNESCO to have carried through its plan for an internationally agreed History of the Civilisation of Mankind is very much to its credit. The plan to have a large number of bilateral committees of scholars to amend textbooks seems now to have run down. All that remains is a tiny effort involving a few countries and one or two school subjects.

The work specifically proposed under the heading 'Education for International Understanding, Co-operation and Peace' for the biennium 1969-70 may serve as a fair example of both the unsatisfying and the more hopeful trends. First, it was proposed that studies be conducted on the content of education so as to identify elements, approaches and methods for promoting peace. One or more sourcebooks for teachers would be prepared on the history of international co-operation for human rights. Now this sounds like a sensible, reasonably large-scale enterprise, world-wide in scope, aiming at getting below the mere surface of things. But then one looks at the budget allocation: $15,195 spread over two years, less than a year's salary for one of UNESCO's higher officials. Big words and little cash. In fact you could hardly produce one thorough study related to one teaching subject, involving several countries and being translated into the UNESCO languages, for such a paltry sum. Even the friends and supporters of UNESCO feel their hearts sink at this sort of thing. It comes, of course, from wanting to do much, being not allowed by member states to do anything commensurate with the problem, and refusing to face them with this fact. The hard truth is that it is sometimes better to say you can do nothing without the means than to hold out promises with inevitably disappointing results. Surely this too frequent combination of high rhetoric and derisory financing should disappear from the published programmes of UNESCO.

A second activity holds out more hope. This concerns the scheme of 'Associated Projects'. This scheme, started as far back as 1953-54, associates schools (and now also teacher training colleges) that will undertake experimental work, within the framework of their present curriculum and arrangements, to promote better international understanding. This has perhaps been the most successful venture of UNESCO in the specific field of education for international understanding. This is because, so far from setting up Education for International Understanding or Teaching about the United Nations as some sort of new subject, it can be taken up by the schools within their own general style and without time-tabling upheavals. It also permits great choice and variety of work. Undoubtedly the Scheme is capable of extension, and it is good that proposals are being made to extend it.

The most expensive activity proposed for 1969-70 in this part of the Programme was a meeting of 'experts' on education for international understanding and peace with special reference to moral and civic education. This was to cost three times as much as was allocated to studies, $45,630. Now you cannot run a meeting of this sort, with up to twenty participants coming from every part of the world, and doing all the relevant paper work, interpreting and translating and so on, for very much less. The present writer took part in this exercise and can therefore report on it (though his views, it must be said, are a little more pessimistic—though by no means entirely so—than those of his colleagues).

First, the level of discussion is bound to be nearer to that of the layman than that of the real expert unless the participants really share a discipline and have basically common and understood terms of technical discourse. If you bring people together from the most diverse cultures and levels of educational development, and in addition from very diverse parts of the total educational field, you will be most unlikely to achieve this. We had, I think, just two psychologists; so, when they spoke to the rest of us they were really speaking to a semi-lay audience. The same was true of those who came from primary schools, or secondary schools, or the universities, or educational administration. The result was that we all performed rather below our normal professional level—and that, without taking into account the difficulties of language. I think nearly every participant felt that, without blaming ourselves, each other, or the Secretariat, the intellectual level was not very rigorous.

Then there is the great difficulty of producing a Report of such a meeting (in at least two languages) which participants can agree to before they go home. At this meeting the result was plainly so far from satisfactory that the meeting very sensibly turned over the draft as raw material to the Secretariat to make what they could of. And in fact the Secretariat did produce a sensible and one would think helpful document. But if they could do this in spite of our fumbling, could they not have done it without spending the $45,000 on calling the meeting at all? They generously said no. It is difficult to be sure.

What was perhaps the best outcome of the meeting was the attempt really to ask what we meant by this awkward phrase 'Education for International Understanding'. Everyone agreed that it was not satisfactory, and largely because it was so plainly ambiguous in its applications. 'Understanding' does not necessarily mean 'liking better' or—in the world context—peace. The reformulated aim suggested for UNESCO and spelt out at some length was to work for the increasing presence of a world dimension in studies at school and university and in adult education. This, it seems to the writer, did help in getting to the heart of the difficulties UNESCO has found in this field of work. Why has its work in this field, in spite of much hard and sincere effort, been more disappointing so far than it might have been?

The significant thing about the Associated Projects Scheme is that it starts from the participating schools' own curricula and simply invites them to take a step forward from there. This, it seems to me, is a very important pointer. Let us change from the posture of the virtuous intruder (Can't you make room for more teaching about the United Nations?') and come in with the teachers and the officials in the continuing process of changing and improving the curricula to match modern needs. Curriculum reform is in the air. The old 'colonial' curricula are being re-shaped to meet national needs, old purposes and methods in all countries are giving place to new. This is the moment to ask whether the content of what is being taught is indeed what is needed to fit a child or young man or woman for living in the later years of the twentieth century. It is good educational sense, not merely 'idealism', to say that we must broaden the curriculum so that the young have that knowledge of the world as a whole that they will surely need, not only as citizens but also often as workers and professional people. We need now at least a degree of world-consciousness to supplement the induction into a national community that schools have traditionally provided and will properly continue to provide. We need to promote the awareness of living in a world-wide human community for practical reasons—because increasingly we do, and cannot operate effectively within it unless we have the necessary knowledge and the appropriate attitudes of mind. For UNESCO this means that 'Education for International Understanding' should no longer look so isolated but should increasingly be fused with the great range of work that is going on for the modernisation of curricula everywhere. This, it would seem to me, should be the key idea for realising the potentialities of UNESCO in all this work. It implies an imaginative jump by those who prepare and those who adopt proposals for UNESCO activities. The concepts that earlier I called twin concepts need to be brought together again, so that the work done for international understanding through education is seen to be work for education itself.

How would this work out? Let us look first at school studies and then at college and university studies. In school studies we might look especially at what is obviously a key subject, history. What history, the history of whom and of what, does a boy or girl now need to know?

First, he needs to know something of the history of his own people. Without this we cannot properly realise our own identity to ourselves. But the phrase 'our own people' is ambiguous. Are my own people the East Saxons (I was born in Essex), or the English, or the British in general? Can we speak of the people of Uganda, or only of the peoples of Uganda? of a Sikh or an Indian? Obviously one's answer depends on the degree to which a community is conscious of itself. It is interesting for me to know something of the history of Essex, but it matters to me much less than it would to know something of the history of the Sikhs if I were a Sikh. And where there is a sound political desire to weld peoples into a sense of common nationhood, one has to think carefully. To accentuate Buganda at the expense of Uganda would be wrong. Yet to suppress it might have exactly the contrary result to the one intended and actually promote separatist feeling. Both pedagogically and politically a blend is necessary, and the balance will have to vary somewhat according to circumstances. The study of the historical progress towards fusion in a common nationhood is of course a proper part of the teaching.

Secondly, the young need a sense of their general world region. This is not always simply geographical. In England it properly includes the English-speaking world overseas, as it also includes

Europe. In the Arab countries of the Middle East it includes the Islamic countries generally. In Africa it should certainly include something of the Pan-African idea.

Thirdly, it is surely patent that all the world's young need now to have some conception of the history of mankind as a whole. Without our personal memory we should lose all sense of personality. Without some knowledge of our collective experience on this planet we shall never have that sense of mankind as a whole that is necessary, necessary now because for certain purposes no smaller unit than mankind as a whole will work for our survival.

It does not necessarily follow that sympathy increases with knowledge: we may strongly dislike what we come to know. But the reverse is true: that ignorance of other peoples is always a breeding ground for suspicion and fear. Those who do not know about other peoples find it hard to conceive of them as sharing a real common humanity, so that when contact brings difficulties hysteria rushes to the surface. If there is 'one world' we must know what that world is and how increasingly there has come to be a common physical and social environment.

This is the mere rationale of such a plan for the teaching of history in schools. But the pedagogical difficulties and problems are immense. Assuming that you want to do it, how do you do it? It is naive to suppose that the sequence of studies should just follow the sequence from the local to the universal (we have never done that with schools teaching national history). Yet there is something in the cliché that you should proceed from the known to the unknown. This has to be worked out, as it can be, and quite sensibly. It is also educationally naive to suppose that you only study one thing once, and then go on to the next thing. There is one level at which you can hear about the story of mankind in the primary school. But you cannot leave it there. You must return to study it more seriously in the secondary school.

UNESCO in its earlier days called together seminars about the study of various subjects in relation to international understanding. But we were then at the earlier stage of thinking to which I have alluded. The Director of the History Seminar in this series told me that he was glad to assume this responsibility but I must know that he did not really believe that there were two kinds of history, history proper and history for international understanding (the former presumably being more historical, the latter more virtuous). Of course there are not: but we almost made it seem as if there were.

Now, it seems to me, UNESCO could launch a series of activities without the risk of this impediment, subsuming the question of the degree of world history in the question of more direct concern to teachers, namely how, in general, should we now teach history? Not much, of course, is to be gained from a single international seminar, certainly not in the old style. What is needed is a series of efforts by individual member states about the teaching of history in their own country, supported not merely by Ministries of Education, but by professional associations of teachers and by historians. The role of UNESCO is primarily to promote such activities and to co-ordinate and supplement them where necessary.

At the college and university level an immense potential field of activity lies ready for action, especially in certain disciplines. Once again the question to put to university teachers is not, what are you doing for peace? but is the content of your syllabuses and curricula what your students now need? It is the university students of today who, in any country, are most likely to be involved later in work with people from other cultural backgrounds, whether they are in commerce, industry, law, medicine, education, administration or politics. On strictly practical grounds I suspect there is strong reason to believe that we are not preparing them properly. We are only on the edge of doing so. How many students of economics about to take their degree could take part intelligently in a discussion of the world's international monetary difficulties or could give a coherent account of the work of the World Bank? How many students of law could say what is meant by the phrase 'the rule of law' in international affairs, or could comment on the significance of the difference between a Declaration and a Convention of Human Rights, and explain the difficulties of moving from one stage to the other? How many students of anthropology or comparative sociology could discuss the difficulties in the idea of 'modernising' a traditional culture? How many future business men with overseas interests understand the problems of starting a factory in a low-income country with a culture different from their own?

Of course the international educational activities on which we should all be engaging must cost money, and we cannot spend what we should be spending to make the world fit for humanity to inhabit while we have the burden of competitive arms expenditure to face. If there were an effective world peace Authority these things could leap forward: a UNESCO Staff College for training international workers in education, a great flow of textbooks and materials for education in world citizenship, a great extension of the concept of voluntary service overseas, of school journeys, of interchange of students and scholars the world over. But I am sure that something more should be done on these lines now, above all in accordance with the idea of curriculum development that I have stressed in this article.

It is obvious that UNESCO, in the sense of a Director-General and a Secretariat in Paris, cannot possibly do all these things by themselves. There is an old and painful saying: that UNESCO is not a headquarters, it is the sum of its member states. If what I have been suggesting is sensible and practical, then, if anything is to happen, the member states of UNESCO will have to believe this and to carry forward most of the action. But there is a limited scope for initiative from the centre. This part of the biennial Programme does seem to me to have got into a bit of a rut and I would like to see it renewed, not on the old basis of virtual separateness, as a thing in itself, but on the basis of fusion with the activity for curriculum reform of all kinds that is now going forward all over the world. As we have seen, there was an apparent fusion of two different ideas, collaboration for education and collaboration for international understanding through education, in the original Constitution. It led not to fusion, but to confusion. What we need now is a genuine fusion, based on the perception that to bring a world-dimension into our studies is work for, and not merely through, education.

FREEDOM AND CONSCIENCE
ERIC BAKER

Quaker, and one time Chairman of the British Section of Amnesty International.

As one of the founder members of Amnesty International, Eric Baker has for many years been concerned with problems of conscience and freedom. In this chapter he discusses the philosophy of conscience and relates it to understanding the problems of peace.

The history of human progress has been the history of the battle against the waste of human life, effort and ability.

It is two thousand years since Aristotle solemnly condemned the slave to little more than a brute existence, declaring that by nature 'the slave is a living tool, the tool a lifeless slave'. He recognized in him only so much reason as would allow him to understand orders, but not sufficient to be able to give them. It is less than two hundred years since Shaftsbury's struggle against child labour in factories and mines. It is much less than twenty years since the realization dawned on our generation that the effect—if not the purpose—of the 11+ examination was to put a gloss on the rate and tax payer's determination to restrict educational expenditure and, in consequence, to condemn many to educational under-achievement and a life-time of wasted potential (a loss to society as much as to the individual).

These three examples are chosen only because they are well-known; the field from which they are drawn is limitless.

What is noteworthy is that there has been, not merely one battle, but two, the one to increase the length of life, the other to improve its quality.

With the first we are well acquainted—the war against physical waste in terms of early death and avoidable disease. It is a war in which the individual battles are universally approved and almost universally supported. The conquest of leprosy, malaria and tubercolosis, the siege of cancer, and the cardiac diseases, are the result of concerted effort in which funds and expertise have been supplied by governments, private organizations and private persons.

More recently new strategies have been developed as we have become more conscious of the effects of environmental pollution. As the public has become more seized of the seriousness of the problem, private organizations and private individuals have again turned to, and by education and propaganda brought pressure to bear on private firms (often wielding commercial budgets larger than the budgets available to some national governments) while government departments have often found themselves enlisted on opposing sides.

The struggle against physical waste is not usually one which calls for martyrs. Although men and women may die of malnutrition, typhoid, or polio, it is rarely (Father Damien apart) that they have deliberately set out to court death in that way. They have, rather, been unwilling victims, and their very unwillingness has argued in their favour. They did not want to die, or die so young, and those who have remained have determined that others should be rescued from the possibility of at least this form of death. Danilo Dolci holding the under-nourished, fever-ridden corpse of a young child in his arms in the village of Trapetto in Sicily, resolved that, though one had died, at least others should live.

But when lives have been physically saved or prolonged, what are they to be used for? A man may live to a reasonable old age, but if his abilities remain under-developed, is he still not the victim of a war in which he has found himself on the losing side? To be well-fed, well-clothed and well-housed is still to have won only one of the battles, not both; it is still to have only half a title to be a human being.

Thus, alongside the battle for a greater quantity of physical life there has been the battle for a better quality of 'spiritual' life, for greater self-consciousness. What is more, as the pace of the former has quickened, so has that of the latter. The achievement of victory in one field leads to realization of the need for victory in the other. But the conditions of the second kind of battle are different from and more difficult than those of the first. It is not simply that the struggle against physical disease is dramatic, not that it is—even in primitive countries—well paid. The victims of physical disease are involuntary and reluctant victims; they are, moreover, victims of a situation so much a part of the human condition that Everyman can identify himself with them. For those involved in the struggle for a better quality of human life, these conditions hold much less certainly.

For instance, anyone who has happened to be on the spot when two cars have collided can see in himself a potential casualty and in consequence consents, however reluctantly, to the laws which regulate the speed and flow of traffic. For the same reason, even the wealthiest man can identify himself with the poorest victim of cancer and give his contribution to the support of cancer research. But with diseases which are non-physical, the matter is different. True, when the statisticians assure us that a certain percentage of the population will spend some time in a mental hospital, we recognize that we ourselves might be among the unlucky ones and are thus prepared to look a little more kindly on mental illness.

On the other hand, however, identification with those who are involved in the struggle for a better quality of life is something which Everyman finds most difficult and comes to unwillingly. It is, after all, quite possible to live more or less contentedly under a dictatorship. More than that, both records and personal experience amply demonstrate that it is not only possible to live contentedly but even with a dignity and a humanity which are entirely laudable under regimes which are restricting and spiritually impoverishing to a degree which would be quite unacceptable at other times and other places. The innate conservatism and timidity of the vast majority not only makes them actively prefer the known which they have made tolerable to that which they fear as a disturbing and threatening unknown, while the habit of obedience to authority will often make them join in deriding—and even in persecuting—those whose only endeavour is to help them achieve that freedom which they fear.

What is it then, that leads men and women voluntarily to take up a stand which they are well aware will not be understood by the majority of their contemporaries and, so far from ensuring them popularity may, in fact, bring only persecution. It is true, of course, that even the most conservative society, in honouring its historic heroes is honouring, not the conservatives, but the revolutionaries of a previous generation. By the same token, and with the same enthusiasm it will condemn the revolutionaries of its own generation. Thus, the true role of the revolutionary is to point out the contradictions inherent in the outlook of his revolutionary predecessors.

The demand of conscience, therefore, which is characteristic of those who make it their task to change society, is the demand for action on a perceived incongruity.

There are some for whom the incongruity is cosmic. Albert Camus pursued Cartesian doubt to its nadir, demonstrating that between man and the world in which he finds himself, there can be nothing but unfathomable incomprehension:

> " . . . The Absurd is not in man (if such a metaphor could have a meaning) nor in the world, but in their presence together."

He does not yield himself to the rhetorical despair with which Russell ended his essay on "A Free Man's Worship" half a century earlier. Instead, like a true Cartesian, he clings firmly to the lucid deliverances of reason—even when all they can reveal is only the depths of the irrational—and declares that nobility lies in living "without appeal". For him, in an incomprehending universe, conscience is still supreme. It is this same conscience which forbids the "great leap" into either suicide or into existentialism. To leap in either direction would be to make as much of a surrender as to leap into the Church, for it would be to subvert or to ignore the one truth which had been discovered, to deny the perceived incongruity—that man and his world were incommensurable.

The perception of cosmic incongruity is parallelled by the perception of the contradictions inherent in society. There is, however, no necessary movement from cosmic despair to social despair and this for one very good reason—that the former arises from the value which man places on himself and his own efforts set in a universe which seems tragically indifferent to the very concept of value itself.

Of all the endeavours which have been made to single out one particular activity which can be said to be characteristic of man and of him alone—homo sapiens, homo faber etc.—none is more appropriate than to describe him simply as 'man who values'. For it is his ability to attach a meaning to the word 'better' which is common and basic to both rebel and conservative. Nor can comparisons be limited to economic and scientific analyses or technologies. They must, in the end, spill over into society itself; social comparisons lead to the recognition of social incongruities and the recognition of social incongruities to social action.

At this point, there emerges one further difference between the modes of action leading to the amelioration of the social as against that of the physical environment. Whatever achievements there have been in the circumstances of our physical life have been the result of man's ability to use Nature against herself. To understand the laws by which Nature works, is to understand the laws by which she may be defeated. The science of flight and the control of epidemics are illustrations of the principle that modern technology has improved both the quantity and to some extent the quality of human life by first setting out to ask why it 'could not' and then using that very answer to provide the reason why it 'could'.

Insofar, however, as the social environment is non-physical, is, in whatever sense of the word 'spiritual', progress has come not by using Nature to defeat herself, but has come by quite a different route. It has been the consequence of pursuing incongruities to their source and of denying contradictions rather than of accepting them. The bird and the aeronaut use the force with which the wind opposes their progress to rise still higher and flight becomes the epitome of contradiction in action, a perpetually successful incongruity which remains successful only so long as both terms of the contradiction are maintained. Let either bird or wind cease to oppose and there is no further progress.

By way of contrast, while Aristotle (to return to an earlier illustration) stoutly defended discrimination against slaves, his position was in the end overturned as a result of the failure of one of the terms of the very incongruity he was trying to defend. To argue that all men were possessed of Reason—but to exclude one class of men was a limitation which it was not in the nature of Reason itself to maintain. The situation was, in fact, made more indefensible by the numerous qualifications which Aristotle ever faithful to observed facts, himself had to introduce—so as to account, for instance, for the fact that some free men clearly had the minds as well as the bodies of slaves and some slaves those of freemen and that, despite the innate disparity of Reason, free men and slaves might, as human beings, enjoy mutual friendship.

"Reason" lost its capital letter somewhere in the course of the eighteenth century, and with it the background of Aristotelian psychology and metaphysics which Aquinas Christianized and bequeathed to Western Europe. Thereafter, it was no longer possible to speak of Reason with Aristotle as that in man which is most akin to the gods, or to say with Aquinas, "Reason in man is rather like God in the Universe", thereby indicating a consonance between the fiat which created the Universe and that which was essential to man himself. What remained was not "Reason" but "reasoning"—the ratiocinative process. Even in this attenuated form, however, it has had a silent and persistent effect on human history. For the one thing which no process of reasoning can accept without question is the exclusive "but": "all men are equal, but . . . ", "war is of course an evil, but . . . ". The contradiction, once perceived cannot, as in physical science be accepted and used; it must be challenged and made to give an account of itself. If the account it gives is found not to be satisfactory, then its denial becomes a matter of conscience and, although the process may be measured in centuries, gradually the exclusion is eliminated so that the universal proposition can be asserted without exception—or at least, with fewer.

Up to this point the argument has been that the improvement of non-physical environment—of what, for the individual is spiritual and for the community, social—has been the consequence of first challenging and then eliminating incongruities, removing the contradictions from universal ethical propositions ("All men, but not women . . . " and so on). This has been the task of conscience and its battle slogan has usually been in terms of "freedom", (a universal slogan could well be "Down with all 'buts'!").

There remains, however, one essential task, that of discriminating between those universal ethical propositions which can properly be adopted and those which can properly only be opposed, of distinguishing between those "All" statements which will improve society and those which will enslave it. "All Jews . . . ", "All Communists . . . " lay claim to the same validity as any other statement beginning with "all". Nor can they be subjected to tests of physical scrutiny such as are available to validate statements such as "All bridges . . . ", "All robins . . . ". Consequently, conscience has frequently proved an ill light to guide and "freedom" become the freedom to move in leg-irons.

In the end, the only criteria are the Aristotelian ones of Reason and of 'virtue' which is the excellence of a function well performed, the function being that of a man in whom not all that is potential is allowed to reach full development, but only so much as is in harmony with his true nature as a creature of Reason.

The concept of man as being of worth in himself has been the liberating concept in the development of education as much as in the dissolution of imperialism. But the endeavour has been not simply to loose what has been bound because in themselves bonds were objectionable. Bonds, or limits on freedom are as necessary as banks to a river and freedom without a purpose to which it can be put may become a slavery of a most destructive kind. Nothing makes this clearer than the history of conscience itself. Those who have protested against restrictions and in the name of liberty are the ones who have most obviously bound themselves to an ideal, who have been most willing to lose their own freedom in order to demand, not that others should be 'totally free' and unrestricted, but that they too might be put to service to the same ideal. The phrase in the Book of Common Prayer which speaks of a master 'whose service is perfect freedom' puts into words nothing less than the desperate truth acknowledged by every revolutionary.

The task of Conscience, therefore, is to challenge incongruities not in the name of unlimited freedom, but in that of a new discipline which will enable all men to realize the potential that is within them of fulfilling their true function.

Footnote:

After reading the foregoing chapter, the Editor remarked that it seemed primarily concerned with the prophets among us. If so, then it has somewhat missed its mark.

'Prophets' are essential, but it is the groundswell, so to speak, of which they are both the sign and part cause, that carries their message from being a slogan to being a cliché.

The phenomenon of moral progress is basically as incomprehensible as any other phenomenon, but the process by which it works itself out can be traced with tolerable ease. It is a process of which the freeing of a colonial country from foreign domination is one aspect and the freeing of one class within a country from domination by another is a second.

Beginning with the insight of a Gandhi or a Dolci what was at first the revelation of a basic truth is then turned into a question mark which hangs over every particular example of the oppressive principle—whether the salt-tax in India or pillar boxes marked "E II R" in Scotland. Constant reiteration of the question may not convert the majority but at least it disturbs. From then on the process is rather like that of extracting the stump of a tree from the ground: constant rocking and an occasional direct chop—then, finally, success!

Success comes when, at last, the minds of the majority no longer question. They have at last accepted the vision of the prophet—but as the light of ordinary day, no longer as a visionary gleam.

It would be a mistake, however, to attribute the final conversion of the majority to the efforts of the prophet alone. The achievement both of sociology and (more by implication) the mass media has been to demonstrate the process of osmosis by which, first doubt, then conviction and, finally the impulse to action creeps through the minds of scores, then hundreds . . . To every Darwin, there is a Huxley; for every leader there are half-a-dozen staff captains—reliable but unspectacular. Their gift is not brilliance, but the capacity to seize the Idea, to explain, organize, apply it in a hundred different ways; to give leadership the educational and organizational strength it so often lacks. What carries the Idea to success in the end is the labour of the unnoticed thousands just as much as that of the great man himself.

The truth of the situation has never been better expressed than by William James in a letter to his brother:

"As for me, my bed is made. I am done with great things and big things, great organisations and big successes. And I am for those tiny invisible, molecular moral forces which work from individual to individual, creeping in through the crannies of the world like so many soft rootlets or like the capillary oozings of water but which, if you give them time, will rend the hardest monuments of man's pride."

STRAIGHT THINKING AS A FACTOR IN PEACE MAKING

ROBERT H. THOULESS

Degree—Sc.D. (Cambridge), Reader in Educational Psychology at University of Cambridge until 1961, now Emeritus. Author of *Introduction to the Psychology of Religion* (1923), *General and Social Psychology* (1925), *Straight and Crooked Thinking* (Revd. Edn. 1974), *Straight Thinking in War-time* (1942), etc.

Dr. Thouless looks at the psychological dangers of emotionally charged languages and suggests an analytical approach.

People, Dr. Thouless believes, must be educated to see through the misuse of language, and delegates to conferences should be taught to approach the conference table as if it were a social therapeutic clinic rather than a verbal battle field.

Man's fighting behaviour is (like the rest of his social behaviour) complicated by the fact that it is tied up with his use of language. It is not only tied up with his use of language for talking to other people and influencing their behaviour, but also with his use of it for talking to himself and modifying his own behaviour. The first of these ways of using language may be called 'communication', the second may be called 'thinking'.

Fighting behaviour is found in man and in other animals. What is peculiar to man is that he can also talk and think about his fighting behaviour. The general tendency of this talking and thinking is to intensify the emotional dispositions that are behind the fighting behaviour and so to make this behaviour more persistent. Two fighting wolves may perhaps more easily end the fight than two fighting men, not only because (as has been pointed out by Lorenz in his book *King Solomon's Ring*) the wolf has instinctive appeasement behaviour as well as instinctive aggressive behaviour, but also because the wolf differs from man in the fact that he has no system of language by means of which he can intensify and prolong his hostile attitude towards the individual or group against which his fighting behaviour is directed.

Amongst human beings, verbal quarrelling is one of the modes of language use, in addition to such modes of language activity as making assertions, asking questions, paying compliments etc. Another mode of language use is pacification or the easing of tensions between individuals or groups. This, however, seems to be more effective as a safeguard against the development of quarrels than as a solvent of wuarrels when they have already started. Those who value peace need to understand both modes of use of language; the quarrelling mode since insight into its nature may reduce its effectiveness, and the pacifying mode in order that it may be used on the occasions demanding it.

The particular kind of fighting behaviour with which we are here concerned is the highly sophisticated and somewhat unnatural activity of war. There is a strong irrational element in this activity (as in all quarrelling behaviour) since it is directed towards the injuring of other men and not towards the rational end of their well-being. Once fighting behaviour has started, however, the injury of the other seems to be a reasonable end, partly because fighting behaviour is accompanied by the emotion of anger, partly because language may be used to reinforce the emotional drive towards injury of the other by causing him to be perceived in the role of the 'hated enemy'.

The use of language for the purpose of creating out of the antagogist a 'hated enemy' figure is one of the purposes of war propaganda. Its methods may be studied in any past war and it may be seen also in various present-day situations in which there is a build-up of tensions between two social groups (as of two racial groups). It contains various elements. First, there is a distinction made between the enemy and all non-enemies by giving the enemy a name which either is from the beginning or which rapidly becomes charged with negative (i.e. aversive) emotion. Secondly, there is a more general use of emotionally charged language to create negative emotional attitudes towards the enemy and positive emotional attitudes towards one's own side. Thirdly, a pseudo-factual case is built up against the enemy by charging him with 'atrocities'. These are unpleasant incidents which, whether true or not, are selected from the total of war behaviour because they serve the purpose of portraying the enemy as a figure to be hated.

These different ways of using language to reinforce and prolong hostile attitudes may be illustrated from wars in which this country has taken part as well as from group hostilities that have not led to war. At the beginning of the First World War, the French had a name for the enemy strongly charged with hostile emotions, 'Boche'; this was sometimes used in Great Britain but not very commonly. The effective hostile label was unwittingly supplied by the Kaiser himself when he exhorted his troops to make reputations for themselves 'like the Huns of Attila'. There does not seem to be any reason for supposing that the Kaiser meant anything except that his troops should have the reputation for being successful fighters, but the term was taken in Great Britain to mean that the German soldiers were to be distinguished for the savagery which was also a characteristic of Attila's followers. So 'Hun' became our hostile label for the enemy, corresponding in function to the word 'nigger' or 'kaffir' in racial hostilities.

This use of an emotionally charged term for indicating the enemy is, however, only a special case of a more general principle that language which appears to be merely pointing to objects or stating facts about them may also be producing emotions and influencing attitudes of approval or disapproval. This is indeed one of the functions of language and it would be unreasonable to find fault with it except when it is used to distort judgment as may happen in propaganda, not least in war propaganda. Sometimes we have to decide what is the right thing to do, sometimes we have to carry out the action decided on. The ideal is that the decision should be made dispassionately, while strong feeling is appropriate as a means of driving us to energetic action in the direction decided on. The emotional use of language is an impediment to the clear thinking which should underlie the initial stage of deciding.

The use of emotionally charged language as a disturber of clear thinking becomes so common in war-time that it is little remarked. In the first winter of the 1914 war, an English newspaper said: "The gorilla of Europe was on the move, glorying in its hairy strength, devoid of conscience, or pity or mercy." The question of the causes of any war, from the first European war to that in Vietnam, is a question on which it is important to come to a right decision. A dispassionate process of judgment is not, however, helped by thinking of the enemy as a gorilla, even if we remind ourselves that the gorilla is, in fact, a much less aggressive animal than is man.

It is not only in the war situation that such emotionally charged language may be used to intensify aversive attitudes and to deflect judgment; it is also a common element in group hostilities such as those between races. Hitler in *Mein Kampf* wrote: "the black-haired Jewish youth lies in wait for hours on end, satanically glaring at and spying on the unsuspicious girl whom he plans to seduce." This passage obviously creates prejudice against the Jewish youth, but the prejudice is seen to be without rational foundation if we take the trouble to replace such emotionally charged words and phrases as 'lies in wait', 'satanically glaring at', 'spying on' and 'seduce' by emotionally neutral words. The passage will then become something like this: "the black-haired Jewish youth watches for hours on end the unsuspicious girl to whom he wishes to make love". The passage obviously loses its anti-semitic propaganda value after this process of emotional neutralisation.

Emotionally charged language may also be used to create favourable attitudes towards one's own side and towards their activities. The approving label for British soldiers in the 1914 war was "Tommies"; and the 'heroism' of our Tommies was contrasted with the 'foolhardiness' of the Huns. One who is aware of the linguistic factors in propaganda will consider that the actual behaviour covered by the words 'heroism' and 'foolhardiness' may be the same, that of going on in the face of danger.

The most dangerous contribution that emotionally charged language can make to war attitudes is that of casting a romantic mist over war which serves to hide its cruelties and wastefulness. This kind of emotional communication may be used in time of war to boost morale amongst those suffering from its dangers and deprivations. In such times there may be a transitory usefulness in the creation of the illusion that the horrors and hardships of war are the dark side of something glorious.

The perpetuation of such illusions in time of peace by emotional oratory in praise of war is, however, wholly bad. The effort then required is that of preserving peace and promoting love and fellowship amongst men. Communication should be helping people to realise the fact that it is more glorious to build than to destroy and that it is at least as praiseworthy to live well as to die well. Then poets and pastors may do much harm by indulging in emotional language to support the romantic fantasy that destruction and blood-shed are more glorious than the co-operative work of construction and of producing food for the hungry.

Another element in the verbal communication that helps to build up the picture of the hated enemy is the atrocity story. Stories of the enemy killing prisoners, attacking hospital trains or ambulances, directing shells or bombs at civilian houses and other actions against non-combatants, are to be found in all wars. They are indeed incidents that happen in all wars and on both sides in wars. When they are told of the enemy, they are not necessarily untrue, although they may be exaggerated and claimed to be more frequent and less condemned by military authority than they really are. They are not necessarily false but they are highly selected for the purpose of creating a picture of the enemy to be hated; similar incidents in our own army or amongst our allies are not reported, nor are the generous and chivalrous actions of the enemy. The selection is made for the purpose of producing hatred of the enemy which can be done as well by selection as by invention.

Invention has also played its part in the creation of atrocity stories. The opening months of the 1914 were rich in atrocity stories about the Germans which later investigation showed to be pure fabrications, some deliberate and some accidental. When, after the end of the 1914 war, the British public learned how much they had been misled by atrocity propaganda during the war, they became generally sceptical about stories of enemy atrocities and were unwilling to believe that the Nazis were treating the Jews as badly as they were said to be by allied propaganda. But if disbelief is a safer attitude to atrocity stories than too ready belief, it is not an infallible guide. Testimony given after the war was over, not merely by the victims of these atrocities, but by those (such as the Commandant of Auschwitz) who carried them out, have shown that the cruelties of mass extermination of Jews and Gipsies was worse than anything that had been imagined. The atrocity story may be true and be about behaviour peculiar to the enemy.

Whether invented, selected, or true, the point of the atrocity story is that it has the function of creating hate. It is part of the linguistic machinery of creating and perpetuating hostile attitudes towards other national groups. From a purely rational point of view, it is obviously irrelevant to the question of whether it is right to be engaged in war with the enemy since, whatever may be the purpose of the war, it is not that of improving the behaviour of the enemy. If we imagine that, in the wars of 1914 and 1939, the Germans had behaved with chivalry and correctness, while the French had committed every conceivable atrocity, we should still have continued to fight on the side of the French and against the Germans: the essential causes of the wars and their immediate occasions in the invasion of Belgium and of Poland would have remained the same.

While atrocity stories serve the psychological purpose of creating hatred, they are to be regarded as linguistic devices for this purpose rather than as a rational ground for thinking badly of the people who are the enemy. When they are inventions they provide no rational grounds for the formation of any attitude, when they are selected they would only be rational grounds for making a judgment about the enemy if one had information as to their relative distribution on both sides of the conflict, which information is obviously unattainable. Even in the rare case that they are true and peculiar to the enemy (like the Nazi extermination camps) one may reflect that those who are responsible are not the whole of the enemy population but a particular group of them under strange social pressures. One may suppose that these horrors appeared as evil and repugnant to the average German non-Nazi as they do to us.

The rational attitude towards all atrocities is to regard them, not as reasons for hating the enemy of the moment, but as reasons for hating war. Part of the resistance against the romantic illusions of those who glorify war is to remind ourselves of the atrocious behaviour engendered by the war situation, and to reflect that, under the social pressures which lead men to commit atrocities, we might ourselves commit the same abominable actions. This question may even be asked about the atrocities of the Nazi extermination camps. Are we certain that, under the same thought system and the same social pressures as those acting on the Commandant of Auschwitz and his subordinates, we should not have done the same? If there is uncertainty as to the answer to this question, the moral must be that we should set ourselves to oppose the formation of such social pressures. One way of doing this is by becoming conscious of the linguistic devices by which such group hostilities as racialism and war are fostered.

We need not endorse the extreme position that, without language, there would be no wars. It remains true that without language there would not be some of the factors that make wars bitter and persistent, there would be no oratorical incantations romanticising the activity of war and creating the image of the hated enemy against whom it seems virtuous to fight. Can we at the language level do anything to combat these factors in war promotion? Two things I would suggest, one educational and the other concerned with the social psychology of international negotiation.

At the educational level, I think there would be great gain if everyone were taught in school an analytical approach to language which enabled them to recognise emotionally charged language and which gave them techniques for resisting its effects, such as that of restating an emotionally charged propaganda statement in emotionally neutral language. A great step would be made towards rationality in international and group relations if a generation grew up that could not be stirred by emotional oratory but who could recognise its devices. Such people could with difficulty be stirred to unreasoned action, and not at all to such unreasonable prejudices as those which refuse respect and love towards people of another nation or of another skin colour.

Until that generation grows up there is much to be done in the way of making more rational the thought of adult populations who are liable to become irrational in their involvement in national, racial or religious rivalries. One cannot, of course, hope to overcome these irrationalities by being equally irrational on the side of peace. The way of peace education is the way of encouraging objective and dispassionate thinking about the causes of group conflicts. The kind of scientific thinking that has led to the control of disease may lead to the control of group hostilities. Our effort must be directed towards getting men to understand that, in the cases of war and race conflict, as in that of disease, the way to get rid of an evil is to discover its causes by the dispassionate methods of scientific research and then to destroy the evil thing by rooting out its causes.

Most especially there is need for the scientific kind of thinking at the level of international conferences. U.N.O. was originally designed as a way of preserving peace. The language use of its delegates is, however, in the mode of quarrelling. They represent eloquently and forcefully the point of view of their own side and point out how much any tension situation that may have arisen is due to the moral defects of the other side. The result of their speeches is the intensification of tensions not their relief. If a delegate, aiming to relieve tensions, used the language of love with respect to the other side, he would be regarded as 'soft' and would quickly be relieved of his job.

The danger is now, however, too serious for the customary use of language between nations to be any longer tolerated. If delegates to the U.N.O. were trained as social scientists to relieve tensions and not to intensify them, if they regarded their task as the objective understanding of the causes of conflict and not the identifying of themselves with one side in the conflict, then the language used in international conferences would be different. It would be the language of pacification not of quarrelling. For this end the education and training of the delegates would be entirely different from what it is now. They would have learned the techniques of the use of language for the reduction of social tensions and would approach the conference table as a social therapeutic clinic, not as a verbal battle field.

These changes in attitude towards language would not abolish war; there are other causes of war than the foolish and quarrelsome things men say. But these are aids to war, and if we could get rid of the part played by language in promoting and prolonging wars, we should make a lasting peace more probable. Let us hope that this will be done before it is too late.

Further Reading:

Propaganda Technique in the World War, H. D. Lasswell, London and New York, 1927.

Falsehood in War-Time, A. Ponsonby, London, 1928.

Report of the Committee on Alleged German Atrocities, presided over by Lord Bryce, London, 1915.

The Great War, W. S. Churchill, Vol. III, London, 1934.

Straight and Crooked Thinking, R. H. Thouless, (revd. edn.), London, 1953.

LOVE AND AUTHORITY
DAVID WILLS

(Born 1903) is the biographer of Homer Lane, and has devoted most of his working life to various efforts to bring enlightened methods to the residential treatment of delinquent and maladjusted men and children. These all involved (among other things) attempts to resolve the conflict that is thought to exist between love and authority. He has written about his work in *The Hawkspur Experiment* (men), *The Barns Experiment* (boys), and *Throw Away Thy Rod* (children). His recent Penguin "*Spare the Child*" describes the conversion of a punitive Approved School to a non-punitive therapeutic community.

Must authority always be associated with the physical power to coerce, or is there a better way?

One of the many tasks that I long ago set myself and put aside until my retirement, was to write a further "travel" of the restless Lemuel Gulliver. I never got as far as thinking of a name for the singular people he discovered on this journey, but their distinguishing feature was this; that instead of being tiny at the time of birth and gradually getting bigger as they got older, they were born enormous—and enormously strong—and gradually shrank to a reasonable size as they approached maturity. They were a very happy, peaceable prosperous people because of the one outstanding consequence of the circumstances of their birth and growth. That consequence, as will readily be seen, was that they did not make the fatal error that is made in less happy civilisations—such as our own—of associating authority inevitably with the physical power to coerce. In this mythical country those concerned with the upbringing and education of the young were inhibited from the use of all but the very mildest forms of physical coercion by fear of the massive resistance and indeed retaliation of which the young were capable. It follows that the young grew up (grew *down* perhaps I should say) amiable, trusting and fearless. Not for one moment did it ever occur to them (why should it?) that one might secure one's own ends by the use of violence, because they had not been shown—as we have—this process in action against them in their own upbringing. *Their* parents, their educators, were compelled by force of circumstance to exercise authority only through love, so that love and authority became indissolubly associated in the minds of all the people who lived in that happy land of fantasy.

But it is not as fantastic as it may at first seem; not nearly as fantastic as some of the other travels which the inventive Dean caused Gulliver to endure. For even in our own civilisation love and authority must inevitably be connected in the minds of the young—whatever happens later—because they both derive from the same source. The very first person to exercise authority over us, and for some time the only person to do so, is that same person who envelopes us in loving solicitude, the person indeed from whom we learn what love is, as she is also the person from whom we learn what authority is. From the moment of birth our mother wraps us in affection and she also exercises authority—often in the form of mild and loving coercion—over us. As the months and years pass we may devise various little ways of evading and resisting that authority, but on the whole we find it acceptable not only because we recognise it as superior—superior in knowledge, in wisdom, in experience,—but also because we recognise it as a loving authority that is wholly beneficent in intention. For every occasion that a child is frankly disobedient there are thousands in which he obeys the authority of his parents—even if reluctantly—because though he cannot see the purpose, or dislikes the purpose, of the thing he is required to do, he knows in his heart of hearts that his parents, because they love him, seek only his good; and because *it is harder to defy an authority based on love than one based on punishment or physical coercion.* Where authority is identified simply with physical power it seems legitimate to seek a similar power to resist it, and "hence come wars and fightings". Even when authority is based simply on superior knowledge and experience one is stimulated to counter it by appealing to the knowledge or experience of others ("quoting other authorities"). But where it is based on love only, where in fact it is identical with love as in the case of loving parents, no such form of resistance springs readily to hand.

Even therefore in our own civilisation we each begin by thinking of love and authority as being much the same thing, so my mythical country discovered by Gulliver is not so fantastic after all. But somehow, somewhere along the line we learn (we are alas taught) to regard them not only as two different concepts, which perhaps they are, but as two contradictory and mutually exclusive concepts, which they need not be.

It is instructive to examine the course of development of those few people in whose upbringing love and authority were separated from the very start. I refer to those children whose parents are, for whatever cause, unloving, or who have no parents. Such children are called "deprived" because they have been deprived of affection. Upon them authority is exercised, often with great inconsistency of operation, sometimes with harshness, and without the ameliorating influence of love, and it is hence a well-known characteristic of such children that they assume all authority to be hostile. They tend to react vigorously against it, become "unamenable to discipline", at odds with society (which they think of simply as hostile authority—*"them"*) prone to assume that they are being discriminated against, anti-social and often delinquent. We may say indeed that the degree to which love and authority have been early associated together in the child's mind is the degree to which he is able to accept normal authority. The child who was not loved finds authority unacceptable; the child who was loved has normally no such difficulty and passes from home to school with little trouble.

It is doubtful even so whether the five-year-old, in spite of his life-long association of love and authority, and his predisposition therefore to accept the latter, will continue for long to accept all authority quite uncritically. I think it may be true to say that he will tend to accept a loving authority, but will tend to react against an unloving one because it differs from the pattern—the secure and familiar pattern—to which he is accustomed. This is a further reason why the child in these days progresses easily from home to school. The modern primary school is, I am glad to say, a fairly loving kind of place, and the authority exercised there is much akin to the authority of home. The primary school-teacher in these days is taught to be kind and loving and tolerant and the child, therefore, readily accepts her authority. For whatever reason (and I am sure there are many) the benign loving approach of the primary school teacher is considered less appropriate as the child gets older, and the upper reaches of the secondary modern school are notorious for their disciplinary problems. These are less noticeable in the grammar school because (I suppose) the grammar school child is on the whole more interested in his studies than is the secondary modern adolescent, has therefore more in common with his teachers, and consequently a more loving relationship is possible. It is too soon as yet to see what will be the effect of "going comprehensive" but I suspect that even within the same school problems of discipline and authority will vary in intensity according to the degree to which teachers and pupils have a common purpose and something in the nature of a loving relationship is possible.

In short, the point I am at present concerned to make is that the degree to which love is dissociated from authority is the degree to which authority finds it necessary to use coercive measures, often of an unpleasant kind; and the degree to which love is dissociated from authority is the degree to which those under authority will rebel against it.

This is a proposition which many people find it hard to accept, and their reluctance is due in part to what I believe to be a very common fallacy. The loving parent (and for that matter the loving teacher) may bring himself on occasion, with great reluctance, to use punitive coercion. This may often secure the desired immediate end, and because it was done so reluctantly, at such cost to the adult concerned ("This hurts me more than it hurts you") and because it was in the nature of a last resort, it is assumed by the punisher to have been the decisive factor and, of course, he is mistaken. When the child has grown into a stable, contributing, compassionate adult, the reluctant punisher will be apt to say "That is because I was even prepared to punish", but he will be wrong. It was not the punishment, which was only an occasional, exceptional thing, but the love, which was constant and continuous and persistent that was the decisive thing. The upbringing might well have been successful without the punishment; it could never have been successful without the love. If the punishment contributed anything (which I personally doubt; but if it did) then that was because it was given by a loving person and not a neutral or a hating person.

It is a fact well known to penologists that a large number of men go to prison once, never to return; and that another, somewhat smaller number, return constantly. There are, of course, many things that account for this, as nothing in the field of penology or criminology is a simple one-factor affair. But there is one factor which which so far as I know has never been investigated, and which I believe makes an important contribution to this phenomenon. This factor, I suggest, is the attitude to society of the men concerned. The one-timers, I believe, are men who think of themselves as belonging to society, identify with it, and tend to regard it on the whole as benign rather than hostile. They see it—if this is not stretching the term too far—as a loving rather than as a hating authority. Hence when society expresses its moral condemnation of their behaviour by punishing them, they are able to accept the authority and mend their ways (I have not time to discuss why in their case the punishment needs to be inflicted and not, as with most of us, merely threatened). Those who return repeatedly to prison are those who tend to see society as outside themselves and hostile to them, and are, therefore, unable to accept its authority. They see society not as caring for them but simply as harming them and as being in general separate from them and opposed to them; and as I implied earlier it is easier to resist a neutral or hating authority than a loving one. So they continue to resist.

(While this was not my purpose, this does high-light the futility of punishing either of these two groups of men. Those in the first group are brought up short not because they were punished but because they have been convinced of the disapproval of a caring society; the recidivist is obviously not helped at all and that is because *au fond* he is not convinced that society cares—he does not think of it as a loving authority).

There is, of course, an obvious biological reason why parental authority must be loving. Insofar as it is necessary for the parent to coerce the child, he is inhibited by affection from doing so in a manner that is harmful to the child. We have all seen the occasional exception to this, due to stupidity or to a mistaken sense of duty, but in general it is true that the loving coercion of the parent is not a harmful one . . . Whereas those who apply coercion without love—as we have seen it applied in the totalitarian states as well as more mildly in our own penal system—are prepared to go to any length, even to the torture and death of the subject, to secure obedience. This is not only because "love suffers long and is kind", but also because those who love see authority as a means, whereas those who wield authority without love are inclined to regard it as an end in itself. Naked authority says "I must be obeyed, or I cease to exist"; loving authority says "It does not matter whether I am obeyed or not so long as my aim, the well being of the subject, is achieved". Loving authority is therefore prepared to discuss the matter at issue, listen to reason, even perhaps on occasion to admit that it may have been mistaken. Under naked authority it is always the function of the subject, never that of the ruler, to confess error; and naked authority, regarding itself as an end, assumes (and rightly on that premiss) that it is destroyed if it is not obeyed.

It may be thought that I have been talking about the acceptance of authority as if that were always a desirable thing, which of course is not necessarily the case. Even a loving authority can make mistakes, and many of us looking back on our childhood with loving parents can remember occasion when they seem to have been in error. But as we have just seen, a loving authority is not concerned with blind acceptance, is more interested in co-operation than in coercion, and in any case is not prepared to coerce to the degree that will cause suffering to the coerced.

It is very difficult to conceive of that remote and impersonal thing the State as a loving authority, and indeed the degree to which it is based on violence is the degree to which such a concept is unthinkable. Yet as we have seen in our own unhappy times there are differences in this matter between state and state, and some are (to put it in the least positive way) even less loving than others. At this moment of time our own state is beginning to move towards the exercise of a less unloving authority over its lawbreakers. There is still a very long way to go, but we are moving, however uncertainly, away from retribution and punishment towards therapeutic care. Men being trained for the Approved School service are taught that one of the prime needs of the boys with whom they will work is affection. Even in the prison service there is the beginning of a crack in the ice. Whereas until quite recently the prison officer was forbidden to address any word to prisoners except in the strict exercise of his duty of supervision, he is now encouraged in some cases to establish something in the nature of a human relationship with those in his charge.

This change is coming about very slowly and is strongly resisted by many in the prison system (and outside it) because they have somehow become convinced that love and authority are two separate and irreconcilable concepts, even though in their private lives they may exercise authority lovingly as parents. It may well be indeed that their presumption about the irreconcilability of love and authority is something they have learned from the prisoners, very many of whom belong to that group to whom reference has already been made, who were denied the experience in childhood of loving parents. To them all authority is necessarily hostile and they bring this attitude to prison with them, demanding from the staff of the prison an attitude consistent with it. As they greatly outnumber the staff it is not surprising if their attitude prevails. That, however, is by the way. For whatever reason the average prison officer is convinced that so far as his work is concerned, naked coercive punitive authority is essential because otherwise the prisoners in his care would violently rebel. In this there is a large measure of truth not only because of the factor we have just noticed—the prisoner's assumption that all authority is hostile—but also because he has ample evidence, in the negative, unconstructive and even degrading nature of imprisonment that in fact this particular authority *is* hostile. But supposing imprisonment were positive, constructive, life-enhancing, and tending manifestly to the prisoner's well-being—would it then be resisted to the degree that it is? Would then a loving authority be feasible? Certainly it would not be as readily acceptable as the more ingenuous idealist might suppose, because it would still be necessary to overcome that prior assumption of many prisoners about the hostility of all authority. In my own experiments in this direction, it has been quite customary for the most loving staff-members to be accused of practising entirely non-existent rigours, not because they *were* practising them, but because it was assumed that people in their position *would* practise them, but with patience this can be in large measure overcome. Just as the young child from a loving family may look critically on an authority that does not conform to the loving pattern with which he is familiar, so I believe the products of the other type of home (or Home), who furnish a large proportion of our prison population, may be persuaded after a time to look again at a kind of authority that does not conform with *their* presuppositions. The immediate response may well be opposition and a demand for the familiar response of harshness and punishment; but when it becomes clear that such a response is not to be elicited—that this is in fact a loving authority—then there may well be a gradual and grudging acceptance of that authority, leading eventually to co-operation in its therapeutic aim. This at least has been my own experience during a lifetime devoted to various attempts to exercise a loving authority among delinquent and maladjusted adults and children.

Lawbreakers are of course only a tiny fraction of our society, and if I seem to have dwelt on them unduly this is because my own work has lain among them, and also because as Winston Churchill truly said, a society is to be judged by its attitude to its criminals. But the state exercises authority in many ways besides this. It exercises authority over all of us, and in that exercise also is to be seen the common assumption that authority is not viable without the threat of punitive sanction, from "Do not spit; penalty forty shillings" to the death sentence (now happily under suspension) for murder. Is it possible for the state to exercise a loving authority— an authority that is without punitive sanctions? The chief inhibiting factor here seems to be that society at present seems only to know one way of expressing condemnation of an action, and that way is to punish its perpetrators. That indeed is one definition of punishment—the expression of society's moral condemnation;* so that we all tend to regard those things as permissible that are not punishable, and conversely. This attitude is much to be deplored because it tends to work against the development in the individual of personal moral standards and imperatives. Experience has shown me beyond any possibility of

* See A. C. Ewing, *The Morality of Punishment.*

doubt that the child who has been brought up by loving parents who say, e.g. "You must not steal because it is wrong; and it is wrong because of the distress it causes to other people" have much firmer and sounder moral convictions than those others, of whom I have met many, who have been brought up by a neutral unloving authority which says simply "Do not steal because I shall punish you if you do". The latter, very broadly speaking, is the attitude of the state. Has the time comes when we can begin to enact laws which instead of a schedule of punishments have a preamble stating in detail why the particular law is necessary? We used to hear a great deal at one time about "courtesy cops" whose function was politely to point out their errors to careless motorists, and only today I read in the paper of a seaside resort that is to appoint "litter maids" to ask people to pick up the litter they have thrown down, rather than to see that they are fined the statutory ten pounds. An extension of this principle might be the beginning of a loving authority exercised by society. I referred earlier to my conviction that the "only once" prisoner is the man who has in some measure identified with society and is therefore—however late in the day—prepared to accept its authority. It is my further conviction that the less harsh and hostile society is, the nearer, that is, it can approach to a loving relationship with its individual members, the more easy will it become for citizens to identify with it and accept its authority.

There can be little doubt that so far as its domestic legislation is concerned, and in large measure so far as the attitude of its officials is concerned, our own state approaches nearer to the ideal of a loving authority than it has ever done. The superficial observer points to student unrest, rioting at protest marches, and above all to the crime statistics, especially those for violent crime, and says that this benign trend must be reversed before the country sinks into chaos (which he miscalls anarchy) . . . It must be borne in mind however that insofar as the state *has* made this advance, it is assuming a new and unfamiliar role. The mass of citizens tend to see it still as naked (unloving) authority and are, therefore, stimulated to resistance in much the same way as the prisoner tends to resist the authority of the prison staff, demanding a harsh and punitive response. If the prison staff continue to resist that demand, continue to show only a caring, loving attitude, the prisoner will in time come to see them as a loving authority and will begin to co-operate. In the same way if the state persists in its trend towards loving care instead of naked authority, its citizens will more and more as time passes come to see it as having the same aims as himself (i.e. the well-being of society and its individual members) and will become more co-operative. But the process is a long and arduous one, and men are impatient for quick results. For some time yet the so-called criminal classes will continue to see the increasing benevolence of the criminal law as a weakness in what it conceives to be naked coercive authority. Not until all legislation is seen as an expression of genuine loving care can we expect an improvement in the crime statistics, and in disorder and violence generally.

In the sphere of international affairs the problem has always been—and still is—to create a supra-national authority that will command universal respect.

The United Nations, which aims among other things at being such an authority, succeeds (in my view) only to the degree to which it is a loving authority. This is perhaps not immediately apparent, and may call for a little elucidation.

U.N. is a "democratic" organisation whose power and authority are derived from the nations which constitute it. They, alas, come to the council chamber with (to say the least) very mixed motives, but in general it may be said that they tend to be more concerned with the pursuit of what they conceive to be the interests of their own nation than with the well-being of humanity in general. Consequently there is horse-trading in the corridors, and when the vote comes to be taken on a specific issue, representatives usually vote not according to the strict rights and wrongs of the matter, but according to the arrangements and agreements and accommodations made among themselves behind the scenes. "You vote with me over this matter, and I'll vote with you over *that*". The final and formal conclusions reached therefore are not an expression of concern for the common good, but a compromise between various self-seeking influences — to say nothing of the veto, which is often exercised on the basis of the crudest self-interest. Insofar, then, as the conclusions reached are not a genuine pursuit of the common good, U.N. is not, in the sense that I have in mind a *loving* authority; and the respect in which it is held throughout the world cannot at the present time be said to be very high.

There are those who say "UN will never be respected until it is given teeth", but God forbid that greater coercive power should be available to enforce decisions reached on the basis of such doubtful motives. It is surely more true to say that UN will be properly respected only when those who constitute it can be brought (impossible as this may now seem) to pursue with integrity the common good instead of the selfish ends of their own nation, thereby making United Nations a loving authority.

Further Reading:

Reluctant Rebels, Howard Jones, Tavistock 1960. Compares "loving authority" with more formal authority in the treatment of difficult children.

Hawkspur Experiment, W. David Wills, Allen and Unwin 1967. An account of the use of loving authority in the treatment of delinquent young men.

Studies in Environmental Therapy Vol 1, 1968. (Environmental Therapy Trust, 27 Marylebone Road, NW1 5JS). Article on the elimination of punishment in the residential treatment of troublesome boys and young men.

The Doukhobors, George Woodcock and Ivan Avakumovic. Faber 1968. A very odd and unaccommodating religious sect, many of whose members emigrated from Russia to Canada. Both in Russia and in Canada they were alternately persecuted and tolerated. It is interesting to see how under a tolerant regime they accommodated themselves to their social environment, but under persecution they became ever more irreconcilably intractable.

Talks to Parents and Teachers — Homer Lane.

They steal for Love — Anthony Weaver.

What is and What might be — Edmond Holmes.

Spare the Child — David Wills. (Love and authority in an approved school).

AUTHORITY AND THE LAW
C. H. ROLPH

C. H. Rolph is the pen-name of C. R. Hewitt, a former Chief Inspector of the City of London Police who is now a staff writer on the New Statesman and a member of its Board of Directors. He is a vice-president of the Howard League for Penal Reform and until July 1969 was a member of the Parole Board for England and Wales.

Where does Natural Justice come from? Does the authority of the police lie in the conscience of the public?

"We are called a democracy. We are prevented from doing wrong" (this is Thucydides in his *History of the Peloponnesian War)* "by respect for authority and for the laws, having an especial regard to those which are ordained for the protection of the injured as well as to those unwritten laws which bring upon the transgressor of them the reprobation of the general sentiment."

We are called a democracy, too. The idea is said to be based upon the conviction, and it has sometimes turned out to be right, that there are extraordinary possibilities in ordinary people. The British police system might be said to depend upon the ordinary: for its authority derives from the conscience of "the general sentiment" and the hope that ordinariness will not get too far above itself in emergencies. The conscience of the people is basically a love of law and order, but the law and order must be, and be seen to be, compatible with fairness, with "natural justice". The veneration of "natural justice" is deeper-rooted than any love of law and order; though only among the best of us does it echo the opinion of Theodore Parker that "democracy means not 'I'm as good as you are' but 'You're as good as I am'."

Where does natural justice come from? Men have always needed to find a mysterious and superhuman source for the laws regulating human conduct, if only that they might feel righteous rather than happy when punishing each other. A good deal of Roman law, as well as Germanic and Norman law, can be found expressed in Holy Scripture. Sir William Blackstone regarded natural justice as "the revealed or divine law, a part of the original law of nature, as tending in all its consequences to man's happiness, and the law of nature expressly declared to be so by God himself". Everyone knows, of course, that other gods than the Christian God have been credited with this declaration, its oldest form being the Code of Laws revealed by Shamash, the Babylonians' sun-god who was also the god of law, to Hammurabi the King of Babylon in 1728 B.C.

In the Paris Louvre there is an eight-foot granite obelisk engraved with a picture of Hammurabi receiving this revelation: it was found by the French in 1902 at Susa, the ancient Persian city called "Shushan" in the Book of Daniel, where it figures as the place of Daniel's imprisonment and vision in the story of Belshazzar's feast. Below the picture there are 51 columns of perfectly carved lettering in 300 paragraphs of civil, criminal and commercial law. This is the Code of Hammurabi, the earliest known written prescription of fair play and "the Golden Rule".

It is enough for many people, probably most people, that natural justice should be no more than this handed-down concept of fair play. Others, myself included, tend to believe in a natural justice that is older than Hammurabi's Code, older than humanity, older than the earth. What is by comparison infantile is its expression as a human appetite for Law and Order. Have you ever wondered, by the way, who first used that overworked phrase? It seems to have been Aristotle in Book VII of his *Politica*—"Law is a form of order, and good law must necessarily mean good order"; but 300 years after that it was Cicero, writing about the famous Twelve Tables of Roman Law, who laid down a principle that deserved to become far more widely venerated—*Salus populi suprema lex esto.*

"The safety of the people shall be the highest law" is thus the theme I borrow from Cicero, himself a lawyer though a great orator and an ineffectual politician, who so identified himself with the Law as to anticipate Mr. Bumble by roughly 2,000 years: "I have behaved," he wrote in 61 B.C., "like a perfect ass". You cannot, of course, dismiss the law as an ass, especially the law of public safety, unless you know the direction in which it is *supposed* to be moving; and there are few people in Britain today who try to find out much about that. To quote Lord Macdermott, Chief Justice of Northern Ireland:*

> "It is still true that most British people take the legal system under which they live, move and have their being very much for granted. They respect and support it, yet they are not curious about its structure or how it works. They look on the law as something that keeps the unruly in place and provides the popular press with a lot of its news, and they have no great thirst, so far, for a fuller knowledge. When life was simpler and the in-

* Protection from Power Under English Law (The 1956 Hamlyn Lecture): Stevens London, 1957.

> dividual had room to manage his own concerns without the constant danger of impinging on the rights of others or of contravening the regulations of some Government Department, this attitude may have been sensible enough . . . But today the situation is so different that the habit of looking askance at the law has nothing left to commend it."

A little learning may, in other words, be a dangerous thing, as Pope would have had his victims believe, but none at all can now be positively lethal.

What English law has really done, in its 1,000 years of misshapen development, is to evolve slower and gentler forms of coercion as the approved means of making the individual conform to majority wishes (or apathies). Killing, mutilation, torture, flogging and the seizure of property were the quick forms, and in England only the last-named survives. The slow forms are the summons, the writ, the solicitor's letter, the fine-with-time-to-pay, the suspended sentence, probation, imprisonment. These are the weapons of authority.

Another name for authority is "the rule of law", a phrase much used among law students and those who teach them. It is said to be the badge of a free people; and what it really means is (1) knowing what the law is or being able to find out, (2) knowing where it comes from or who made it, (3) equality before the law, which is generally known to be an unattainable ideal, (4) law courts which have complete independence of the government, and (5) everything being done by "due process". Moreover, there has to be a moral superiority about the law. It must stand for what is good, and fair, and just: it must reflect "natural justice". We have heard many warnings lately about the dangers of passing laws that are not likely to be enforced, for this, it is said, "brings the law into disrepute". Undoubtedly there are Acts of Parliament which are expected to operate by the mere fact that they exist, they are mere declarations of disapproval. Examples are the Litter Act of 1958, the Restriction of Offensive Weapons Act 1959 (more sensibly known as the Flick-Knives Act) and the Oil in Navigable Waters Act 1963. No-one seriously supposed that these were going to be enforced, and a multiplication of such statutes could eventually lead to a condition where the law's prohibitions and requirements were as ineffectual as those of an absent-minded mother mechanically rebuking her child without knowing what for.

When the law of a country is indeed "brought into disrepute" among a majority of its people, that country is losing the means to govern. This is true however smooth and sophisticated may be the means of enforcement; but still, even in England, the means of enforcement is commonly taken to be (in the very last resort) the exercise of violence. In the past half-century this fact has been skilfully exploited by "protest" and reformist movements, whose organisers have grasped that "non-violent resistance" really means using the violence of the authority resisted to call attention to your campaign. The process was brought to perfection by the Mahatma Gandhi, who was repeatedly taken off to prison for doing no more than sit cross-legged in the wrong place or at the wrong time. The origin of civilisation, as H. C. Bailey once wrote, is man's determination to do nothing for himself which he can get done for him.

We have to admit, then, that authority often resorts automatically to force, *some* kind of force, when it is absolutely defied; and that this is true whatever the nature of the government in power. A dictator will use his violent resources secure in the belief that no-one but himself and a few sycophants knows what the public thinks or wants. A democratically elected government will use it more riskily, in the knowledge that a large minority of the voters doesn't approve of it at all. (Sometimes, our electoral system being what it is, there may even be a majority disapproving of it). And a democratically elected government must be prepared to tolerate and contain the "devoted and eccentric individuals" whose methods could lead to its downfall. In such a country, the problem confronting the police but seldom, if ever, formalised for them, is the dilemma stated by Wells in his *Outline of History:**

> "We see an educational system meanly financed and equipped, badly organised; . . . we see popular information supplied chiefly by a venal press dependent upon advertisements and subsidies; we see farcial methods of election returning politicians to power as unrepresentative as any hereditary ruler or casual conqueror; everywhere the executive is more or less influenced or controlled by groups of rich adventurers, and the pursuit of political or social science and of public criticism is still the work of devoted and eccentric individuals rather than a recognised and honoured function in the State."

Wells was writing 50 years ago, almost to the day. How much of that would he have to change today? He saw international relations,

* 7th Edition, Cassell, London, 1932, p.972.

moreover, in terms of a balance of terror, the scale of which would grow uncontrollably; and though here he was more pessimistic than some of us, would he himself see it in any different light now? I believe that "authority", which in this country—and in my context—so often means the authority of the police, lies in the conscience of the people and therefore demands the people's moral approval. Unconsciously, the public of Britain expects a police service that is normally impeccable. There are countries in North Africa and Latin America where police brutality and corruption are part of the order of nature and where everyone, accordingly, makes allowance for them in his daily dispositions. "In Mexico City", I was lately told by a friend who has been living there for years, "when a policeman tells you that yesterday you drove past a yellow light, you do not reveal to him that yesterday you were confined to bed. You pay him 50 pesos, or 100 if he seems kindly and likely to be useful in the future. It is utterly useless, and in the end much dearer, to argue. But at least you know *exactly* where you stand". And yet even if (as he believes) the great majority of British policemen are restrained and honest, how is he to recognise the occasional one who is dangerously different?

The police of this country have always been the victims of a public that expected too much of them. To be frank, I have always known policemen who (in public) would hold up and burnish this perfectionist image of themselves, whatever their personal conduct might be; and they have sometimes gone to the extreme of obstinately rejecting stories even when, after full investigation, everyone in the country knew them to be painfully true. There are some who still say that the Challoner affair was a "put-up job", without saying who put it up and why. At about the time when H. G. Wells was writing what I have just quoted, European immigrants arriving at British Ports of entry were given a printed notice that began: "The Police of This Country are Your Friends". The police of the countries they came from were not their friends. The new idea took root in their wondering minds with the greatest difficulty, but once it was established they would go to the police about everything from a frozen water tap to a dispute over a game of cards. It is odd that those have always been the kind of people who knew most about the police at work in this country; and inevitable that, by contrast, the police should be judged by their countrymen mainly on what happens to those who break the law. In a useful booklet published in October 1969 by the National Council for Civil Liberties,* citizens and

* *The Police and the Citizen* N.C.C.L. London, 1969. 4s.

policemen are thus defined:

> Citizens, in modern usage, are people living in a society with its own rules and customs. Policemen are persons employed to ensure that the citizens observe the rules.

Simplicity itself. No word about social service or the role of the police in accident rescue work, or what they are able to do in softening the limitless tragedy of poverty, bereavement and loneliness in the modern State. They ensure that the citizens observe the rules.

And as to this, there are many who will say that the authority of the police rests solely on the threat of ultimate violence. If the police themselves thought their strength was based on violence alone, they would have to leave out the word "ultimate". For the violence that they can call into use would, in really grave circumstances, inevitably provoke the counter-violence that only military intervention can crush. Police violence, or even the offer of it, is always seen as provocative when its recipient is staging a protest about something. The role of the policeman, as symbolised by his carrying no more than a short and concealed wooden stick (which in fact, as often as not, he leaves at home—and sometimes gets into trouble for it) should be to persuade and negotiate. This is a lesson which, in the past, has been repeatedly learned and forgotten by the police themselves: but consider how well it was currently known by the time of the "great demonstration" against the Vietnam War, in Grosvenor Square on 27th October 1968. Turn again to the National Council for Civil Liberties,† an organisation not noted for any unreasoning pro-police bias:

> The change of police tactics was wholly successful as far as the main march was concerned. The behaviour of individual police officers was, with very few exceptions, exemplary. The good humour of the demonstrators and the determination of their organisers to prevent disorder made the occasion a responsible and peaceful protest. Much of the tension which arose before the demonstration can be attributed to the press in general and to two newspapers in particular. If the press indulges in fantasies about the prospect of violence it is quite conceivable that the more irresponsible protesters will indulge in the same fantasies. On this occasion certain reports occasioned alarm amongst

† Monthly Bulletin of the N.C.C.L., December, 1968.

> members of the public and those intending to demonstrate, and placed quite unfair pressure on police officers selected for duty that day. When violence did not occur on the main march many commentators were visibly disappointed. Peaceful protest is not merely a matter for police and demonstrators . . . A hard core determined to provoke the police into violent retaliation. That they did not succeed is a great compliment to the police officers on duty at that spot, who showed commendable restraint.

What was the "change of police tactics"? It was in fact a return to the ancient tactics of talking before instead of after the event, and doing it in offices instead of in hospital wards and court-rooms. And it was made possible by the readiness of the demonstrators, no less than of the police, to say beforehand what they wanted to do and, in the case of the demonstrators, to identify the enemy by whom they expected to be exploited.

A domestic police force, like a United Nations Police (from whose title the word "Force" might suitably be dropped) can be as effective as its moral authority will allow, and no more. And in a country like ours it must watch and contain, but may never suppress, those minorities by which a democracy is eternally threatened and unintentionally nourished. I suppose the police will never really love, or be loved by, H. G. Wells's "devoted and eccentric individuals"; and those are more numerous, or perhaps they are more articulate, now than in Wells's day. They have changed the face of England; and Gandhi (whom my police colleagues once execrated) changed the face of India. It is difficult not only for the police but for anyone to believe, though it is the truth, that the future is in the hands of such men. Senator Robert Kennedy once declared that "one fifth of all the people are against everything all the time". This is how it seems to the police, too; and learning to live with it is bound to take a long time.

Further Reading:

Social Science and Social Pathology, Barbara Wootten. Allen and Unwin, 1959.

Crime & Punishment in Britain, Nigel Walker. Edinburgh University Press, 1965.

The Idea of Punishment, Lord Longford. Geoffrey Chapman, 1961.

Keeping the Peace, David Williams. Hutchinson, 1967.

Individual Morality, James Hemming. Nelson, 1969.

TRUE NATIONALISM LEADS TO TRUE INTERNATIONALISM

PETER MANNICHE

Founder and Director, until his retirement, of the International Peoples College, Elsinore, Denmark. Now chairman of the Scandinavian Executive Committee Short Summer School Courses in Norway, Sweden and Denmark for International Understanding c/o 3060 Expergaerde, Denmark.

Denmark provides a living example of the practical nature of an educational policy which could change the prevailing philosophy from that of "power" to that of "life". Upon such a foundation may the authority of the U.N. grow without violating man's sense of dignity.

"One of the foremost educators of the world is Denmark's poet Bishop N.F.S. Grundtvig". This claim, made by Prof. Robert Ulich is supported by Prof. J. A. Lauwerys when he says "it is certain that the radical transformation of rural Denmark in the last hundred and fifty years from a poor and rather backward area would not have taken place if a wise and foresighted educational policy had not been pursued."

What can we learn from this educational policy which has so transformed Denmark and made her into what many people talk of as a "Social laboratory" and a "Co-operative commonwealth"? Are any of the lessons applicable to the work of the United Nations?

To answer these questions we must first look to the ideas of Grundtvig and to the conditions then and since.

What do people mean when using the term "co-operative commonwealth" about Denmark? This term is actually not correct for private business is still the rule in most of the Danish urban industries and commerce, and the farmers, who are the chief promoters of co-operation, are eager to maintain an open market. Nor is it true, as several observers have intimated, that the co-operative movement in Denmark is wholly the produce of the folk high schools. Co-operation was practically forced upon the Danish farmers by an *external* factor: dependence on foreign markets, especially England, for sale of their agricultural products. The necessity of wholesale transportation, steadiness of supply and uniformity of quality, put before the comparatively small Danish farms the choice between handing their products over to a big commercial firm or—what they did—joining a Co-operative society, *selling their own products,* and thus avoiding the middle-man's profit.

It was at that point that the folk high school entered the co-operation pictures. Led by pioneers of idealism and practical enterprise the farmers were able to carry the co-operative movement through. That they could do so by themselves, without help from the universities was due to the influence of the folk high schools which not only supplied the pioneers of the movement, but educated the whole peasantry to an understanding of their problems and a trustful appreciation of their leaders. Though the folk high schools will have to adjust themselves a good deal in the next generation to the increasing urban population, the movement has shown some quite remarkable accomplishments. Roughly 7,000 students have attended the folk high schools each year for a three, four or five months' course. Foreigners find it difficult to understand the dynamics which for generations sent between one third and one fourth of the whole rural population to these schools at their own initiative to some extent at their own expense and for the sake of education without obtaining degrees or direct material return. But the money they spent, and the money their government spent on their behalf, proved to be a very fruitful national investment.

THE RESULTS OF THE FOLK HIGH SCHOOLS

When some of the more utilitarian-minded farmers objected, that the students of Kristen Kold's pioneer folk high school were getting no practical results from the teaching, Kold told them: "If you are putting drain pipes in the soil, you have to mark the places where you put them, but when you sow corn you need no markers. In time of harvest you will see the results."

The results did come, material as well as spiritual. Director Anders Nielsen, a leading figure in the Danish co-operative movement, says of the folk high school: "It has filled in and levelled the clefts in society and thereby paved the way for working together. It has sent students out into life with an added love for the country and its achievements, riper and more thoughtful, more receptive to life's teachings, and therefore, well equipped to understand and make their way where less developed persons run aground. This significance of the folk high schools has now been emphasised and affirmed so often, and from so many sides that it can well be stated as a fact, that not only the co-operative movement, but the cultural position of the Danish farmers on the whole rests on its foundation. We must remember with gratitude the great religious and educational leaders, Grundtvig and Kold, and their many co-workers and followers who have called forth a higher culture and feeling of solidarity and who have taught the people to think and use their powers . . . so that not only the individual, but the whole community is benefitted."

That such individual growth has great social and economic consequences is the lesson taught not only by the experience of the folk high schools, but many other spiritual awakenings. Economic prosperity followed in their trail when the French Huguenots spread all over Europe. The Jews, the Parsees, and the Jains in India, Quakers, Wesleyans, Mennonites and Haugians in Norway, can be mentioned as other examples.

A rough examination made some thirty-five years ago, of the available information for the whole country, showed that of all the chairmen of co-operative dairy associations 54 per cent had been students at a folk high school, 23 per cent at an agricultural school (which gives purely technical instruction, but has been called a "child of the folk high school"), and 2 per cent at a dairy school. The figures show clearly that the folk high schools in particular have supplied the farmer's co-operative movement with its local leaders.

The growing political influence of the farmers helped to secure increasing State support for them. Though the schools have always been voluntary efforts there is considerable help from public funds, both to the schools themselves and their students, and the State sees that the accounts are in order, besides keeping an eye on the work, with which, however, it rarely, if ever, interferes. The Ministry of Education insists on its right to sanction the appointment of the Principal but he is free to choose his own fellow teachers. The Government and the Parliament realises that success depends more on personal devotion than on any system. As with the folk high schools so with the co-operatives, the Danish farmers are free to patronise private concerns, but the fact remains that in course of time the Danish farmers have been so thoroughly organised that they are conditioned by co-operation. A farmer who wishes, may get his mortgage loans from a kind of co-operative credit society, he may electrify his farm through co-operatives, he may sell his milk, pigs and eggs through co-operative dairies and export societies, and buy household wares as well as seed, fertilised in village co-operative or mutual savings banks. Of roughly 150,000 Danish farmers possessing more than half of the land, 50 per cent are members of, as a rule, several co-operatives, freed from the selling requirements of their calling. The farmers have not only increased the production of superior crops and livestock, but have also adapted their production to changes in the foreign markets. The co-operatives have made possible the development of more highly standardised products and the consequent reduction of their selling costs.

Through the administration, with its bulky organisation and democratic methods may sometimes make for slower management and initiative, the co-operatives have, on the whole operated economically and have furnished a healthy competition to private business. They have eliminated the possibility of exploitation of the farmers, and they have enabled these to unite individualism and socialism, freedom with social responsibility.

Can the Folk High School Serve the Developing Countries?

That the movement has been able to expand, and—to some extent—maintain its original enthusiasm for over a hundred years is a sure indication of a wise combination of voluntary and national efforts. Now, in the last third of the twentieth century, many countries find themselves in a situation analogous to pre-industrial Denmark. The question is therefore: Can the Scandinavian folk high school be imported by the developing countries? What are its characteristics, irrespective of the time of its origin?

The Grundtvigian folk high school has been called a historic-poetic and a typical national form of adult education. An emphasis on the study of history and literature, and a worship of the national was characteristic of the period of romanticism, in the last decades of which in Denmark the first folk high schools arose. These were influenced by the times. Their teachers sought to learn from the great past and—through a sense of national fellowship—to inspire great deeds. They largely succeeded because they concentrated their efforts on the inner development of their countries. So long as nationalism is fellowship in *life,* it can be a powerful motivator of fruitful efforts. This happened, as we have seen, in Denmark particularly after the defeat by Germany in 1864. It happened in Russia for Russia after 1917 was greatly influenced by the nationalism of Dostojevsky and other "slavophiles": in Japan, where nationalism was personified in the emperor, and we see it now everywhere in the developing countries. It is deadly in earnest for the new populations struggling for a place in the sun. The sense of national fellowship has released enormous energies.

But we in the West have realised how fellowship in life has often turned into fellowship in *power,* and that when this happened nationalism became the scourge of our time, the greatest cause of war. To be sure, Hitler and his men did not really worship their nation as much as they did "the State", but the nationalism of the ordinary Germans was utilised by them to strengthen the power of the German State inside as well as outside its historical borders. Grundtvig warned against any such misinterpretation. "What I call *"folkelighed"*, he wrote, "is considerably different from the un-Christian and anti-Christian nationalism" which (also in his time) was preached in Germany. The terms he used *(folkeligt* and *universelt)* referred respectively to a genuine community consciousness within regional borders, and to matters concerning humanity as a whole. To him, narrow-minded nationalism was a reflection of the fact that the people who nourished it had but a superficial knowledge of their own people's life and culture. Delving deeper they would discover the links that bind the peoples of the world together in universal fellowship.

To understand the lasting essence of the Grundtvigian folk high school, the best way may be to point to three of its features, namely: its personal method, its individualistic principle in education, and its socioreligious purpose.

If these features are truly characteristic of the Grundtvigian folk high school, the developing countries can benefit very much from it.

The Personal Method is important, because of the social structure of these countries. To be sure, the new countries are now developing very rapidly, but the average African and Asian citizen is still a member of an extended family or of a caste. This gives him protection and social security. It is dangerous to move a person from his or her natural environment into the loneliness of big cities. Deep love among human beings and true human wisdom cannot be fully developed within *large* units. The "personal school" can, much better than a large educational institution, lead the Asian and African peasants organically into the modern type of society which they hope will emerge from their "revolution of rising expectations."

Education which builds on individuality is the educational principle of the folk high schools. Grundtvig inveighed against the hunt for degrees. This would, if it were carried over from the university (where it may function) to the farmer's own school, take the farmers away from their jobs. There is hardly any folk high school ending with an examination. Gandhi likewise condemned examinations, which standardised Indian education and made university degrees lead to city careers, the universal goal of all forms of higher education. Education of Indians should be adapted to, and therefore vary with, the local environment and the individual needs of the students.

"The State", he said, "would do the greatest harm to mankind by destroying individuality, which is the root of all progress." Other of Gandhi's writings do modify this statement, but not its principle. It was "unity in the manifoldness" he hoped for—a society in which the individuals work together for the whole of society without thereby losing their individual character. To serve humanity was Gandhi's main desire which knew no national frontiers. By serving India as best he could, he felt that thereby he served also humanity and God.

By uniting, in education, regard for the individual with a social goal, Gandhi and Bishop Grundtvig were in full accord with one another. Grundtvig did not want instruction in the folk high school to be based on an examination with questions to the young, but wanted it to help to find answers to their own questions. He believed that the greatest of all questions was the question about life itself. The age of youth, therefore, is the proper time for enlightenment. When the farmers and the artisans in Denmark were later called upon to take an active part in the legislation about condition for life and the social aspects of it, they were educated for this duty, not primarily through children's schools, but through schools for adults.

He held that the child should rest and grow in its rest. The child has first of all the right to be a child, and the education given to children must be adapted to their needs. Nor is adolescence the proper time for the development of such social responsibility, and education for a true and living democracy. The youth between fourteen and eighteen need physical activity and familiarity with the work they may later have to do. The best schools for the average person in these difficult years of human development are the workshops of capable artisans and the farms of good farmers. It is not until men and women reach adult years that they are mature enough to understand fully the life and society in which they are to thrive. Then the religious life, the sex life, the feeling for poetry and for fatherland are fully awake. The soul of the full grown youth is far more filled with questions than it was during the transitional years. The method of answering these questions to be used by the folk high school teachers. Grundtvig thought, was to tell their students about the life of the human race in the light of history, and send them back to their farms or workshops with an increased interest and a clearer understanding of citizenship.

In connection with the idea of improving the folk high school in the developing countries, it is important to bear in mind that in several of these countries, not least in Latin America, where they are most needed, they may not—for several years to come—have sufficient financial resources to provide most of their citizens with more than three or four years of schooling. The question then arises as to what period of their lives would be best for them to receive this education. The quickest way of creating an enlightened democracy might be, according to Scandinavian experience, to provide for young adults the opportunity to spend at least five months of their lives in Folk High Schools.

Experience taught Grundtvig that he who does not love his near-by neighbour does not love the distant ones either. But this as already emphasized, was not narrow nationalism. He thought that each nation had the duty to make its special contribution to the life of the whole human race.

K. G. Saiydain, when he was Education Secretary in India, said about Mahatma Gandhi: "His teaching has illuminated the way not only for his own country, but for the whole world", may also be said about Grundtvig.

The three characteristic features of the folk high school were basic to the work of the International People's College at Elsinore, which was started in 1921 and in course of time have received students from about 20 nations. The present principal is Poul Kjaer, and it can now accommodate 110 students. These cannot but learn to develop the same qualities as must the nations in order to enter the United Nations, or any form of international, political organisation in the right spirit. In all probability these features will prove still more essential in the Rural Development College which was started in 1964 at Holte, near Copenhagen, with the task of adapting the folk high school to the new developing countries and of finding a pattern of behaviour that will make continued collaboration between the races possible through mutual understanding.

This College which was supported by the Ford Foundation and the Danish Government, receive students selected by governments which were almost all in the developing countries. Since 1960 we have also arranged short international vacation courses in July and August for the study of the Scandinavian countries, and underdeveloped countries in particular. We must concentrate on building up a channel of human internationalism, a prerequisite for an efficient United Nations. Now it is no longer the relations between European peoples which will decide whether humanity is to die or survive. We must set out again, not as formerly to explore the geography of the new countries, but to meet with human beings of races other than our own and in fellowship with them try to find a common denominator among conflicting ideas, a pattern of behaviour that will make continued collaboration possible through mutual understanding. The United Nations cannot thrive unless each member nation realise that it has its particular, and consequently limited part to play, and that no single nation or group of nations possess all qualifications for leadership.

In a competitive society the failure of your neighbour may be the cause of your own success. but co-operatives can only be furthered by people and nations who are ready to share their successes and failures with others. It is this spirit of fellowship which the folk high schools helped to foster among the independent farmers in Denmark, and it is this spirit which UNESCO and other forms of international education are to foster within the United Nations.

Further Reading:

Denmark A Social Laboratory Peter Manniche. Consult Mr. Strandberg, Monrads Alle 35, Copenhagen, Valby 2500 Denmark.

Rural Development and the Changing Countries of the World Peter Manniche. Pergamon Press, Oxford, 1969.

Grundtvig Koch Hal. Antioch Press, U.S.A. 1932.

The Danish Folk High School Thomas Roerdam. Copenhagen, 1966.

Education for Life Noelle Davies Williams. Morgate, London, 1931.

Education in Democracy Moeller and Watson. Faber and Faber, 1944.

IS THE "DANISH MODEL" APPLICABLE TO THE WORLD LEVEL?

KNUD NIELSON

Teacher at the International Peoples College, Denmark, in Political Theory, Philosophy and International Problems. Chairman of the Council of "World Association of World Federalists."

To what degree could the Danish experiment be used in the international scene or at the world level? Is there some analogy between the national development and what could happen internationally? On the world level we have, due to an explosive development, technically become *One World* in *Interdependence*.

This chapter is supplimentary to the preceeding one.

Nations have *together* advanced in the development of peaceful things: tools, fuel-power, "division of labour", social organisation, administrative areas, effective and frequent representation of the people, social rate of advance, types of goods produced, weapons of war, and organisation, strategy and tactics. The more important fields of interdependence are (1) communications (traffic, T.V., radio, etc.); (2) production (industrial and agricultural), and (3) security or military techniques.

Paradoxically enough this growing interdependence in the world has focussed upon the differences between peoples. When neighbours keep apart, differences do not matter so much and therefore the aim should be to retain and harmonize independence, but within a framework of co-operation in which these differences may be reconciled for the good of all.

Into this background the co-operative principles of Scandinavian origin could perhaps be used as a sort of "inspiring model". Education is of the first importance. We need universities dealing with (1) *international problems* of coexistence and economic co-operation, and the preservation of natural resources from pollution and destruction; (2) *transnational problems* in the field of business organisation, co-operation; among citizens' organisations, cultural exchange co-operation etc., peace-making and "trouble-shooting".

Some problems such as the execution of world-laws raises problems of *supra-national organs* and their functions. We need *international colleges*—a sort of "World Folk High Schools" for a more popular study of, and a practical training in, living the above problems. One thing is to study and understand—another to make "real—to "live" these things.

Another field of "co-operative-techniques" is the *unavoidable negotiations* between "Big business", international expertise, representatives of different ideologies, which must come together to solve the extremely complex problems of overpopulation, hunger, economic growth, development, public health and the preservation of resources. As international co-operation will probably neither be entirely "state" (whether world,—regional or national state), or entirely "private" (whether capitalistic, ideological or in the field of private international companies), the lessons of the Danish/Scandinavian co-operative-techniques and experience may again be of use.

One day in the future the society of nations—regional and global alike may be governed without depriving nations and other groups of their "rights to be different" and "administer" themselves as much as possible within the community (of states). Here,—all the limitations in such analogies taken into account—the "Danish experience" might, be if not helpful directly, then perhaps, rightly understood act as an inspiration. These techniques will partly begin on the practical level and partly in education. In education because this in itself must support reform, but also because we must be educated for all the other forms of co-operation in a complex world to create a world based on "Unity with diversity", tomorrow.

PLANNING FOR HARMONY
SIR CLOUGH WILLIAMS-ELLIS, C.B.E.

Architect, Town Planner and Pioneer of the countryside protection movements. Past president of the Design and Industry Association. Vice-President Institute of Landscape Architects and Councils for the Protection of Rural England and Wales. First Chairman of the First New Town Corporation (Stevenage), Consultant Planner to various municipalities and creator of Portmeirion township and other development schemes.

Sir Clough Williams-Ellis stresses the importance of beauty, believing that by providing a beautiful environment a healthy society will be encouraged. But such beauty implies co-operation, planning, unity and diversity.

It is often said that, now-a-days, architects and planners are no longer proper practitioners in their respective professions but, as government or local-government employees have become, rather, social engineers and welfare officers. Heaven knows we need such, both more and better, but I am concerned to extend the concept of welfare to include "that Strange Necessity" beauty, lacking which I hold that any man is deprived and defrauded of his greatest possible source of happiness, if he did but know it.

Mostly he doesn't know it and puts up with ugliness and squalor as fatalistically and patiently as with the other infelicities of his life on earth that he accepts as inevitable.

And whose fault, as Ruskin asked, is that crippling resignation? That of the defrauded untaught or of the unteaching elect,—those of us who know and care, yet do little about it?

I was once involved in a more than usually fierce controversey about a large scale industrial development that proposed to dump itself down on a long settled and well integrated community, purely for the convenience and profit of its promoters and without any genuine concern for its environmental human consequences, still less its harmful impact on the natural amenities of the place.

But what was disheartening was the almost unquestioned acceptance by the locals of this alien intruder on the score of work and wages *alone* without care for anything else at all and quite regardless of such side effects as added ugliness, traffic, noise and the fumes invading their homes, all under the persuasive banner of "Full Employment" as if that was everything. Of course we all want work and wages and it is hard for amenity to flourish and survive without nourishing economic roots, but it is surely abject and pitiful to accept and welcome "Full Employment" as sufficient when "Enjoyment" might have been demanded and largely provided for had the citizens concerned been alert enough to insist upon it.

Controversial planning issues are generally settled at ministerial enquiries, where the main witnesses for and against a project are professional planning experts, like counsel in a court of law. Amenity bodies are generally well and ably represented, but why are the people directly concerned generally so passively mute, so apparently indifferent to the issue being fought above their humble heads?

True, the amenity champions have done their best (so far a poor best) to rouse the masses to a realisation of that fuller enjoyment of life that might be theirs if only they would really and resolutely press for it. The trouble is of course that they have no idea, poor souls, how different things *could* be or what they are missing—no idea at all of how to enlarge and better their lives if they do come to suspect deficiencies. I will confess that I have myself an instinctive, illogical, and quite indefensible feeling that seemly architecture and a gracious landscape are sufficient ends in themselves, self-justified, regardless of their social implications, of the conditions that have produced them, or even of their own repercussions on humanity. That view, treating mankind as a mere foreground to inanimate beauty, as just figures in a landscape, cannot, I own, be intellectually defended. I have to admit that no sensible person is likely to concern himself about visual beauty, its creation or preservation, save with reference to its human values.

Not without difficulty, I too have at last persuaded myself into that more reasonable if utilitarian belief, which I suppose might be baldly stated somewhat thus: "That the mere existence of beauty is of no importance, it is only its enjoyment by man that signifies". It follows, it seems to me, that admitting that much one must go yet further and allow that what really matters is that the appreciation and enjoyment of beauty shall be as widely diffused and shared as possible—for the greatest happiness of the greatest numbers and *that* must mean popularizing and democratizing the enjoyment of such beauty—to make lovely buildings and artifacts of all kinds as well as lovely places generally accessible and familiar, without — somehow — thereby imperiling their very existence.

With the overwhelming mass of our teeming population town-bred, and barbarously reared in far other than splendid cities, having had little contact with beauty of any kind (including literature and the arts) and therefore knowing or caring little for it, the introduction is inevitably hazardous, for one is unlikely to respond appropriately when presented to the hitherto unknown. Yet it is a risk that must be taken. We must perforce put up with the inevitable misunderstandings and gaucheries that will mark the first contacts of the uninitiated with their hitherto unrealized heritage.

But in order that this very heritage itself may be spared, and shall not dissolve utterly away at this unaccustomed touch, this overdue presentation must assuredly be made, for it is altogether too dangerous that the vast majority of its heirs should be insensitive to its intrinsic loveliness, ignorant of its pleasure-giving potentialities or its historical value, that they should still be without pride in its possession and careless of its preservation. To ensure that at any rate our chief national treasures, both of landscape and of architecture and the rest, shall survive these difficult transitional times, that they may give pride and pleasure to our possibly more civilised successors, they must now attract to themselves a general popularity and appreciation—a wide democratic good will, that will protect them from neglect and injury and maintain them against the Philistine. The greatly increased leisure that is forecast for most of us through automation and a shortened working week, will need to be filled by pursuits and interests of SOME sort and we shall be concerned to see that these are civilized.

Yes, yes! but HOW? Well, to begin with, obviously by education of a kind that we seem to have largely neglected. I recall years ago inducing a few enterprising schools to run essay competitions in response to some such suppositions as this:

"Imagine yourself on the roof of your home with an-all-round view of a couple of miles and in your hand a magic wand by the waving of which you could alter all you see to any extent. What changes would you make and why? Remember that if you are moving *people*, you must think where to and how, not forgetting that they may not want what you want—but must put up with whatever you arrange for them until they can themselves change things, which may take a long time."

A simple enough little exercise that could obviously be varied and improved in a hundred different ways and widely used if only enough of us cared enough about sowing the seeds of good-citizenship in our children.

Meanwhile all our efforts at planning for harmony, or indeed planning meaningfully at all, are bedevilled and distorted by the need to sacrifice quality to quantity—providing at best a mere veneer of "Amenity" instead of a basic comprehensive graciousness.

How often now, do or can those concerned with housing, live up to the old definition of "Right Building" as that providing "Firmness, Commodity and Delight"?

As things are, all we can do is to make a pretty desperate situation as tolerable as may be by such palliatives as concern and ingenuity can contrive, which, given our present economic and political uncertainties, is likely to fall far short of our hopes.

Certainly the magnitude of the problem facing us is now well recognized and such eminent social scientists as Ebenezar Howard, Raymond Unwin, Geddes, Abercrombie, Buchannon, Lewis Mumford, Doxiadis and the rest have all had a stab at an answer, but we still seem to be stuck. Partly because their several recommendations have not been studied, understood and approved by enough of us to get popular backing, partly because they are thought unrealistically long-term, ambitious and expensive, but largely because we still lazily accept muddle and meanness as inevitable.

But is it? If it is, our civilization is surely a failure and life much less worth while living than it might have been.

I recall a letter from Lewis Mumford in which he wrote to me, "I would die happy at any time if I could count on this inscription on my tomb stone:

"This Man was a Fool
The dire things
He foretold never happened"

For many years and in many great books he has long been warning America and the world at large of the consequences of machine worship and a too mechanistic outlook generally when man himself is so very much more than a machine.

That would seem to have been forgotten by some of our *avant-garde* modern architects. If my so impressively capable successors could only descend from their clinical and negative abstractions to the level of warm humanity—could build with more loving-kindness—could bring back delights to rejoin the firmness and commodity wherein they so excel—then we should surely be on our way to something better—something pleasurable. Most modern buildings seem to have so wantonly thrown away obvious chances of interest and distinction—to have wilfully withheld opportunities for delight—for imaginative, sensitive detailing and for the appreciation of arts, skills and craftsmanship as well as overall harmony. A sharp reaction to the feeble elaboration and vulgarity of most late Victorian and Edwardian architecture was certainly overdue and a thorough purge was certainly called for and has been now achieved. But don't let us go on reacting so aridly, so drearily, so emptily—let us dare to be a little more friendly—even a little gay. Let us use our wings.

The Festival of Britain gave us a glimmer of hope in 1951—where is it now? If a heretic deviationist such as I were allowed to offer a prayer on behalf of British Architecture, it would be this, GOD, GRANT GRACE.

But our traditional pattern of living has been largely destroyed by a new scale and a new speed of development that is producing chaotic conditions that seem hostile to civilized life as we have known it. Perhaps we may contrive to adapt ourselves to this bleak-looking future but only I think by the sacrifice of some of our humanity.

Of our attempts to set higher amenity standards there is now an encouraging plenty, including the Government—sponsored New Towns, various well devised new neighbourhoods established by municipalities, and one of London's official '51 Festival enterprises, Lansbury.

This baby townlet, peeping hopefully out like a little kangaroo as it were from the pouch of its old mother borough of Poplar, the child of her shabby old age—there was something poignantly inspiriting about its own fresh vigour, its well articulated little body with all its parts properly proportioned and functioning as they should. I should like to have been able to applaud an infant grace holding more than a hint of further beauty yet to come, but though this stripling neighbourhood is seemly indeed by our lamentable East-End and suburban standards, and a pattern of livable layout still well worth our closest study, it cannot be pretended that it uplifts the spirit by any radiant loveliness. But, it may be asked, does it much matter if the public does vote it all a little dull, so long as it satisfies its enlightened sponsors and pleases its actual inhabitants? Surely yes, for the Lansbury project might easily have had a gracefulness that would have ensured it a popular esteem and provided the east London boroughs with a standard of amenity that would stretch their imaginations and keep them on their cultural toes instead of remaining just flat-footedly and conscientiously competent. In short, to be entirely the layman's cup of tea—or mine—it needed just a little more sweetening.

Only love (*with* intelligence) can make a gracious town, or keep it so, a vigorous civic pride justly founded on a confident knowledge that all changes made are for the better, aesthetically as well as practically, any undue complacency being kept in check by the acceptance of a high standard based on the very best that has been, is being, or could be done elsewhere, and not merely on local comparisons between bad and not-so-bad.

All this implies PLANNING which simply means proposing to do, and then doing, certain things in an orderly, premeditated, related and rational way, having in view some definite end that is expected to be beneficial. It is the reverse of opportunism, of the day-to-day solving of problems as unrelated phenomena, without care for the final pattern that will result.

Examples of both ways of life have occurred at different times in the world's history, and in many different countries; sometimes one way has been dominant, though never to the complete exclusion of the other.

Even prehistoric man had to plan and co-operate to some extent, as do the primitive peoples of today; otherwise he could scarcely have survived the hazards of his hostile world. Only by sharing-out of tasks—hunting, food-gathering, defence, cooking, child-minding, shelter-contriving—could even the simplest society be kept alive.

Whether the whole tribe in conference, or the elders, or the chief alone settled the actual division of work, the 'action taken' would be the result of PLANNING. Indeed, the very existence of a tribe presupposes some sort of planning. You cannot live long in a group satisfactorily without an agreed set of rules or customs. Agreements to such rules is a condition of survival. What we call 'civilisation' really means a way of life pretty thoroughly planned in some at least of its aspects.

All sorts of injustices, hardships, deprivations, wastes and follies that were accepted with a shrug as inevitable only a generation or so ago are now regarded as an intolerable blot on our civilization and there are a multitude of alert good citizens and reforming bodies all concerned with assuring peace and using that peace for the enhancement and enriching of our lives.

Highly intelligent proposals of all sorts are constantly being propounded and even tried out, but for all our efforts, we still seem unable to do much more than patch and tinker where a radical recreation is really called for. But not called for loudly enough by enough of us, and until it is, it will never get the attention, so desperately needed, from ANY government striving as all must, to meet its electorates most clamant demands. True, there has been some excellent planning legislation and the Government sponsored New Towns, schemes for new cities, linear and other—National and County Parks, the Lea Valley new deal, and so on, but, if and when all have been fully realised there will still be endless details to be filled in with grace as well as practicality where alert and civilized good citizens should have their say.

Don Marquis held that "The world exists to produce artists in order that they may produce new worlds. They should have charge of this world and govern it, because they and they alone understand something of what it is all about". If, as I take it, he means that we need poets as well as plumbers, I am certainly with him.

Too much? So thought, apparently a friend who held that I was over-stressing the claims of landscape against the basic needs of my fellow-creatures and so sent me this on a postcard:—

"Pomona loves the orchard
And Liber loves the vine
And Clough he loves a fine facade
And an unspoiled skyline
But the citizen wants gasworks
Electric wires on high
And light and drains and telephones
God help me, so do I!"

How right she is—and how right am I!

As in my contribution to this symposium I have made so bold as to discuss BEAUTY, some of its aspects in nature and in art, its relevance to our lives and indeed its very reality. I might well have been expected to attempt an acceptable definition and some proof that, aware of it or not, it does (or should) play a powerful part in our whole human make-up and existence.

I confess myself incapable of doing either, and wonder indeed whether anyone else has been fully successful, though many wise men have believed and lived and written as though their aesthetic assumptions were axiomatic, as I too hold them to be.

In his book ART & TECHNICS, Lewis Mumford personifies these two concepts as respectively Orpheus and Promethous, holding that it was the music-maker rather than the fire-bearer who was man's first teacher and greatest benefactor in that, by means of symbols, he was enabled to express fellowship and love:—

> "He who goes daily into the world of aesthetic emotion returns to the world of human affairs equipped to face it courageously and even a little contemptuously. Surely there can be no reason why almost every man and woman should not be a bit of an artist since almost every child is. Can't we save that potential artist?"

That was Clive Bell, himself most highly responsive to visual beauty, as Bernard Shaw was not, though he was intelligent enough to realize its tremendous importance in the lives of others, as witness the death-bed speech in "THE DOCTOR'S DILEMMA":—

> "I believe in Michael Angelo, Velasquez, and Rembrandt; in the might of design, the mystery of colour, the redemption of all things by beauty everlasting, and the message of Art that has made these hands blessed. Amen. Amen."

A generation ago there were those who affected to think so vehement a devotion to beauty so expressed, almost a blasphemy. Today, there are, I think, many of us who, not being painters, yet feel as profoundly moved by visual beauty, whether God-made or man-made, as did Shaw's disreputable but dedicated artist.

If that great champion of beauty, the historian G. M. Trevelyan failed in precise definition who shall succeed?

> "This flag of beauty, hung out by the mysterious universe, to claim the worship of the heart of man, what is it, and what does it signal mean to us? There is no clear interpretation. But that does not lessen its value. Like the universe, like life, natural beauty also is a mystery. But whatever it may be, whether casual in its origin as some hold, who love it well, or whether as others hold, such splendour can be nothing less than the purposeful message of God—whatever its interpretation may be, natural beauty is the ultimate spiritual appeal of the universe, of nature, or of the God of nature, to their nursling man. It, and it alone, makes a common appeal to the sectaries of all our different schools of poetry and art, ancient and modern, and to many more beside. It is the highest common denominator in the spiritual life of today."

That, sincere, eloquent and moving as it is, of course, *proves* nothing. But it may still make some, as yet un-alive to beauty, alert to recognize and cherish it as the great vitamin that can enrich their existence beyond conception.

Further Reading:

The Myth of the Machine, The City in History, and the numerous other relevant books by Lewis Mumford.

Landscape in Distress Lionel Brett. (Now Lord Esher).

Tomorrow's Landscape Sylvia Crowe.

Designed for Recreation Elizabeth Beasley.

The Anatomy of the Village Dr. Thomas Sharpe.

Architect Errant (Autobiography) Sir Clough Williams-Ellis. Constable.

Portmeirion — The Place and its Meaning Sir Clough Williams-Ellis. Blackie.

Roads and Landscapes H.M.S.O.

England and the Octopus New (1975) and revised edition of the 1928 book with an introduction by Lewis Mumford.

NATURAL LAWS IN PRACTICE

STRUCTURE

The importance of *structure* in a world organization is of the utmost importance and insufficiently recognized. One of the first essentials for peace is for power to be controlled; the following chapters discuss this problem.

THE PHYSICS OF POLITICS

LEOPOLD KOHR·

Professor of Economics, University of Puerto Rico. Author of many books on the decentralization of power. (See end of chapter). Author of weekly column in EL MUNDO, San Juan, Puerto Rico. *Extra-Mural Tutor in Political Philosophy,* University College of Wales, Aberystwyth.

The idea underlying this essay is that many of the difficulties of modern life could be solved, by replacing the current bad balance of power with a good one. Since, in a dynamic world, a food balance depends on the parts of a system being both numerous and small, the essay suggests a return to what the Germans call Kleinstaaterei, the Augustinian ideal of a political universe composed, not of well meaning heavy-weights, large powers, groupings, alliances, or of a second Tower of Babel with the fate of the first one still in mind, but of a society of mobile small nations physically unable to disturb by their interaction the general equilibrium.

There is a clipping in my wallet, cut out from an English Sunday paper, the name of which I cannot recall, of a review whose author I have forgotten, discussing a book on Milton published in Summer 1968 by a scholar whose name I cannot remember. But I know why I kept the clipping so negligently cut without reference. It says:

"Blake was right. 'The reason Milton wrote in fetters when he wrote of Angels and God, and at liberty when of Devils and Hell, is because he was a true Poet and of the Devil's party without knowing it.'

"Except that Milton was of God's party too. His triumphant poem is an arch, and such an arch, divided against itself, cannot but . . . "

Now everyone would expect the sentence to end: "but crumble." This is what *we* would say of a society divided against itself, or of a nation divided against itself. But actually the completed image reads that "such an arch, divided against itself, cannot but stand."

Indeed, were the arch *not* divided against itself, with both its parts standing united on the same side, *then* it would crumble. For stability requires not unity, but balance, and balance requires parts at opposite ends, maintaining the system by pressing *against* each other, as Government and Opposition do in a democracy, not *with* each other. This is why Aristotle warned "that we ought not to attain greatest unity even if we could, for it would be the destruction of the state. A state is not made up only of so many men, but of different kinds of men; for similars do not constitute a state. It is not like a military alliance." Like an arch, it must be divided against itself if it is to stand.

So balance, and the harmony that results from it physically, aesthetically, and politically, rests on division, not unity. The only question is: how can this balance best be achieved? How can we distinguish between a bad balance and a good one?

The answer to this is very simple. A good balance is one that rests in itself; that needs no outside interventor to prevent the system from collapsing. An arch is *well* balanced. It does not need its builder to continue propping it up once it is completed. And a galaxy of stars is well balanced. It does not need the Lord in order to preserve its equilibrium. But a bicycle is *badly* balanced. Like a punishment invented by wrathful ancient gods, it must forever be ridden if it is to be prevented from falling to the ground. And so are modern great powers badly balanced, not only singly but also as parts of a universal equilibrium. In both instances they require the constant direction, supervision, and intervention of huge national governments or international agencies only to discover that not even the most strenuous pedalling insures them against collapse.

On the other hand, a small-unit system as exists in Switzerland, or a small community such as an individual Swiss canton or the tiny Yorkshire parish of Markenfield (which was able to read, digest, debate and reject the Maud Report on county fusion in less than 24 hours), are so self-balancing that they hardly need a controlling agency at all.

This leads to a second question. If a well-balanced system is one that requires no outside interventor, what is the secret that makes it function? The answer to this is a little longer than to the first question but hardly more difficult.

It is longer because there are *two* types of world each of which requires a *different* type of structure to bring about the *same* result: an equilibrium that, by definition, needs no outside regulating force. One of them is the world of dead, non-moving matter. This is governed by a *stable* balance which is the better the *fewer* the parts and the *larger* its divided elements. As examples we may think of an oaken table and the ground on which it stands, a mountain and the plain from which it rises, or the two sections of an arch. A heapful of small papers on a desk, on the other hand, constitute a bad balance. They must be kept in place by a third force such as a paperweight lest a mere breath of air scatter them all around.

The opposite applies to the second type of world: The dynamic world of moving particles. This is represented by a galaxy of stars, a system of water drops such as constitutes a lake or ocean, a system of firms in an economy, a system of states as in the United Nations, or a system of men as exists within every society. Here a *mobile* balance is needed allowing for the constant readjustment to parts constantly on the move to different positions.

But in contrast to the stable balance of the rigid and the dead, a mobile balance co-ordinating the living and the moving can be successfully achieved only if the component parts are not large and few, but numerous and small. They must be numerous so that their inevitable meetings and collisions resulting from their ceaseless random movements are of a statistical frequency that permits their enrollment in the orderly pattern inherent in every system. And they must be small so that, in the absence of an external controlling force, their collisions do not lead to destruction but, as in an artist's mobile, release on their own the forces tending to restore the overall equilibrium by the chain reaction triggered off by the latter's very disruption. When tanks collide, the result is disaster. But when couples collide on a dancing floor, it is part of the fun. No watchful authority needs to warn them that they are on a collision course—unless they are five-hundred pounders. For collision here is both cause and correcting force of every disrupting interaction.

Now the world of man being so obviously a *mobile* universe, it follows that it is well balanced only if its divided and opposing units are both numerous and small—small not necessarily in relation to each other but to the system as a whole. In a small-business system, there may indeed be some units conspicuously larger than others. But this does not matter as long as their *number* is small. And so it is with systems of states. The Swiss canton of Berne is very much larger than Uri, and the state of New York very much larger than Rhode Island. But in both cases they are so small in relation to the overall federations in which they are embedded that their size can neither dominate nor significantly disrupt the rest. The central power necessary to ensure stability and peace of the whole is therefore both minor and easily within the financial reach of the members of the system who must contribute to its upkeep.

This was by and large true also of the international scene. Until close to the end of the 1,000-year old Holy Roman Empire, as long as there existed a great multitude of smaller states, they engaged in numerous but infinitely smaller conflicts, suffering lesser complexities, fighting shorter wars, and snapping faster out of depression than is possible in the simpler world of modern monster states. Though the gradual emergence of great powers had inescapably a disturbing effect on the "concert" of nations, until the beginning of this century they were still sufficiently numerous to keep each other in a self-balancing condition of equilibrium that may have required an occasional Congress as in Vienna or Berlin, but as yet no permanent secretarialized supra-national authority in the form of a League of Nations or United Nations.

However, once the great powers *did* appear on the scene, there was, as in the case of cancerous cells, no natural barrier left which could have stopped their further growth. The consequence of this was the gradual wearing-out of the *mobile* mechanism ensuring the type of *automatic* balance of power whose proper functioning in a dynamically moving world demands the side-by-side existance not of a few large but of a great multitude of small units. Nor could it be replaced by a *stable* balance which, true enough, is the better the fewer and larger its component units. But it works satisfactorily only if the parts have stopped moving and become dead—a condition for which unfortunately not even the bulkiest of great powers does as yet qualify. Hence the inevitable emergence of the current bicycle of two superpowers which, no longer able to preserve their equilibrium automatically, leaves us with but two alternatives: either the bicycle must be constantly ridden by a third force greater than that concentrated in its parts—if the two wheels are to be aligned in the same direction. Or it must crash if, as at present, the two wheels remain alligned against each other like the two halves of a divided arch. For while the lock produced by the immobile opposing parts of an arch is hardened by pressure, the lock of wheels divided against themselves, and oscillating at the slightest touch, is loosened by it until it parts. Nor would the picture change as a result of the emergence of China and a United Europe considering that tandems are as unstable as ordinary bicycles, and it is unlikely that either of them could do anything except side with one or the other of the existing superpowers.

What then is the way out of this disastrous situation which compels us to choose between two alternatives leading to the same ruin? One solution offered is to turn the bicycle of uneasily balancing superpowers into the monocycle of a world-state embracing the unsurveyable mass of all mankind. But this makes barely more sense. For even a monocycle must still be ridden—unless it is mounted in concrete on top of a sepulchre. Moreover as Aristotle would say: "Law is order, and good law is good order; but a very great multitude cannot be orderly to introduce order into the unlimited is the work of divine power—of such power as holds together the universe."

This is why, as Arnold Toynbee has shown, every civilization achieving the monocycle of a universal state discovered that its success invariably turned out to be the penultimate step towards its collapse. It made no difference whether it had worked out its grand design in Hindu, Islamic, Western, or ecumenical Christian terms. Nor did it matter whether the aspiration leading to its establishment was political as in the Tower-of-Babel of a United Nations, or economic as in a Common Market. The human mind simply cannot encompass such magnitudes.

This seems to leave us only with the opposite alternative. That is: if we are to achieve an enduring structure of order, harmony and peace, we must restore the self-adjusting mechanism of an automatically operating mobile balance. We must apply not the imaginings of man but the laws of a nature which hold the universe together with the help not of a power of divine proportions but of a device which explodes and fragmentizes that very power wherever it threatens to coalesce into magnitudes disruptive of the scheme of things.

In other words, what is needed is neither a giant monocycle ridden by the Lord in unopposed speed through the endlessness of space and time; nor a bicycle brought to total standstill by Gabriel and Luzifer furiously pedalling eyeball to eyeball against each other. What is needed is a flexible polycycle resting not on four or six large but on countless little wheels capable of twisting into all directions without the danger of ever tipping over, and thus releasing Lord, Gabriel, and Luzifer to devote themselves more constructively to performing their fascinating roles in Marlowe's *Faustus* or Goethe's *Faust*.

In concrete terms, the polycycle solution implies the dissolution of the current structure of superpowers and great-nation states in favour of a return to a world of small communities. This may sound utopian. May be it is. Yet, it has been advanced again and again as a means for eradicating the havoc wreaked by the realists. It has been advanced by St. Augustine who proposed "a society of small states living in amity" to take the place of the fear-ridden unitarian system of ancient Rome. And it was suggested by the Duke of Sully who encouraged Henry IV of France "to divide Europe equally among a certain number of powers in such manner that none of them might have cause either of envy or fear from the possessions of the others." So noble was the latter's concept that it became known as the *Great* Design. But it failed to convince the feet-on-the-ground politicians who, unlike bricklayers working on great cathedrals, seem never able to grasp that large blocks must first be broken up before the size is obtained at which obstructionist components can be grafted into systems larger than their own.

But not only theorists of the past have expressed their faith in the "natural-law school" of political organization which favours a return to a self-balancing cancer-free small-state system in the international sphere and a cantonal small-community system for the domestic arena. The hopeless bankruptcy of modern big-block fusionism has widened its appeal also among many contemporary leaders in politics and thought. In Great Britain alone, they range from "devolutionists", "city-regionalists", and the growing number of defenders of "nationalities" rather than of "nations", to national independence leaders such as Gwynfor Evans, the inspired Member of Parliament for Carmarthen and President of *Plaid Cymru,* the party of free Wales, to Dr. E.F. Schumacher, the originator of the idea of *Intermediate Technology*. The latter has drawn the same conclusion from his position as Chief Statistician of the British Coal Board, the worlds' largest enterprise, which St. Augustine has drawn as a citizen of Rome, the world's largest empire, namely that man is not made for bigness, and bigness not for man. And finally, one might mention in this connection phenomena such as the movement for a *Fourth World* which is trying to rid the *Third World* of the conceptual tumor of religious, economic, and political oecumencism which the inexperienced liberators of the post-war period have so eagerly absorbed from the *Second World*.

Erwin Schroedinger, the Nobel-prize winning Physicist, showed in his fascinating little book, *What Is Life,* why atoms must be numerous as well as small if order is to be preserved in the vastness of the material universe. Similarly, I have tried to show in these pages that also states and nations must be numerous and small if order is to be preserved in the political universe which, after all, is material too. This explains the insistence of the founders of modern economics, the *Physiocrats*, that the best preparation for sorting out the messed-up world of man is by studying the laws not of man but of nature. For only then is it possible to grasp that, when flaws develop in our political structure, we must eliminate the flaws to satisfy the structure, not stretch the structure to satisfy the flaws.

In other words, if social overgrowth disturbs the equilibrium among communities and states in one part of the system, it makes no more sense to correct it by fostering a counter-balance overgrowth in another part than does the idea of curing the elephantiasis in the right leg by raising it also in the left. The only answer that makes sense in that case is not the fusion but the fragmentation of things that have become too big. As this reduces friction mechanically, as in ball-bearings, it does so also politically among states. Moreover, as the term *miniaturization* implies, contraction to smaller units reflects not a romantic hankering for the lost bliss of the Middle Ages but the most successful principle of survival and progress.

In order not to end this essay on a note of gloom, let me point out that, by reducing the size of nations to manageable proportions, the stage will be set for a United Nations government to perform its function of enforcing the laws of peace, not oratorically, but for the first time, effectively. For it is in the nature of things that only small states are modest, sensible and above all, weak enough to accept an authority higher than their own. For the real question of our time is of course not: How can *little* states survive? They *are* surviving in glory and splendour, as we see in Switzerland, Sweden, Norway, Iceland, Luxembourg. The real question is: How can the *big* survive? If China invaded Tibet, Russia Czechoslovakia, Nigeria Biafra, it was not for fear that the little could not stand on their own feet. It was because the monster powers felt *they* could not afford to let the tiniest nation go free without endangering their own security. For *they,* not the small, are the ones who are in constant trouble with their currencies, their economics, their population pressure, their growth, their lack of it, their armaments, their youth, their universities, their garbage disposal, their pollution, their crime waves, their hopeless fears of aggression and futile efforts of finding peace among themselves. *They,* not the small, must answer that question.

Further Reading:

Customs Unions — *A Tool of Peace* by Leopold Kohr. Washington: Foundation for Foreign Affairs, 1949.

The Breakdown of Nations, London: Routledge & Kegan Paul, 1957; New York: Rinehart, 1957, out of print; Milan: Edizioni di Comunita, 1960. Swansea: Christopher Davies, republished in 1973 as paperback.

Weniger Staat (Freedom from Government) Düsseldorf: Econ Verlag, 1965.

Die Uberentwickelten, oder Die Gefahr der Groesse (The Overdeveloped Nations). Düsseldorf: Econ Verlag, 1962; Barcelona: Editorial Luis Miracle, 1965. Paperback 1970.

The Breakdown of Great Britain, London, Ethical Society, 1971.

Is Wales Viable, Swansea: Christopher Davies, 1971.

Development Without Aid (The Translucent Society), Swansea: Christopher Davies, 1973.

THE ECONOMIC VIABILITY OF SMALL NATIONS

JOHN PAPWORTH

The author, who until 1972 was the Editor of Resurgence, and who now works as Personal Assistant to President Kaunda of Zambia, believes that many of our problems are the consequence of an excessive growth of the size of our political and economic units, a development which puts their workings beyond their control and hence beyond the compass of people's effective moral judgments. He is the author of *Economic Aspects of the Humanist Revolution of our Times.*

It is not often realized that the Biafran War of Independence, even though it ended with Biafra's military defeat, was part of a world-wide pattern of events, a pattern which is coming to oust many other issues on the political scene. People seldom linked the Biafran struggle with that of the Catalonians and the Basques in Spain, the Bretons and the Alsatians in France, the Montenegrans in Yugoslavia, Greece and Albania, the Nagas and other hill tribes on the borders of India, the Aborigines of Australia, the Indians of the Americas, to mention only a few of the many ethnic groups around the world which are seeking either independence or new forms of expression of their common desire for self-determination. Yet this world-wide phenomenon, which embraces the many subject nationalities of the Russian Empire as much as the movements for Scottish and Welsh independence nearer home, is one of the most pronounced and, curiously, least remarked revolutions of the 20th century.

It is not always a revolution by war and bloodshed, even though nearly everywhere it is confronted by implacable and well armed forces of repression which seldom hesitate, as in Biafra, to unleash the most harrowing forms of suffering on those who oppose their suzerainty. Frequently, as with the Indians of the Americas, it is a matter of tenacious holding on, as this case for generations, despite every kind of repression which in this case has reduced their numbers to a mere rump. The weapons of survival here have been a firm refusal to abandon the culture, language and the religious beliefs of their forbears, so that now, after generations, a new spirit of renaissance is growing, numbers are increasing and there is a new mood which insists on nothing less than full and equal recognition — not as Americans subject to Federal laws, but as Indians subject to their own. In the long run the forces of repression will be of little account, for essentially this revolution is one of the mind and spirit and it indicates that men are changing one of their most basic assumptions about the nature and form of government.

Hitherto, in modern times at least, the question of the *size* of a political unit has either been regarded as subordinate to other issues, such as whether it is governed by capitalists of socialists, or it has been assumed that there is an innate virtue in the factor of bigness. So that every increase in growth, of size and with it, of course, of centralization of power, has been assumed to be 'a good thing', and any attempt to resist or reverse the process condemned as being the delusions of backward-looking, sentimental political Luddites. So that when Bismark unified Germany (as recently as 1863) or when Napoleon unified Italy or when Alexander the Great unified the former City States of Greece, everyone who was anyone applauded the deed as being an indelible sign of the march of progress.

And yet, and yet . . . The same forces that have broken down the social framework of the 18th century, which have led men to reject the class stratification of society, and to reject with it the presumption of the innate inferiority of the majority and the assumption of the superiority of a powerful ruling minority, have been at work in group and ethnic terms. So that the widening of horizons of individuals about the nature of democracy has inevitably led to a similar widening of horizons by groups, or even nations which have been previously incorporated, generally by force, in another.

Who decides? On what basis? And for what ends? These are not questions which have been decided for all time by our Henry Tudors, Bismarks, Richelieus and Stalins, and which need no longer concern us; they have become the central and key questions of politics, if only because an increasing number of people in every part of the world are insisting on making them so.

People who are comfortable with old assumptions have a considerable resistance to making, or accepting, new ones, especially in political affairs, and resistance to the idea that small nations have a right to their independence is usually expressed with the solemn pronouncement that such small countries are 'not economically viable'. Since this is assumed to be the case, it is further assumed that there is nothing more to be said, and that anyone who insists on saying it is merely a crank making propaganda for a cause which is obviously a non-starter.

Yet what are the facts about 'economic viability'? 'Viability' we need to remember, means 'the ability to live', and clearly in discussing this question we also need to take into account the standard of life at which a nation can live. In the business of getting a living there is always a certain amount of consumption of finite and irreplaceable resources, there is always some pollution of one element or another (and frequently several) of the habitat, and there is always some degree of waste of resources, or the production of goods or services for which there is not sufficient effective demand. So that any estimate of economic viability or economic efficiency will need to ask to what extent a small nation will increase or diminish these factors, as well as to what extent it can create a satisfactory level of consumption for its citizens. Indeed it will need today to go further and find an answer to a question which has been sedulously avoided since the dawn of the industrial revolution; to what extent is its standard of consumption and its general level of economic activity viable not simply for itself, but for the grandchildren and subsequent generations of those now living?

The importance of this question stems quite simply from the rapidly accumulating evidence that much of the economic activity of the developed, or perhaps more accurately, the overdeveloped, nations, is based on a rapacious consumption of irreplaceable resources and a heedless and irreversible process of despoliation of the elements of our planetary habitat which are likely to impoverish our posterity to a quite awesome degree.

An examination of the evidence here, the rate of consumption of oil and other fossil fuels as well as of relatively scarce ores, the lowering of water tables, the pollution of waterways, lakes and oceans, the pollution of the atmosphere, the savage assault on natural forms of soil fertility by modern methods of cash-crop farming, to name but a few factors which must be set against the current population tidal wave and the revolution in economic expectations which ensure that current demands or economic resources are bound to increase prodigiously, suggests to some experts that there is still nothing to worry about and that if we modify this or that aspect of our lives all will be well. The present writer believes such experts to be wrong and that in fact our way of life is itself a disaster course; he believes that there are disasters now looming which can only be avoided by a revolution in human outlook and in the manner in which men approach their habitat and its resources. He further believes that, at heart, this question is a moral one, a matter of seeking good as an absolute and rejecting evil, and that whilst it cannot be argued that small societies will always choose what is good, it is *only* in small societies that that choice is open at all. In monster societies it is not morality, but power and profit which determines the course of events, which is why people in such societies feel so utterly helpless when confronted by the monstrous evils of our time. Since, however, so many experts appear to be of another mind, let is at least be said that the possibility of the sheer unviability of large nation states is a factor which wise men will not ignore.

But if it is difficult to measure the viability of nations by extrapolating current trends into the obscure future, we can also do it very easily by looking around us. Economic viability cannot be measured in a vacuum; it must be related to the present state of human affairs and to the larger questions of peace and war, and in this context it can be said that the *only* countries which have managed to remain free of involvement in wars, which have kept their currencies stable and which have virtually abolished poverty and illiteracy are not big ones at all, but quite small ones. It is true that there are not many names one can add to those of Switzerland and Sweden, but this is largely due to the fact that the big nations have been behaving so insanely that the involvement of a great many small countries in their irrational courses has been inevitable.

I do not suppose the inhabitants of either Sweden or Switzerland feel any special virtue in having achieved these things and they would be right in feeling so, for their achievements are a product of their size as much as their virtues. If Sweden were simply a territory in a country called Scandinavia (embracing all the countries in that geographic expression) we may be sure that sooner or later.it would have been involved in a major war, its currency would be tied far more closely to the fluctuating fortunes of the 'big powers' and the problems of poverty and illiteracy would prove to be as insoluble as they have in other large countries.

It may be noted in passing that no really large country has solved the problem of poverty. It is true that the *average* income of the United States is *the* highest in the world, but averages, like a young lady's clothes, are more important for what they conceal than what they reveal, and in this case it helps to conceal the fact that some of the worst examples of poverty in the world are to be found in the U.S.A. Nor are these examples confined to a small minority of people. Would that they were! The late President Kennedy used to talk of one third of the American people going to bed hungry every night, and for a country which once had a greater, more accessible and less exploited degree of natural resources than any other in the world, this must surely be taken to be an achievement of some kind. How is it possible for so much squalor, both civic and personal, to exist side by side with so much wealth as the U.S. possess? It is difficult not to refer back to the question of size and to suggest that because of the personal nature of the problem of poverty (to the individual afflicted by it) anything so ponderous as federal government machinery is simply too large to grapple with it. This failure to find a solution does not spring from a lack of will or of resources, for the money required is a mere flea-bite compared with the sums lavished on war, 'defence' and moon rocketry, and so ludicrous has the gross disparity between national wealth and mass poverty become that the idea of a minimum income for everybody to cover all basic necessaries of life is being seriously discussed as an alternative to the continued outpouring of Federal funds, to such demonstrably little effect, on poverty programmes and the like.

Is it possible that world wars, transoceanic military adventures such as Korea and Vietnam, and the folly of lunar journeys are things appropriate to the scale of a Federal Government, whilst matters of health, welfare and social progress are not? In the fable of La Fontaine it may be useful to recall that it was the lion, the king of the jungle, which was trapped in the hunter's net, whereas it was the mouse, by nibbling patiently at the strands of the net who effected the lion's release. Scale, clearly, is all, at least as a starting point.

It may, of course, be argued that the defects of American life are due to capitalism and that under another system of government . . . Curiously enough, in the communist world it is again the large nations, such as the Russian and Chinese Empires, which appear to be doing so badly, whereas quite small ones such as Yugoslavia, appear at least to be finding their problems manageable.

And what should one say of the Indian sub-continent? Before the British imposed a single form of rule upon it, its different parts were flourishing and prosperous. "Indian society of that period (i.e. the second half of the 18th century) was far more highly developed than the local American empires encountered by the Spaniards; indeed, in some respects it was more rather than less developed, than the contemporary European States with which it collided. It is true that India was relatively backward in certain respects which turned out to be decisive. On the other hand Indian industrial and commercial techniques in, for example, the production of textiles and in some respects in banking and public finance were ahead of Europe". P.12

John Strachey 'The End of Empire'. Victor Gollancz 1959.

We may note that not only did economic activity reach a high level, so too did dancing, music, sculpture, carving, architecture, poetry, philosophy and many other fields of creativity. Where is all that excellence today? It is dying out under the blight of an overlarge centralised form of government. It is dying out as it has died out in the U.S.A.

Yet these defects do not arise from any particular defects in American or Indian people, any more than the advantages of living in Switzerland arise from any particular virtues in the Swiss character; it is mainly that both peoples are living in the kind of political environment that tends to produce these consequences.

Nor is it any product of mere chance that it is the small countries which tend to acquire a greater degree of political tolerance. It is the United States which sends its young men half way round the globe to murder Vietnamese peasants, whilst it is the small countries such as Sweden and Canada which give young Americans sanctuary from conscription. It was Russia which murdered nearly all its intellectuals along with about 20 million other of its own people under Stalin, yet Stalin remained in power and died quietly in his bed 30 years later, and his ghost still stalks the empire he ruled; the shooting down of six workers, largely from panic and military wooden-headedness, during a demonstration in Sweden at the time when Stalin's terror was already under way resulted in the downfall of the Swedish Conservative Government and it has taken a generation for the Swedish conservatives to recover from the disgrace.

It may well be pleaded that these factors are out of place in a consideration of economic matters. The justification of such a view is surely more apparent than real, for no country can move forward to goals of economic betterment of its people, and live in a climate hostile to tolerance and freedom, even if it is because only in such a climate that the true nature of those goals can be determined.

It may well be too, that even a survey of the prevailing world scene will fail to convince some that not only are small nations as viable in economic terms as large, but that they are even more so and that there are inbuilt factors which make large nations unviable. The world economic crisis of the twenties and thirties originated not in Luxemburg but in the United States. It is big nations such as Germany, France, Italy and Britain which have been plagued with crises and wars which have destroyed the value of their currencies or their democratic institutions (and frequently both). Yet whoever heard of a chronic state of crisis in the numerous independent states of pre-Bismarkian Germany or pre-Napoleonic Italy? or in Liechtenstein?

As we go back into history another truth emerges which suggests that the basic and central question of economic and political democracy has yet to be fully comprehended, far less answered, and in brief it is this: What is the maximum size to which a country should attain in terms of the well being of its citizens? It is a modern conceit to say simply 'the bigger the better', but there is much in history to indicate that our forbears acted on a quite different assumption. They were not so foolish as to argue that the smaller it was the better, but they did have a very firm idea of the limits to which a unit might grow without creating more problems for its members than it could solve. Partly these limits arose from the type of transport and weapons of war that prevailed, nevertheless those limits existed and they had the most spectacular results.

Europe, before the age of mass technology, was linked in all directions by chains of independent cities or city-states. These cities were not mere aggregations of mud huts, nor were they vast sprawls of uniform edifices whose forms were a betrayal of nearly every instinct of architecture man had ever acquired or practised; in comparison with what had gone before and what has followed since they were jewels of civic and private splendour. Venice, Florence, Salzburg, Munich, Hamburg, Chartres, Avignon, Oxford, Cambridge, Chester, Salisbury, Winchester, Dresden, Lisbon, Barcelona, Warsaw, Dubrovnik, to name but a few, were not peculiar rarities to which people flocked simply to gape, they were not afflicted with a 'tourist' problem at all, for they were part of a general pattern of civic excellence which dominated European civilization and which, even when their power was broken, enabled Europe to retain a pre-eminence in matters of invention, research, technology, trade, war, conquest, missionary enterprise and much else for centuries. Nobody at that time was fool enough to wonder whether a city state was 'economically viable', if only becuase the evidence that it was, was so abundant and so apparent that it is doubtful if such a question ever crossed anybody's mind.

One very important point about these city states is of vital importance. Nearly all their achievements were based not on a brute exploitation of the habitat as now prevails nearly everywhere, but on a process of economics that was largely self-regenerating. They did not use the achievements of their forbears to rob their posterity, they acknowledged their debt to the past and lived in ways that left the world a more beautiful and richer place for their posterity than it might have been. Millions of us in consequence visit their cities just to look at them, and galleries and museums around the world count as their greatest treasures those works of art they produced. It is difficult to envisage our posterity three or four centuries hence visiting with any similar sense of awe and joy our own major cities. What will Manchester, Chicago, Turin, Düsseldorf, Lille and such places signify other than that we lived ugly lives, making ugly things for ourselves without a shred of concern for *their* well-being or for their heritage that was temporarily and so disastrously in our care?

It is true that there are some dour, blinkered minds that refuse to see this former era of history in terms other than some doctrinaire class struggle, and who insist in believing that all the palaces, the churches, the cathedrals, the universities, the hospitals, the monasteries, the statues, the bridges, the furniture, glass and silverware, the tapestries and silks, the paintings, the frescoes, the clothes, the gondolas and the enormous numbers of spacious private mansions and lesser dwellings of Venice, for example, were all the product of some grim, joyless, downtrodden class of exploited serfs toiling away in dim unheated and verminous dens in a state of chronic semi-starvation. In point of fact this was probably the condition of numerous workers *after* the independent cities and city states had largely disappeared. Art can *exist* under the most varying conditions but for art to *flourish* as it flourished in mediaeval Europe it needs relative freedom and relative material abundance. It is true, of course, that mediaeval Europe was so short on sanitation that grim plagues of infection were not uncommon, but how was it ordained that we should sacrifice the magnificence of renaissance art for flush lavatories and the mass production of machine-made goods? Why could we not have both?

This surely is the challenge confronting us today; clearly either we must civilize technology or it will destroy us, is in fact already destroying essential artefacts of our material culture as it has in fact destroyed much of our spiritual culture. The question is not whether small nations are economically viable, but how we can escape the death trap which large ones have created for us. This means, I take it, scaling down technology to genuinely human dimensions and with it our politics as well.

We need not assume that if even our villages are made free and independent, as I believe they should be, they will not combine and co-operate with others for such purposes as seem to them necessary.

To co-operate is a vital part of man's social nature and no man questing for social solutions can be unaware for long of both the virtues and the necessity of many forms of co-operation. This need exists quite independently of the power of central governments and can be met very often without any recourse to them at all. This is particularly true of many forms of co-operation which involve a strong element of personal relationship between citizens such as health, education, the control of delinquency, police and many aspects of what is called 'welfare' but which nowadays is often synonymous with a great deal of needless, centralized, bureaucratic bossing around and ordering of citizen affairs.

Education may be taken as a good example of this. Since education policy is now handed down from the top, all prospects of local variations of schooling and of educational excellence are being stamped out. Yet why should there be a 'national' policy on education at all? Since the subject is 'people', and since people everywhere are different, why should there not be thousands of localized educational policies according to the lights and wisdom of the parents, the teachers and the local taxpayers? This does not preclude for a moment the most far-reaching forms of co-operation to whatever degree may seem appropriate to the people involved at the base. If they had the power to make decisions at parish, village and city-ward or precinct level, it is not difficult to see how they would soon devise varied forms of co-operation for teacher training, recruitment and payment, for group purchase of educational equipment, the conferences they would institute at various levels to thrash out key questions of educational practice and experience, the exhibitions they would arrange for new buildings, new methods, new apparatus, and so on and so on. Think of the enthusiasm that would be generated! Think of the sense of involvement in real matters that would flourish! Think of the fun people would have! At present all this is sacrificed on the altar of sterile centralized bureaucratic conformity.

It is possible to apply a similar analysis to many other facets of politics, all of which indicate that what we experience now is not free citizen co-operation but the *force majeure* of top people in the establishment who find this spirit of involvement wholly irrelevant to their purposes. Yet clearly there are some forms of co-operation which need to be centralized; Mafia type gangsterism is growing in Britain, and it would clearly be absurd if such elements could commit crimes in Middlesex for which they could obtain immunity by skipping over the border into Surrey simply because the local people in both places were too jealous of their prerogatives to achieve a common mode of legal redress.

Again, there is the vexed question of the democratic control of money and currency. Clearly a common currency is desirable and clearly some centralized control of the mechanism is indispensable. Why not local banks under local control and whose boards elect the Board of, shall we say, the Bank of England? Why not? Unfortunately so great are the abuses of the money system that quite a number of simple souls are driven to suppose money can and should be abolished altogether. The prevalence of such pipe dreams tends to deflect attention from a consideration of more effective measures of control. For example, I am not aware that anyone has proposed that there should be local control of credit required for local purposes, but such a measure would transfer considerable power from unrepresentative and centralised hands where it is frequently used for purposes inimical to local well-being, such as helping chain stores to push local traders off the High Street, when in representative hands it might well do the reverse.

With such measures we need have no fear at all of the spirit of constructive probing, questioning and determining which might well flourish in every parish given a chance; our real enemy is the silent, passive, gullible spirit of inertia and acquiescence which today pervades huge masses of people, and which enables a few power-hungry politicians to wreak what mischief they will so long as they do not diminish the existing availability of bread and circuses. On this basis there can now only be a dramatic decline in the fortunes of our potential world civilisation from one disaster to another, and the principal result of which can only be a steady proliferation of quite needless misery and suffering for millions of people.

Yet if men will now refuse any longer to be slaves of technology, refuse for example, to allow the motor car to despoil life any further, refuse to accept mass production of anything as a norm, refuse to eat factory processed food, turn their backs on such inanities as space travel, such excesses as the Concorde aeroplane, and such insanities as modern wars and such delusive mechanisms as modern political parties, to make a bare start on a very long list; if instead they will insist on making technology their servant, scaling it down everywhere to human size and insisting it follow the needs of human purpose, then surely, the powers of technology allied to the exercise of genuine democratic power can enable man to achieve such splendour as even yet they have never known.

Can? But will they? This is a discussion about economics, yet it was more than three hundred years before Christ that Aristotle* was moved to observe that 'The real difference between man and other animals is that humans alone have perception of good and evil, right and wrong, just and unjust. *And it is the sharing a common view in these matters that makes . . . a city.*' (My italics)

I believe this to be even more pertinent today than when it was written. I believe further that however logical and desirable it may be for men to act as I have suggested they should here, mere logic and desirability will not lead them to sacrifice comfort, either of body or mind, or habit, convenience, the general desire for a quiet life or a good time, or the sheer spiritual inertia in which most of us are content to wallow. The vital spark will be missing so long as men feel unable to acknowledge with humility and joy the beauty and the majesty of God and the transcendent nature of His power in the universe. I truly believe that if men can bring themselves to that act of humility and acknowledgement they will themselves acquire a power to act for truth in a spirit of rightness against which no forces, however evil and seemingly omniscient, can prevail.

* 'Aristotle — The Politics'. Penguin Ed. 1969, p.29.

ORGANIZATION FOR PEACE IN THE GRAECO-ROMAN WORLD

JOHN FERGUSON

British Classicist and Theologian. Dean and Director of Studies in Arts, The Open University.

Formerly Professor of Classics, University of Ibadan, Nigeria; Professor of Classics, University of Minnesota, U.S.A.; Professor of Humanities, Hampton Institute, U.S.A.; Vice-Chairman (formerly Chairman) British Fellowship of Reconciliation; Chairman, British Council of Churches. Author of numerous books and articles in the fields of classical studies, international affairs, division of community affairs, and Christian social commitment. Recent writings include: *Utopians of the Classical World; The Religions of the Roman Empire; The Place of Suffering; The Politics of Love; Sermons of a Layman;* and the anthology, *War and the Creative Arts.*

In *Alternatives to War and Violence* John Ferguson essayed a brief survey of attitudes to war and peace in the Graeco-Roman world. Here he looks at the practical question of organization for peace, the extent of its success and the reasons for its failure.

Among the Greeks of the classical and post-classical period there were four main types of organization directed to the attainment of peace. These were *amphictionies* or religious associations, *symmachies* or semifeudal alliances, *sympolities* or federations, and treaties for *koine eirene* or general peace.

Religion did in fact set some bounds to the militarism of the Greek states. Thus the period of the Olympic Games was a period of Sacred Truce. Hostilities were dropped during the period. When, during the Peloponnesian War, the Spartans attacked Lepreon in the period of the Truce, they were fined the formidable sum of 2000 minae, to be paid to the treasury of Olympian Zeus, and when they refused to pay, were blackballed from the Games. A monarch as powerful as Philip of Macedon was compelled to make full restitution when his mercenaries robbed an Athenian named Phrynon on his way to the Games. Alongside Olympian Zeus the main religious force for unity was Apollo of Delphi. The Delphic Oracle was the centre of a league known as the Amphictionic League. The Oracle itself carried considerable political weight, and political consultations play a major part in our records of it; in general it is just to say that the weight of the Oracle was on the side of moderation and peaceability. In this way its political influence extended far beyond the League. In addition the Pythian Games, like the Olympian Games, were a period of Sacred Truce. The League itself from an early date attempted to check the excesses of war by what might be termed Geneva Conventions. The members took an oath, known as the Amphictionic Oath, not to destroy the city of a League member, not to reduce it by starvation, or to cut off the water supply. This is, for its date, more radical than it sounds; it does not cut at the sinews of war, but it does attempt to assert that morality and religion have their say in political conflict.

A symmachy was a permanent alliance of free states. The motives for such an alliance were political and military, not religious. The root-meaning of *symmachy* is 'union in battle', and it might seem paradoxical to call it an alliance for peace, but it can be justified. For in the first place, a symmachy was naturally concerned to keep the peace among its members, and, in the second, a symmachy might extend sufficiently to be an instrument for a wider peace, somewhat as the U.N. was formed out of a limited military alliance. In the Greek world such a symmachy is to be seen in the Peloponnesian League, founded in the latter half (perhaps right at the end) of the sixth century B.C., of which Sparta was the leading state. It was in origin a military alliance, and no meeting could be held without the authority of Sparta, but all states had an equal voice and voting was by simple majority. It was in fact a compromise, at once an instrument of Spartan imperialism and a check upon it. But when in the early years of the following century the whole of Greece was threatened by Persia, at the first onset, in 491-0, Athens appealed to Sparta to settle her difference with Aegina, and ten years later a Hellenic League was formed to face the more formidable attack. It was never fully comprehensive, but it performed a remarkable feat in achieving peace among its members: so much so that when Athens was occupied by the invaders, the women and children were evacuated to to the recently hostile island of Aegina. It fell apart, partly because Spartan internal politics would not allow her to pursue policies of 'liberation' across the sea, chiefly because the Spartans and Athenians were ultimately concerned with their own aggrandisement. The Hellenic League broke into the old Peloponnesian League dominated by Sparta, and the Delian League, dominated by Athens. They clashed, and in 404 Athens succumbed through her overreaching ambitions. A second Athenian League was formed in 378-7. This was a remarkable instrument. Athens freely conceded precautions against the dictatorship she had exercised in the previous century, and was making financial sacrifices instead of feathering her own nest. But the history of the fourth century was too volatile, and the League too clearly directed against Sparta for it to be an effective instrument for peace. Yet there was to come a Hellenic League, which might have worked. It is true that it was militarily imposed, by Philip II of Macedon in 338. The League was a symmachy and was called a symmachy. The constituent states were free and autonomous, and their constitutions, good, bad or indifferent, were guaranteed. They were required to contribute soldiers to a central army, money to a central treasury, and representatives to a central parliament, on the basis of proportional representation; the central assembly had the right to inervene in internal affairs if there was unconstitutional interference with person or property. Philip's League was overtaken by his death and the new world opened up by Alexander; but for centuries, right up to the time of Hadrian, it remained the sort of instrument which the Greeks felt they needed.

Four things will be noticed about this concept of the symmachy. First, it is probably the most effective means of union between states which will not renounce their sovereignty. Second, historically it has depended on an external enemy; so the U.S.A. and the U.S.S.R. united against Nazi Germany; so the simplest short-term solution to the Nigerian Civil War might have been a take-over attempt by Britain uniting the tribes against them! Third, it was in Greece dependent, for good and bad, upon the initiative of a single strong power; this state, Sparta or Athens, provided the driving force for union—and the ruthless ambition which led to disaster. Fourth, the constitution of Philip's League shows that a symmachy of autonomous states is not incompatible with some "interference" with the "internal affairs" of each: one wonders if the UN should not take far more seriously infringements of the Universal Declaration of Human Rights by its member-states.

The great period of federation was the Hellenistic Age. It was both fostered and hampered by the shadow of Macedon. The Achaean League during the third century B.C. remains the most famous of these federations nurtured as it was by the statesmanship of Aratus of Sicyon. "Nowhere", said Polybius of it, "could be found a system and a principle more pure and unalloyed of equality, freedom of speech, and, in a word, true democracy, than among the Achaeans." No single city dominated it: all member-states were on equal footing: all had to be democracies: all shared common laws, common weights and measures, a common government and a common deliberative assembly. Unhappily the Achaean confederacy turned into a more powerful nationalism: and hostility to Sparta where Cleomenes had revived Spartan jingoism against the background of left-wing revolution, and to the contemporary Aetolian confederacy, where a remarkable statesman named Agelaus was proclaiming a more comprehensive Panhellenism, were its undoing. There were other important confederations, not all of them in Greece. In Lycia a non-Greek people under Greek influence developed an interesting constitution in which the central assembly was representative (in most federations any citizen of a constituent state might attend: Greek democracy was direct) and in which the federal police were highly developed: women were influential economically and perhaps politically. Lycia, however, was notorious for internal class-warfare. In general, the history of Greece, like that of subsequent federations, shows that, while a federal constitution may enable states to retain a measure of independence and yet grow together, there remains the possibility of internal conflict and of a more comprehensive violent nationalism in external relations; the history of the U.S.A. offers signal examples of both.

The concept of *koine eirene* is much that which Woodrow Wilson intended when on 22 January 1917 he declared "There must be not a balance of power, but a community of power, not organized rivalries, but an organized Common Peace." In the war-weary world of the fourth century man began to replace phrases like "cessation of hostilities" or "truce" with "peace"; a Common Peace was an extension of this throughout the Greek world. Its features were: first, the achievement of agreed peace and cessation of war: second recognition of the autonomy of all states concerned; third, an implicit defensive alliance among all the states; fourth, the fact that it was deemed to apply to all Greek states, whether or not they had sworn to it, unless they explicitly contracted out. That the treaties of *koine eirene* were markedly unsuccessful in their purpose is shown by simple historical fact; there were such treaties in 387-6, 375, twice in 371, 362-1 and 338-7. We should, however, not forget historical perspective: 362 and 337 seem somehow closer than 1919 and 1945, but the interval is about the same, and Ryder, our greatest expert on this field, compares the record of *koine eirene* favourably with that of the League of Nations. We see the wars which were not averted; we do not see those which were.

To those four organizations we may add the institution of arbitration. Arbitration was known before Greek times, as when the King of Kish was called in to define the frontier between the Sumerian cities of Shirpurla and Gishku, but the Greeks gave it fuller and wider scope.

Not merely was arbitration invoked in recalcitrant disputes, but it became a part of treaty terms that the states agreed to employ arbitration rather than violence in future disputes. It did not always work, but out of 41 cases where we have full knowledge, 33 were settled by arbitration, and in only 8 was there further trouble. The arbitrator was usually an independent Greek state, but after Rome impinged on

Greek affairs, she was in increasing demand as an arbitrator. The speed of action might be astonishing: 18 Magnesians were appointed to arbitrate between Itanus and Hierapytna. They took evidence on the spot, sat the clock round and gave their decision within twenty-four hours. Many of the disputes concerned frontiers, but no occasions of conflict were outside the sphere of arbitration. Plainly arbitration was not, and is not, an infallible means of reconciling states in conflict. Its decisions cannot be enforced. It rests on moral sense and good faith. Yet these are stronger forces in human relationship than we sometime allow, as the achievements of arbitration among the Greeks may remind us.

Still, for all the high vision of Greece, it was Rome who achieved peace, peace, as it is sobering to recollect, over a wider area of the world for a longer period than at any time in the history of man before or since; this is one reason out of many why Rome merits our continuing attention. Of course she conquered by violence. The conquest was sometimes reluctant: witness Rome's relations with Greece in the second century B.C.: but when the violence came it was ruthless. But she did not rule by brute violence: she ruled by consent. For example, the whole of North Africa from the Atlantic to the borders of Egypt were policed by one legion (III Augusta), nominally 6,000 men but in fact rather less. This includes as a very small part the modern Algeria, where in the twentieth century a small guerrilla force humbled the might of France. Spain had one legion, France and the Low Countries effectively none, though four were strung along the Rhine frontier. No, Rome ruled by consent, a consent the more striking in view of the initial violence. It is worth enquiring how that consent was achieved.

Its basis was the institution of double citizenship. It must be remembered that citizenship was membership of a city, not of a state in the modern sense; further, that except for Rome (perhaps 1,000,000) and Alexandria (perhaps half a million) there were no cities to approach our modern conurbations. A city was a place where a man could feel he belonged. The Roman Empire was in fact the great age of the municipality, *municipium.* "The city" wrote Mattingly "is not only a place for security or trade; it is not simply the centre of a country district. The fully developed city is also the beginning of something quite new—a new unit of consciousness, the unit of man as a social and political being. The city is the place in which man as such a being exists." Natural, essential that such a city should have a high measure of autonomy, and that its citizens should bear, and be proud to bear, genuine responsibility. Interesting, encouraging that our planning experts should be turning from amorphous agglomerations back to Trendon or Milton Keynes.

The Romans had been, and in measure remained, citizens of Rome in this sense. But as Rome spread, two things happened. First, citizens of Rome themselves emigrated, as soldiers, settlers, traders. This is the analogy the writer to Hebrews has in mind when he says "Here we have no abiding city", or Paul when he describes the Christians as a "colony of heaven". All over the Mediterranean world and beyond were pockets of people who had no abiding city where they were; they were Roman citizens, and they stood for Rome before the world. But secondly, the very citizenship of Rome itself was extended to individuals who had merited well, or to whole communities. It was a cherished privilege, as the story of Paul reminds us, and even when in A.D. 212 (or 214; a current dispute) by the *Constitutio Antoniniana,* it was extended to virtually all the free inhabitants of the Empire, its meaning was not lost. The combination of local with world loyalty proved a healthy one. Regional loyalty was far more suspect, and we who have inherited the violent divisiveness of European nationalism may feel that the Romans had something. Regional units, known as provinces, were necesary to administration, and there were regional councils with local representation; their prime, though not their sole, function was religious. Nationalism was avoided. It is significant that the little island of Britain had three legions: there were frontier problems, but there was also the danger that natural geography might create its own nationalism. And Rome succeeded. *Urbem fecisti quod prius orbis erat:* "you made a city what was once a world".

With the extension of citizenship went the extension of law. Through the Stoics the Romans had been long aware that the actual civil code, *ius civile,* was continually being challenged by legal practices used by mankind generally, *ius gentium,* and by natural law, *ius naturae.* Bryce showed how under these pressures the old law of the city of Rome was expanded and improved till it was fit to be applied to the provinces; at the same time the various laws of the various provinces became assimilated to the enlarged and improved law of the city; the two streams, in his image, flowed together and merged. Law was the most lasting of Rome's gifts to posterity; for their contemporaries it provided the cement of community. Here too there is a lesson.

The basis of these practical developments lay in Rome's extraordinary powers of assimilation. Even Latin literature was continually recreated from outside Rome: in the first century B.C. from the area we call North Italy but they called "Gaul this-side-of the Alps"; in the first century A.D. from Spain; in the second from Africa; and at the end from Africa and France. One thinks of Senghor and Achebe! Tolerance, a readiness to learn from others, and a corresponding reluctance to impose on them were the secrets of Rome. "Unity of sentiment was what Rome attained; and it was the only unity worth attainment. Uniformity was neither sought nor secured" wrote Hugh Last in *The Cambridge Ancient History,* and went on "Each in its own way the provinces progressed; their advance was made possible by the Pax Romana; and their fidelity was an outcome of the gratitude commanded by a power which established peace throughout the world and then was wise enough, despite the growing temptations of paternalism, to leave its inhabitants free to enjoy the measure of self-government which they could exercise with advantage to themselves and without damage to their neighbours."

Further Reading:

"Federation for Peace in Ancient Greece" J. A. O. Larsen *Classical Philology 38* (1944) 145-62. This splendid article is the direct source of the first part of my paper.

History of Federal Government in Greece and Italy E. A. Freeman London and Cambridge 1863. An old book by a fine scholar. We know more about the facts: it is much to be wished that we could recapture his vision.

Greek Federal States J. A. O. Larsen Oxford 1968. An immensely learned, scholarly and rather dull work. It brings Freeman up to date but cannot replace his breadth of vision.

Koine Eirene T. T. B. Ryder London, 1965. A pleasant study by a young and upcoming scholar.

International Arbitration amongst the Greeks M. N. Tod Oxford 1913. The standard work in English.

Roman Imperial Civilization H. Mattingly London 1957. There are many general introductions to the Roman Empire: this is one of the best.

The Cambridge Ancient History vol. XI The Imperial Peace A.D. 70-192 Cambridge 1936. The standard English reference work on the great period of Rome's peaceable rule.

Pax Romana and World Peace L. Waddy London 1950. A book by a schoolmaster who is deeply concerned with the relevance of what he studies.

The Roman Citizenship A. N. Sherwin-White Oxford 1939. The standard work.

The Roman and the British Empires J. Bryce London 1914. Outdated in its attitudes, this is still the work of a great scholar, and lays proper stress on law as an instrument of unity.

Politics and Culture in International History A. B. Bozeman Princeton 1960. An excellent general historical study of international affairs.

NATURAL LAWS IN PRACTICE

CO-OPERATION

Co-operation is seen as the instrument for abolishing fear and distrust. The first chapter in this section deals with the psychological implications, and the second and third with the practical economic and financial ways of co-operation as a means of strengthening the U.N.

TOWARDS A WORLD COMMUNITY*

JEROME D. FRANK

Dr. Jerome D. Frank is a practising Psychiatrist with the Henry Phipps Psychiatric Clinic in Baltimore and Professor of Psychiatry Emeritus at the John Hopkins University School of Medicine. Member of the National Board of S.A.N.E. a citizens' Organization for a sane world.

From the psychological standpoint, the task is to find ways of diminishing distrust and fear amongst members of different nations and foster their sense of belonging to a world community.

During the last few centuries the nation-state has emerged in the Western world as the most suitable political structure for protecting its members and promoting their welfare, aims best accomplished on the whole by each nation's trying to promote its own interests as much as possible without regard to other nations' interests. But this is becoming increasingly unworkable, because national boundaries are losing their significance: nuclear fallout circles the globe, regardless of its origin; the deliberate production of massive changes in the eco-system is now practicable—for example—melting the polar ice cap, thereby raising the level of the northern oceans several feet. This would drown all maritime nation's coastal cities. Observation satellites have opened all nations to military inspection, and delivery systems can send intercontinental missiles thousands of miles.

These are portents that in the future probably no nation will be able to guarantee its citizens' safety or unilaterally advance its national interests. The freedom of action of even the most powerful is already sharply curtailed—it is scarcely an exaggeration to say that America's foreign policy is made as much in Peking and Moscow as in Foggy Bottom—and the people of all nations will soon share a common fate.

From the psychological standpoint, the task is to find ways to use those forces that are making the nation-state obsolete—communication, transportation, and technological advances—to diminish distrust and fear among members of different nations and foster their sense of belonging to a world community. This would facilitate the expansion and modification of existing international organizations

* Extracted from *Sanity and Survival,* Barrie & Rockliff, Cresset Press, London, 1968. By kind permission of the author and publishers.

and the invention of new ones. While the relative merits of various proposals for achieving these ends depend on political, legal and economic considerations that lie beyond the scope of this enquiry, a few psychologically.oriented comments may be in order.

Many people believe that the way to start is by strengthening the United Nation's peace-keeping activities, and plans for world governments stress their peace-keeping functions. Peace-keeping seems especially attractive to nations like the United States which would gain most by maintaining the status quo, but while peace-keeping would be an essential function of any world government, this obviously would not be sufficient in itself to gain the allegiance of most of the peoples of the world, especially those who wish to challenge the current hegemony of the United States. No domestic government consisting only of a police force and judiciary and having only punitive powers could long survive; to win their citizens' allegiance, governments must perform positive services, and maintaining order is only one. In fact, to give a world government only peace-keeping powers initially might impede its development by making it so unpopular that nations would resist giving it other functions. Such allegiance as the United Nations commands among the developing nations, for example, probably derives mainly from its health and economic development programs and not from its peace-keeping struggles, whose value is by no means negligible but whose success has hardly been spectacular enough to account for the organization's vitality . . .

One powerful force for group formation is the existence of a common enemy. As scientists become increasingly convinced that the universe contains innumerable other societies of intelligent beings, the fantasy of a possible invasion by one of them takes on renewed life. Such an event would probably bring about overnight the unity of mankind, but even definite proof that we were under surveillance from another planet—and not all sightings of unidentified flying objects have been adequately explained—might give world government a powerful boost.

But a common enemy, which is not the only basis for group formation, is also a poor one, since groupings formed to fight a common foe fall apart once the enemy ceases to be a threat. Other types of interdependence offer better inducements with more enduring effects. As technological advances such as communications satellites and international mass transportation create an ever increasing number of activities requiring international co-operation, all nations' self-interests will demand their increasing investment in a world government.

International mass communication is creating a world public opinion, which all nations' policy-makers will increasingly have to take into account. Existing rudimentary world opinion already exerts some restraint on the use of violence by the Great Powers. The United States, for example, could blow Cuba off the map and is certainly not well disposed to Castro, but it has been deterred from destroying his regime by force primarily by the adverse effects of such a move on its relations with the other Latin American nations. And I cannot but wonder whether this new concern was not reflected in the strong emotional reaction of American leaders at the thought of a war crimes trial of American fliers in North Vietnam. The quiet execution of some twelve fliers created no uproar, but American leaders were apparently upset by the prospect of a public trial in which American soldier's actions would be displayed before the world as crimes.

Having to keep in mind the multiple audiences of the world public puts a great premium on ambiguity of expression and may sometimes act as a disadvantageous constraint on policy-making. But the constraint will probably work against war-like policies more often than not. The potentialities of a mobilized world public opinion suggests that there may be great merit in the imaginative proposal for a "Court of International Delinquency". Such a court would be empowered to try individual national leaders for offences against mankind's peace and security, as defined by the UN International Law Commission, and if a leader refused an invitation to appear, he could be tried "in absentia", if necessary without his government's consent. The court would have no power to impose sanctions on states, thus circumventing one of the main current obstacles to an effective World Court; and since it could not punish those found guilty by imprisonment or fines, there would be no problem of trying to enforce its decisions if a nation backed the accused leader. It could, however, hold the offender up to public disgrace and also recommend that other nations treat him as "persona non grata" by refusing to recognise his credentials of office, grant him a visa, and the like. In an extreme case this would amount to banishment from the world community: the convicted leader would be a prisoner within the borders of his own nation. A leader held up to international obloquy would have trouble maintaining his position at home—even today national leaders work hard to appear in a good light, not only before their own countrymen but before the rest of the world. The sanctions at the disposal of such a court might thus be considerably more powerful than is immediately apparent . . .

For all their impact, however, mass communications, as indirect forms of contact, have less potential for improving international attitudes than personal interchanges and contacts, for these, too, have become possible on a vastly greater scale than ever before . . .

Using as subjects students who come to the United States to study and stay for a least a few months, psychologists have been observing international personal contacts with a view to learning how to use them more successfully to promote the sense of world community.

Although their personal characteristics undoubtedly affect visitors' receptivity to impressions from the host country, only age has received systematic attention. Among adults, whose identities and roles are relatively fixed, intensified allegiance to home reference groups often result from visits to foreign lands. The most-travelled American businessmen, for example, most uniformily represent the standard business view—that of the Republican Party. Youngsters, however, are more impressionable and their identities are not yet fully formed, so they are particularly receptive, provided the experience of meeting foreigners occurs in a setting that counteracts anxiety. Furthermore, it is easy for them to form new reference groups from among their age mates and teachers; hence the success in promoting international-mindedness in their participants of programs like the Children's International Summer Villages and the Experiment in International Living. In the former, eleven-year-olds from several nations attend camp together for a month, either in the United States or another country from which some of the members come; in the latter, late adolescents and young adults live for a month as members of families in other lands and then travel for a month in a group, including the youths from their host families . . .

The types of personal contact most likely to create favourable impressions and therefore heighten accessibility to each other's views are those the visitors regard as useful. There is a good illustration in a thorough study of a group of young adults from West Germany who were students at American universities for six months to a year. They seemed especially receptive to features of American society that either helped them implement both societies' shared values or provided information they regarded as useful. Thus, they responded favourably to American patterns of give-and-take discussion and to methods of child-rearing, because they saw both as fostering the individualistic orientation they shared, and were particularly interested in American forms of democratic processes and voluntary participation in civic activities, which they believed would make their own society function better . . .

If cross-cultural contacts are to have any real value, the new attitudes they engender must persist after the visitor returns to his home. An indirect measure of the permanence and degree of the impact of the visit on the visitor would be how much difficulty he had in readjusting to his home country—presumably, the more difficult the readjustment, the more significant the impact of the cross-cultural contact. There are generally no problems after fleeting visits, but after longer visits students, especially those who have not "found themselves" before leaving, have the hardest time, as might be expected—the very characteristics that made them the most accessible to the impact of their visit make their return difficult.

The readjustment, actual or anticipated, may be so difficult that the student does not return and thus defeats the whole purpose of the program. This problem is particularly widespread in technical fields: the United States is technically so far advanced that visitors from technologically less developed countries cannot use their American training when they return to their own lands, which lack the necessary expensive, highly specialized equipment; and to make matters worse, they are usually assigned to administrative jobs, where the need is greatest. One way to meet the problem might be to send American teachers to schools abroad instead of bringing the students to the United States.

A direct way of measuring a visit's lasting effects is to ask the visitors about it some time after their return home. When the immediate reactions of the German exchange students were compared with those six months after their return, explicit positive comments on democratic values and procedures were highest just before departure, but dropped after six months at home. Such expressions as statements favouring tolerance, civic responsibility, and give-and-take discussion — suggesting that the values had been internalized—increased through their stay, and increased further after their return home.

The findings suggest that well-managed extensive and massive visiting programs—in which stays would be long and visitors would be allowed to perform useful functions, including studying— could powerfully promote world-mindedness. In this connection, two bold and imaginative proposals for interchanges between Americans and Russians deserve mention. One plan—initially conceived as a kind of hostage-exchange to guarantee that neither would launch a nuclear attack, but since cast in more constructive terms—envisages a million people from each country, preferably as prominent as possible but of different ages and walks of life residing and working in the other. Its sponsors have been able to activate only a small visitor's program, but someday conditions may be suitable for fanning the spark into flame.

The other proposal—which has elicited expressions of interest from American and Russian leaders, although it is still only on paper—would have thousands of American and Russian high school students attend school in the other country for a year. The youngsters would be particularly suited for exchange programs since in addition to being especially accessible to new experiences and able to make friends easily, they are by and large too young, inexperienced, and untrained to make good spies, and so would be less likely than adults to arouse suspicion in their hosts . . .

The Peace Corps is still too minuscule to have a perceptible effect on the course of international events, but as a demonstration of how the mutually beneficial effects of cross-national personal contacts can be successfully increased, it may prove to be a major achievement of our time and a powerful moving force toward world peace.

The next step, and it is around the corner, would be for the United States to become the recipient of help from other nation's "peace corps" in handling certain types of problems. Americans might learn a good deal from members of Israel's 'kibbutzim', for example, or from directors of co-operatives or those who rehabilitate prisoners in certain Scandinavian countries.

There are more efficient ways to reduce international tensions than through the use of mass communications, personal contacts, and aid-giving. If methods were available, the nations themselves could engage in co-operative activities through their representatives. Increased mutual friendliness of their citizens would inevitably follow, for group members' attitudes toward each other depend primarily on the circumstances of the group's interactions— a generalization, as firm as any about human nature, applicable to all groups, from small artificial ones in psychological laboratories to nations.

The results of an experiment performed some years ago at a boy's camp illustrate that friendship or enmity between members of groups are the products, not the causes, of group interactions. Eleven-year old, middle-class, American, Protestant, well-adjusted boys, all strangers to each other, were brought to the camp and divided into two groups, which were isolated from each other during the first six days until each had become a cohesive organization with definite leadership structure, local customs, and a name. In the following week the two groups—the Eagles and the Rattlers—were subjected to a series of competitive activities in which one side's victory inevitably meant the other's defeat: this produced a high level of mutual hostility, analogous to that displayed by nations at war. To their own groups the children attributed self-glorifying qualities, but to the other they assigned those traits which justified treating it as an enemy. They improvised and hoarded weapons, raided each other's property, and indulged in other shows of power.

Attempts were then made to restore peace, one spontaneously by a high-ranking member of one group who tried to open negotiations with the "enemy". They took his overtures as attempts to deceive them by pretended expressions of reconciliation and his departure was accompanied by a hail of "ammunition"—green apples hoarded for use in case of attack. And his own group, far from receiving him as a hero, chastised him for making the attempt. The analogy to the fate of certain international peacemakers is obvious. Nor were there any effects from camp leaders' direct attempts to overcome the mutual stereotypes of the two groups by appeals to fair-mindedness or justice—as would be expected, since the stereotypes were the product, not the cause, of the mutual hostility. Bringing the groups together at meals or movies was equally ineffective for in such settings the warring fractions sat apart from each other, and hurled taunts and spitballs.

But the mutual hostility was finally resolved (measured by one group's members choosing friends from the other) by a series of experiences in which the groups had to co-operate to attain goals that neither could achieve alone. For example, a very inviting movie could be rented only if the two groups combined their treasuries; more compellingly the camp water supply, secretly interrupted by the counsellors, could be restored only by co-operative action; and when the truck carrying food and supplies for an overnight camping trip ran into a ditch and stalled, both groups had to get on the tow rope to pull it out.

There are similar "superordinate goals" at the international level that could promote co-operative attitudes among nations and combat hostile ones, and the most obvious, one would think, is survival— a goal surely shared by all nations, and one increasingly jeopardized by the arms race. If threats to survival in the boy's camp were the chief means of drawing the warring factions together, by inference the threat of nuclear annihilation should be useful to draw nations together. Unfortunately, an essential difference between the boy's camp and the international arena is that the boys' joint measures for survival did not weaken them with respect to each other, while nations still regard other nations, not modern weapons, as the main threat to their existence. All want to survive and recognize that disarmament is necessary to achieve this goal, but none is willing to risk reducing its armed power relative to other nations to get the process started—each nation perceives as immediately endangering to itself the steps it must take to achieve ultimate universal security.

Survival as a goal also presents other psychological difficulties. It is not compelling because the danger of modern weapons is not experienced as very real—it is too problematical and too new. Moreover, survival in itself is not especially rewarding, it is merely a prerequisite for the attainment of all other goals. Nevertheless, a more widespread and concerted effort to dramatize the common danger facing all nations would be worthwhile. The inhibitions affecting leaders of major nations in this respect would not apply to the small, militarily weak ones, who could take the initiative. And the UN affords a readily available platform.

Perhaps the most hopeful area for co-operative international research is outer space, including the moon and planets. The payoff in terms of knowledge and therefore potentially in human welfare would undoubtedly be enormous, and the resources necessary for an adequate job are beyond even the richest nation's reach. Since the area is new, no nations have any vested interests and none of those co-operating would start with enough advantage over the others to breed suspicion. Space exploration could also substitute for some aspects of war, because it meets the need of many young men to prove their manhood by undergoing dangers and risking their lives. And space heroes already reap at least as much glory as military heroes.

The opening of outer space to exploration is somewhat analogous to the discovery of the New World, an event that probably helped extinguish the religious wars that had devastated Europe by introducing a new type of national hero, the explorer, and more attractive bones of contention. The area of conflict shifted from idelogical differences to division of spoils, and the participant's emotional investment gradually followed suit. It was several centuries before Catholics and Protestants could even begin to resolve their religious conflicts, which often intensified the wars over colonies, but actual fighting over religious doctrines died away. It cannot be claimed that

Columbus's discovery reduced the numbers of wars between European nations, but the decline of the idelogical component may have reduced their destructiveness for a time.

Competition in outer space may have a similar effect on the intensity of the ideological conflict which is today's main source of danger. Gains in knowledge about outer space do have military implications, of course, and this is the most serious obstacle to international co-operation in this area, but nations so far are willing to forego possible military advantages, as the unanimous United Nations resolution against the orbiting of weapons bears witness. And the potential military implications have not prevented the universally favourable reception given the Russian and American space triumphs; both nations can sincerely congratulate each other on new space feats, a response that would be unthinkable to an improved nuclear missile.

In the experiment in the boy's camp all members of the contending groups were involved in the co-operative enterprises to achieve superordinate goals. It is obviously impossible to involve all citizens of co-operating nations in similar fashion, but thanks to the human capacity for identification, all members of a group can participate vicariously in its representative's activities. Entire student bodies of colleges or large segments of the citizenry of cities become emotionally involved in the fortunes of their athletic teams, and the hero's receptions accorded astronauts and cosmonauts indicate that the public at large shares the thrill of their achievements.

These considerations all suggest that if co-operative international ventures are to have the greatest beneficial effect on international attitude, the fact must be dramatized that the participants are their nation's representatives, and not individuals.

Each successful co-operative international project would generate trust and create habits of co-operation that would smooth the path for the next one. In addition, the international agencies that would have to be formed to conduct some of these enterprises would set up rules of procedure and precedents which could gradually become sufficiently extensive and powerful to withstand international antagonisms as well as to supply part of the foundations for effective peace-keeping international organizations and world law.

The upshot of these speculations is that the same scientific activities that threaten to destroy humanity could be powerful forces for saving it. Modern scientific developments and the new forms of communication and transportation could be exploited to break down international misunderstanding and distrust and to increase mutual appreciation and the sense of community among nations. The formation of a genuine world state, presumably the end result of these processes, is a necessary condition for an international system of enduring peace. Whether it would be sufficient, no one knows. States can maintain order within their borders most of the time, yet there are still occasional crime waves, riots, and civil wars.

But there is still the most challenging problem of all—how to create conditions that will permanently keep the human propensity for violence within acceptable bounds.

TRADE AND DEVELOPMENT — INSTRUMENTS TOWARDS HUMAN RIGHTS

GORDON EVANS, O.B.E.

Executive Secretary, Society for International Development (United Kingdom Chapter). Clerk to the United Nations Parliamentary Group. Member of Lecturing Panel, Institute of Bankers.

This Chapter is one of hope, based on the wide area of co-operation already achieved within the United Nations family of international organizations and agreement in principle between virtually all its member nations upon what the next steps forward should be.

The challenge before us, particularly the rich nations, is whether we care enough, whether we have the political will animated by sufficient strength of moral purpose, to take these crucially important next steps, and to make good the targets and policies, well within our power, for which we have voted.

The Universal Declaration of Human Rights provides the world community with its basic morality, "as a common standard of achievement for all peoples and all nations". The first twenty-one articles set out the civil and political rights to which people everywhere should be ("are") entitled. Articles 22 to 27 set out their economic, social and cultural rights. These two different types of rights were incorporated into the two International Covenants which were unanimously adopted by the United Nations General Assembly in 1966, and are now before the governments of all States Members for ratification. The Covenants, when ratified, will be legally binding.

It is essential that both types of rights shall be fully observed if a world community of peoples is to be created "in which human beings shall enjoy freedom of speech and belief and freedom from fear and want". But whereas civil and political rights can be achieved through the adoption and enforcement of appropriate legislation, the economic, social and cultural rights require a high level of economic development before they can be achieved.

For example, the Universal Declaration Article 25 (1) states that "Everyone has the right to a standard of living adequate for the health and well-being of himself and of his family, including food, clothing, housing and medical care and necessary social services, and the right to security in the event of unemployment, sickness, disability, widowhood, old age or other lack of livelihood in circumstances beyond his control".

Article 26 (1) states that: "Everyone has the right to education. Education shall be free, at least in the elementary and fundamental stages. Elementary education shall be compulsory. Technical and professional education shall be made generally available and higher education shall be equally accessible to all on the basis of merit".

Plainly the realization of these and similar rights pre-supposes a high level of economic development. It is well understood that economic and social development march together and are mutually dependent. The civil and political rights set out in the Declaration are the end product of slow centuries of both kinds of development in the industrialized Western countries from which it mainly derived. Yet both these kinds of rights have now been generalized to and accepted as standards by all Member States of the United Nations, most of which are still in the pre-industrial stage. Many of the economic and social rights have been recognised and implemented in the industrialized West only since 1945. They are now held to be the rights of all people everywhere.

This fundamental situation is recognized in Article 22 which states: "Everyone, as a member of society, has the right to social security and is entitled to realization, *through national effort and international co-operation* and in accordance with the organization and resources of each State, of the economic, social and cultural rights indispensable for his dignity and the free development of his personality".

Such "national effort and international co-operation" are legally obligatory upon States Members of the United Nations. Article 56 of the Charter, the world's master treaty to which all others are subordinate, states: "All Members pledge themselves to take joint and separate action in co-operation with the Organization for the achievement of the purposes set forth in Article 55". These purposes are the promotion of:

(a) "higher standards of living, full employment and conditions of economic and social progress and development;
(b) solutions of international economic, social, health and related problems; and international, cultural and educational co-operation; and
(c) universal respect for, and observance of, human rights and fundamental freedoms for all without distinction as to race, sex, language or religion".

With the emergence of many new, self-governing nations consequent upon the dissolution of the colonial empires after World War II came the discovery that political independence was not enough. Along with the new independence came the realization of inescapable dependence upon a world trading and financial network into which they were inextricably woven. This network had grown up unplanned and piece-meal over more than two centuries. Its functioning brought benefits to many in all countries, stimulating development wherever it took root, planting in many the beginnings of modern economies. But its purpose was not social. Both within and between nations its distribution of benefits was grossly unequal and often, as in the slave trade, it operated with fearful cruelty. Its breakdown in 1929 was a major factor contributory to the collapse of the League of Nations and World War II.

The United Nations was created in 1945 with the aim of organizing the world as a community of nations for the achievement of agreed common purposes. A major new organ was the Economic and Social Council, operating under the authority of the General Assembly, charged with the responsibility of promoting international action for the purposes set out in Article 55 of the Charter (see above). ECOSOC's tasks included those of initiating reports, studies and conferences; and making recommendations to the General Assembly, to Governments and to the specialized Agencies. The specialized Agencies, each with its own independent constitution, governing body and sources of finance, provide world services. If the United Nations may be considered as constituting the beginnings of some kind of world government, the specialized Agencies may be seen as embryonic departments of state for such a government. Each Agency corresponds at the international level to a department of state within individual nations. For example, the Food and Agricultural Organization of the United Nations corresponds to Britain's Ministry of Agriculture, Fisheries and Food; the UN Educational, Scientific and Cultural Organization corresponds to our Department of Education and Science; the World Health Organization to our Ministry of Health, etc. ECOSOC's task includes that of co-ordinating the work of these Agencies.

Probably the greatest single service performed by the UN family of organizations has been that of providing the world with a continuous stream of information on all aspects of international affairs, presenting the world to the world, bringing its priorities and needs into focus and measuring its economic and social trends, thus illuminating problems and opportunities ahead and enabling governments to steer rational courses. The main facts about the world social situation which the United Nations and its Agencies have brought to the world's notice are:

(a) One third of the world's population living in the industrialised countries enjoys 87.5% of the world's gross national product, leaving 12.5% for the other two-thirds, whose people are still mainly in the pre-industrial stage;

(b) More than half the world's population is underfed or undernourished and is illiterate;

(c) It is estimated that world population, which reached 3,420 million in 1967, will reach 7,000 million by the year 2,000, increasing more in the next 30 years than in the previous 500,000 years.

(d) The lines of poverty and underprivilege everywhere coincide with the lines of race and colour.

The First Development Decade

These facts and what they imply, taken together, constitute the 'time-bomb' in the not-far-distant future of human history which could bring about an explosion which would be as ultimate in its consequences for civilization as all-out nuclear war. It is not too much to say that if the nations, acting together through the United Nations system, do not quickly establish an effective world order of economic and social (and hence, political) priorities and produce and implement a world plan capable of bringing present trends progressively under humane and responsible control, there is likely to be a complete and hopeless breakdown of civilization before the end of the century.

The fact that this situation, brought to the world's notice by the United Nations, is common knowledge to all governments, constitutes the best hope that effective action will be taken to deal with it. It was in the light of this situation that in 1961 the decision was taken to designate the 1960s as the United Nations Development Decade. A programme for international economic co-operation was unanimously adopted aimed at bringing about "a minimum annual rate of growth of aggregate national income of five per cent" in the developing countries by 1970. The developed countries were called upon to pursue specific policies designed to help them to achieve this goal.

Achievement would have meant that, allowing for the estimated increase in population in developing countries, their income per head by 1970 would be increasing twice as fast as in 1960. Each developing country was called upon to set its own target. Whilst the aim was that the economic and social advancement of each country would be self-sustaining, the whole emphasis of the General Assembly resolution was upon the necessity for a special, concerted programme of international co-operation, involving both national and international measures, in order to achieve it.

Four main lines of action were agreed:

(a) Using a proposal of the World Council of Churches in 1958, the General Assembly in 1960 adopted a resolution calling upon the industrialized countries to ensure that the flow of private investment, public loans and grants to developing countries should reach 1% of their national income.
(b) Countries were requested to increase contributions to technical assistance and pre-investment so that by 1970 the programmes of the United Nations would reach an annual expenditure of $300 million.
(c) International trade was recognized as the "primary instrument for economic development", whereby developing countries earned most of their foreign exchange requirements. Measures were to be taken in both developed and developing countries to bring about the expansion of developing countries' trade.
(d) Measures were taken to mobilize science and technology for the benefit of developing countries in order to make available to them the most efficient techniques of wealth production as rapidly as possible.

On the food and population fronts, the Food and Agriculture Organization in 1960 launched its Freedom from Hunger Campaign. Together with the Population Commission of the United Nations and the World Health Organization it wanted to bring the quality and quantity of world food supplies into balance with the projected increase in world population. FAO estimated that in order to provide barely adequate diets, world food production would have to double by 1980 and treble by the year 2000. In 1969 after five years' intensive work, FAO published its monumental *Indicative World Plan for Agricultural Development*. This sets broad lines of strategy for the Second Development Decade. It has two time-horizons, 1975 and 1985 and sets targets, suggests alternative policies, economic inputs and incentives and describes institutional changes country-by-country that will be necessary. Already sharp increases in agricultural production in many countries are being reported, the so-called "green revolution", due to the use of improved strains of seed and fertilizer. As a result, local gluts are occurring and attention is being drawn to the need for increased storage and marketing facilities.

The World Food Programme was established in 1963, administered jointly by FAO and the United Nations as a multilateral food agency. Its purpose is to utilize food surpluses as emergency food aid but mainly as a form of capital investment for development. The workers in industrial development projects spend a high proportion of their earnings on food. If the supply is static the effect is to raise its price, thus adding to the difficulties of the rest of the community. With the help of the World Food Programme governments are able to steer food supplies, as a form of capital investment, into industrial complexes to meet the increased demands of wage-earners without disrupting markets or price structures. The General Assembly has recommended a target for the WFP of $300 million for 1971-72.

A major mobilization of scientists and technologists took place in 1963 with the United Nations Conference on the Application of Science and Technology for the Benefit of the Less Developed Countries. (UNCSAT). The UNCSAT Report, in eight volumes, was a kind of Mrs. Beaton's cookery book of development problems, together with their scientific and technical solutions. The first volume, *"World of Opportunity"*, edited by Professor Lord Ritchie Calder, contained a summary of the scope and proceedings of UNCSAT. As a follow-up the Economic and Social Council established a permanent Advisory Committee on the Application of Science and Technology to Development, composed of high-level experts. This Committee has worked out a world plan in this area and established a set of priorities tailored to the needs of developing countries. The report entitled *"A World Plan of Action for the Application of Science and Technology for Development"* has been published, and will be considered by the UN General Assembly in September 1972.

UNCTAD I

In 1964 the United Nations Conference on Trade and Development (UNCTAD) was convened, attended by some 2000 delegates from over 120 countries and scores of inter-governmental bodies, UN agencies and non-governmental organizations. UNCTAD sat continuously for three months. It was hailed as the beginning of a new era in the evolution of international co-operation in the field of trade and development, and later that year was established as a new organ of the General Assembly. The main basic document was the report *New Trade Policies for Development* by UNCTAD's dynamic then Secretary-General, Dr. Paul Prebisch. He showed that if the 5% growth target for the Development Decade was to be achieved, import programmes for the developing countries would be required which would open up an increasing trade gap between them and the developed countries which by 1970 would be running at an annual rate of $20,000 million. Therefore, the concrete problem which the governments assembled at UNCTAD had to solve was how this gap was to be covered.

It was recognized that by far the most satisfactory means would be through policies of both developed and developing countries which would enable the latter progressively to earn the foreign exchange to pay for their requirements by increasing their exports to developed countries. There would be an unavoidable time-lag before this balance could be achieved which would have to be covered by increased financial transfers from the developed countries in the shape of governmental grants and loans and private investment. Aid and trade were seen as having complementary roles which together would be indispensible to the success of the Decade. The long-term goal would be to expand the trade of the poorer with the richer countries so as to bring about a new international division of labour.

It was shown that a major weakness in the position of most developing countries was their dependence on a narrow range of primary export commodities, often only one or two, such as coffee, cocoa, cotton, tea, rubber. These were subject to unpredictable price fluctuations with a generally downward trend and Prebisch showed that over many years the terms of trade of the developing countries had steadily deteriorated so that in real terms they were having to trade increasing supplies of their primary products in return for the developed countries' manufactured products which steadily rose in price.

In order to counter this trend UNCTAD made a number of recommendations. A proposal from the United Kingdom and Sweden was adopted for a scheme of "supplementary finance" to compensate developing countries whose development plans were disrupted by unforeseen declines in commodity prices resulting in falls of export revenue beyond their control. This proposal was submitted to the World Bank which in due course produced a feasibility study, but no further action has so far been taken. Britain has nevertheless continued to press for a scheme on these lines.

A major obstacle to expanding the trade of the poor countries was shown to be the difficulty of access to the markets of the rich for some raw materials and for manufactured and semi-manufactured goods. The structural bias of the whole market was towards the interests of the rich, which absorb over 70% of the poor countries' exports. Tariffs are so designed as to discourage processing of raw materials and industrial exports from developing countries. On most raw materials the rich nations' tariffs are low or nil. On semi-processed goods and manufactures they are much higher. When, despite these, poor countries' goods still manage to find a way into Western markets they are often confronted with rigid quota systems which place a fixed limit on quantities that may be admitted. The prices of tropical products such as tea and coffee in some European countries are increased by internal excise duties.

The most important proposal to emerge from UNCTAD in 1964 was that of introducing a generalized preference scheme for the exports of manufactures and semi-manufactures from developing countries on a non-reciprocal and non-discriminating basis. The General Assembly target of financial transfers of 1% of national income from developed to developing countries was confirmed, adding that it should apply to individual developed countries and be calculated net of capital repayments. Attention was drawn to the fact that more and more aid was being used up in the servicing of past loans and developed countries were urged to increase the proportion of aid made in the form of grants or long-term low-interest loans.

One of the remedies persistently sought by the developing countries for unremunerative price fluctuations of their exports and for the instability of their markets was through international commodity agreements, covering such primary products as coffee, cocoa, sugar, tea, cotton, bananas, rubber, tin, copper, lead, zinc and many others. Already some of these commodities are covered by agreements, operated by such bodies as the International Tin and Coffee Councils. Agreements to cover other major commodities such as sugar and cocoa are in the 'pipe-line'.

UNCTAD I was notable mainly for the coherent group of 77 (now 96) developing nations which emerged, which enabled them to concert their policies and on most issues to speak as with a single voice. The degree of unanimity among the developed countries was markedly less. The Conference of 1964 left behind it, to carry on the work, a 55-member Trade and Development Board which meets twice a year, and Committees on Commodities, Manufactures, Shipping and on Invisibles and Financing Related to Trade.

Development of International Organs

As the decade advanced new machinery was called into existence and existing machinery was modified. An International Trade Centre was established by UNCTAD and the General Agreement on Tariffs and Trade and the work of GATT was orientated to take increasing account of the needs of developing countries. The United Nations Industrial Development Organization (UNIDO) was established, with its headquarters in Vienna, with an "action-orientated" mandate. At UN Headquarters the Centre for Development Planning, Projections and Policies, and the Centre for Housing, Building and Planning were established; and the UN Institute for Training and Research (UNITAR). The main move towards consolidation was the merger in 1965 of the Expanded Programme of Technical Assistance and the Special Fund into the United Nations Development Programme (UNDP).

Whilst UNCTAD was the main organ for promoting international understanding of trade and development problems and endeavouring to negotiate relevant policies and agreements among governments; and the UNDP was the main organ for promoting international technical co-operation and pre-investment among governments and the UN family of Specialised Agencies; the main international organ for the investment of capital for development was the World Bank in Washington and its affiliates, the International Finance Corporation and the International Development Association, all three being Specialized Agencies of the United Nations. Their role was to act as a bridge across which increasing supplies of capital could flow from the developed to the developing world. Whereas the Bank lends at economic rates of interest to governments or against government guarantees for development projects, the IFC provides risk capital for development through private enterprise. IDA makes grant-like, long-term, interest-free loans. Under the dynamic leadership of Robert S. McNamara, President of all three agencies, the work is rapidly expanding. In 1971 the level of loans and commitments amounted to $2,600 million compared with $1,004 million in 1968 and $1,900 million in 1969: the Bank's money being raised by increased sales of its bonds on the markets of developed countries. In addition to conventional project lending the Bank in recent years had made loans for agricultural development, in particular irrigation projects, and for education, emphasizing projects which increase trained manpower.

UNCTAD II

The second meeting of UNCTAD at New Delhi in February 1968 was notable above all for its revelation of the lack of political will among the larger developed countries to make good the modest adjustments and sacrifices that were necessary for carrying out the recommendations of UNCTAD I. The aid target of developed countries was raised from 1% of National Income to 1% of Gross National Product, representing an increase of about 25%. Nevertheless the performance of the rich countries, even under the lower target, had been disappointing. It was clear that as a ratio of GNP the general trend of contributions was downwards, though in absolute terms it was continuing to rise, thanks largely to the upsurge of private investment. The most considerable step forward was a unanimous agreement in favour of the early establishment of a generalized non-reciprocal and non-discriminatory system of preferences for manufactures. But this was an agreement only in principle, heralding an indefinite period of detailed negotiations with no date-line for implementation. No progress was made on the UNCTAD I proposal for supplementary financing for commodity price fluctuations, the developed countries taking the view that they needed more time to consider the joint World Bank-International Monetary Fund study on international commodity policy.

Nevertheless, as with the first UNCTAD, UNCTAD II performed the great service of casting a clear, if lurid, light upon problems and trends in the relations between the developed and developing worlds. UNCTAD III will be held in Santiago, Chile, April-May 1972. It is well timed to focus world attention on the international development strategy of the Second UN Development Decade, launched in December 1970. In preparation for UNCTAD III, 96 developing countries meeting in Lima (November 1971) unanimously adopted "The Declaration and Principles of the Action Programme of Lima."

UNDD I reached its target

The United Nations Development Decade of the 1960s was the world's first attempt at making and carrying through a concerted programme of economic and social co-operation with the specific social purpose of raising the rate of economic growth of the poor countries to 5% annually by 1970. Despite the many general and particular short-falls and failures, this over-all target was achieved. In 1968-69 the developing countries taken together added approximately $15 billion to their combined gross national product, thus reaching almost exactly the 5% annual rate of growth target. But the increase of incomes per head was less than had been expected, due to the increase in population which had not been taken sufficiently into account in 1961 when the targets for Development Decade I were set.

Amongst the many causes of DD I's success, one that was indispensable was the continuing growth of economic activity in the developed countries with consequent continuing expansion of international trade. Although the share of developing countries as a proportion of world trade fell, their export earnings steadily increased as a consequence of the general expansion. Such expansion will continue to be necessary if the Second Development Decade, with higher targets, deeper understanding of problems, greater experience and more refined and precise methods is to succeed in doing the far more effective job that must be done towards abolishing poverty, hunger, disease and ignorance in the developing countries.

The Second United Nations Development Decade

The International Development Strategy for the Second United Nations Development Decade, adopted by the General Assembly in October 1970, is based on the experience—the successes and failures—of the first Development Decade. The main goals of the Decade include an average rate of growth in gross national product of the developing countries of at least 6 per cent. If population growth can be held back to 2.5 per cent, then gross product per head will increase by 3.5 per cent a year—sufficient to double the average income per head by 1990. These figures in turn imply an average growth rate of 4 per cent a year in agricultural output and 8 per cent in manufacturing output.

The success of the developing countries in reaching these goals will depend mainly upon their own efforts. But to an essential degree success will depend on the developed countries providing financial resources of at least 1 per cent of their gross national products, of which at least 0.7 per cent is called for in the form of official development assistance. In addition, and of at least equal importance, are measures to provide expanding markets at remunerative prices in the developed countries for the goods, primary, semi-manufactured and manufactured, of the developing countries, since it is by means of their exports that the latter earn by far the greater part of the foreign exchange they need to sustain their import programmes.

There are two main distinctions between the First and Second Development Decades. The latter places far greater emphasis upon social development, recognizing that, although economic growth is essential, it is not enough. Its benefits must be clearly distributed among all sections of the population. This involves special provision for rural development, in areas where the vast majority of people live, together with measures to provide employment opportunities to overcome the growing mass unemployment and under-employment.

Secondly, provision is made for regular, systematic review and appraisal of objectives, policies and progress, nationally, regionally and globally. The over-all appraisal will be made biennially, by the General Assembly, through the Economic and Social Council, the second biennial appraisal (1975) being in the nature of a mid-term review.

Three Major Reports

Reviewing the global development enterprise, the efficiency of the UN System, and planning ahead for the Second Development Decade, were three major reports. *"Partners in Development"*, the report of the Commission on International Development, set up by the World Bank, over which Mr. Lester Pearson presided, analysed the failures and successes of the past twenty years of international development effort, and put forward guide-lines and recommendations for the future. The report showed *inter alia* that the rate of progress of the developing countries is far greater than was that of the rich countries at a comparable stage in their development; and that some 85 per cent of the capital being invested in the developing countries is generated from their own resources.

At the same time, the *"Study of the Capacity of the United Nations Development System"*, commissioned by the UNDP, with Sir Robert Jackson of Australia as Commissioner, produced a detailed analysis of the pre-investment and technical co-operation work of the whole UN system, and made many radical and far-reaching recommendations. The most important recommendation was that the activities of the system, the UN and the Specialised Agencies, should be more strongly co-ordinated at the international level, and should be directed towards providing assistance to country programmes, helping developing countries at their request, in integrated development in accordance with their own planning priorities.

Thirdly, there was the report of the UN Committee for Development Planning, of which Professor Jan Tinbugen was the Chairman. This did the main preparatory work for the strategy of the Second Development Decade. A major feature of this report was the emphasis placed upon the need to take special measures for assisting the least developed countries. Criteria were drawn up for identifying such countries, and thirty-three countries were listed as qualifying for this category, based upon the proportionate contribution of manufacturing in their gross products and their literacy ratios (manufacturing ratio, more or less than 10 per cent; literacy ratio, more or less than 20 per cent).

INTERNATIONAL CREDIT CREATION

Probably the greatest stride forward for facilitating world development based on the continuing expansion of world trade and investment was the agreement reached in September 1967 by the members of the International Monetary Fund for the world's first experiment in the deliberate creation of international credit. This takes the form of a new reserve instrument called "Special drawing rights", journalistically known as "paper gold", issued by the International Monetary Fund, with the intention that the central banks of member countries will accept SDRs as if they were gold for augmenting their foreign exchange reserves. The first experiment took place over a three-year period beginning in 1970. On 1st January 1970, SDRs to the value of $3,500 million were allocated among members of the IMF in proportion to their quotas. Britain's share was $410 million. This represents an unearned increase in Britain's stock of international purchasing power. Similar allocations were made in 1971 and 1972.

This scheme, which represents a revolutionary step forward in international monetary co-operation, has great potential value for the struggle against world poverty. Probably its main service will be to provide essential additional means for financing the continuing expansion of world trade, upon which more than anything else the development of the poorer countries depends. In addition, SDRs could provide a means of channelling internationally created purchasing power from the richer countries to the poorer ones, without creating budgetary or balance of payments problems for the former. This could be done in several ways: by stepping up bilateral programmes; by additional contributions to multilateral agencies such as the International Development Association, the United Nations Development Programme, international funds for compensating commodity price fluctuations, or the purchase of bonds of the World Bank. An international expert group convened by UNCTAD (United Nations Conference on Trade and Development) meeting in September 1969 has produced a report on *International Monetary Reform and Co-operation for Development* advocating the establishment of a direct link between international credit creation and international aid, and describing the ways in which this could be done.

There can be no doubt that the inauguration of this new, costless facility of international credit creation, in the allocation of which vastly the greatest proportion has gone to the developed countries, removes from the latter all genuine reasons for their failure hitherto to comply with the recommendations for which they have voted in UNCTAD, that they should contribute 1 per cent of their gross national products (net) towards assisting the development of the poorer countries. The recommendation made in the Pearson Report *(Partners in Development)* and in the International Development Strategy for the Second United Nations Development Decade, that the rich countries should contribute 0.7 per cent in official aid by 1975 is one which now could and should be complied with forthwith.

"Who can now ask where his country will be in a few decades without asking where the world will be?" asks the Pearson Commission. U Thant, in May 1969, summarised the issues with sober realism: "I do not wish to seem over-dramatic but I can only conclude that the members of the United Nations have perhaps ten years to subordinate their ancient quarrels and launch a global partnership to curb the arms race, to improve the human environment, to defuse the population explosion, and to supply the required momentum for world development efforts.

If a global partnership is not forged within the next decade then I very much fear that the problems I have mentioned will have reached such staggering proportions that they will be beyond our capacity to control."

Further Reading:

Power to End Poverty: Background to the Manifesto of Action for World Development Derek Walker. (Action for World Development, 69 Victoria Street, London S.W.1.)

Partners in Development: Report of the Commission on International Development Lester B. Pearson (Chairman) Pall Mall, London.

A Study of the Capacity of the United Nations Development System Sir Robert Jackson, H.M.S.O.

International Targets for Development Edited by Richard Symonds, Faber & Faber.

State and Society in a Developing World David Blelloch, The New Thinkers Library, Watts.

Science and Starvation: An Introduction to Economic Development Donald J. Hughes, Pergamon Press.

Social Policy in Developing Countries Arthur Livingstone, Routledge and Kegan Paul.

An International Development strategy for the Second United Nations Development Decade (H.M.S.O. Cmnd. 4568, 45p.).

Britain's Role in the Second Development Decade (V.C.O.A.D., 25 Wilton Road, London, S.W.1. 10p.).

PART THREE
MAINTAINING PEACE

The understanding of peace is of little value unless there is machinery in being for preserving it. If war is seen to be futile what are the alternatives?

The following chapters examine non-violent resistance in Czechoslovakia, non-violent peacekeeping operations in the Congo war, the Charter of Human Rights and the International Courts. World Order, the need to reconsider our assumption that nations can be coerced and to substitute the rule of law to individuals. A U.N. peacekeeping and peacemaking force.

CZECHOSLOVAKIA: A BATTLE WON, A WAR LOST[1]

ADAM ROBERTS

Lecturer in International Relations at the London School of Economics; co-author with Philip Windsor of *Czechoslovakia 1968*; editor of *The Strategy of Civilian Defence* (Faber 1967). Has visited Czechoslovakia several times.

This chapter discusses the impact and ultimate failure of the resistance in Czechoslovakia after the Soviet-led invasion of August 1968. It raises the question as whether civil resistance can succeed in circumstances where it demands national unity.

There is no other word for it but 'defeat'. In the seven years since the invasion of their country in August 1968 Czechoslovakia's leaders have abandoned most of the principles of the 1968 reform movement and have capitulated to the main Soviet demands. Centralized dictatorial control of all aspects of political, economic and cultural life has been re-established.

The defeat occurred in the wake of a remarkable and in some respects unique campaign of civil resistance waged by the Czechoslovak population against the occupation—a campaign which was particularly intense in the period 21-27 August 1968.[2] Because this resistance was followed by defeat it is natural that there should be many serious arguments to the effect that civil resistance was bound to fail; and that some forms of military resistance should have been used. These two arguments both have considerable force, and they deserve to be considered carefully and sympathetically.

The Argument for a Military Threat

The argument is increasingly put that the Czechoslovaks should have attempted to deter a Soviet invasion by issuing a clear military threat; and that small nations in such exposed situations must look to their defences either through nuclear deterrence, or through a partially guerrilla type of defence on the Swiss or Yugoslav model.

Even if such options were not really open to the Czechoslovaks in 1968, these might be the lessons that other countries would draw from the Czechoslovak tragedy: any judgement on this broader question, however, is outside the scope of this chapter, which is a preliminary attempt at assessing the position of Czechoslovakia *vis-a-vis* the Soviet Union.

Would it have been possible for Czechoslovakia in 1968 to have had some kind of *defense a tous azimuts?* When one asks Czechoslovaks why no preparations of any kind were made for resisting a Soviet occupation, they often preface their reply by mentioning the allegedly indecisive role of Alexander Dubcek, whose failure to believe in or prepare against the threat of invasion is easy to condemn in retrospect. They also tend to refer to the widespread faith in friendship with the Soviet Union, the historic relationship between Czechoslovaks and Russians. Behind these rather general causes of the Czechoslovak failure to prepare for the worst, however, was a quite specific political obstacle. It is easy to forget that Czechoslovakia's patriotic unity really built up only around the time of the invasion. Before August 1968 any move to introduce an explicitly anti-Russian element into Czechoslovakia's defence policy would have created the danger of a split in the three bodies that would have been most involved in any such effort: the Communist Party, the Army, and the Interior Ministry.[3] Such a move might merely have precipitated the invasion it was intended to deter.

Even if preparations for some kind of territorial defence had been made in Czechoslovakia, would they have deterred? It is frequently suggested that the Rumanians and the Yugoslavs have escaped Soviet invasion because they have made it clear that they would wage war against any attackers. A national road to socialism, it is argued, can only be pursued once the flanks are secured by efficient military preparations. In the case of Yugoslavia the threat of resistance by prolonged guerrilla warfare certainly has some credibility, conforming as it does to the country's character and history. But whether such a policy would have prevented the invasion of Czechoslovakia is quite another question.

Two special factors—ideological and geographical—put Czechoslovak political developments in 1968 in a different category from the earlier heresies of the Yugoslavs and the Rumanians. These factors reinforced each other and greatly increased the Soviet concern about Czechoslovakia.

The Russians in 1968 viewed the ideological challenge posed by the Czechoslovak progressives quite as seriously as, twenty years earlier, Stalin had viewed the Yugoslav heresy. Perhaps the alarm over Czechoslovakia was even greater. Whether the Russians were right to regard the Czechoslovak challenge as a real threat to their empire, their security, and their political system will long be a matter of conjecture, but the indications that they did regard it so are numerous and convincing. Certainly the free press which the Czechoslovaks enjoyed for some months in 1968 was an implicit reproach to the controlled press of other socialist countries; moreover, it contained a number of explicit comments on such sensitive and explosive matters as the Soviet role in the Czechoslovak purges of the early 1950's, and Kadar's role as a Soviet collaborator in suppressing the Hungarian revolution of 1956. In an empire with a common political creed, a redefinition of so basic a part of the catechism as the leading role of the party was bound to have implications outside the frontiers of the country where the new road to socialism was being explored. For the Russians there was the ominous precedent of 1956, when relatively peaceful changes in Poland led to a violent upheaval in Hungary. Rightly or wrongly, the Russians in 1968 regarded the Czechoslovak revolution as a dangerous virus, and it appears that they considered it far more serious then the earlier heresies of the Rumanians or Yugoslavs.

Soviet ideological fears were reinforced by the facts of Czechoslovakia's geography. Czechoslovakia is unique in having common frontiers both with the Soviet Union and with West Germany; and the extraordinary importance of its geographical situation is heightened by the fact that it also lies between the northern and southern Warsaw Pact countries. To the north it is contiguous with East Germany and Poland; and to the south with Hungary as well as with neutral Austria. It is evident that for the Soviet Union the strategic importance of Czechoslovakia is far greater than that of Yugoslavia or Rumania—especially when the Soviet Union's deep historical fears of Germany are borne in mind. Czechoslovakia, along with Poland and East Germany, formed a defensive military structure known by the Russians as the 'iron triangle'. Fears that the 'iron triangle' would be broken help to explain the disproportionate attention paid to Czechoslovak events not only in the Soviet Union but also in Poland and East Germany.

The geopolitical argument for the invasion was made by the East German party daily *News Deutschland* on 21 August 1968—the morning on which troops of the five Warsaw Pact powers were entering the cities of Czechoslovakia:

> Every citizen of the German Democratic Republic will understand, by a glance at the map, that an intolerable situation would have been created for our republic and for other fraternal socialist countries if anti-socialist forces, especially those inspired by West German imperialism, could have pursued their

counter-revolutionary activities from the south, that is, from our very flank.

If Czechoslovakia's geostrategic position made intervention seem all the more necessary to the Soviet Union, it might conceivably also have had the opposite effect: it might have deterred the Soviet Union from any action which risked war. Some Western commentators have suggested that the Soviet leadership would have been especially reluctant to intervene if it knew that it would have to fight the Czechoslovaks, because it would not wish to have a war on its hands in a country bordering on West Germany; the Soviet leadership, according to this argument, would have feared that a war against the Czechoslovaks might have 'spilled over' and involved NATO, thus producing a wider and more dangerous conflagration. If this argument were a convincing one it might possibly reinforce the case for saying that Czechoslovakia should have threatened to fight its attackers. But it is not wholly convincing. A Soviet-Czechoslovak war in Bohemia would certainly have involved NATO in some agonizing decisions, but it is hard to see that it would have been likely to drag the NATO powers into direct military hostilities with the Soviet Union.

Whether a Czechoslovak threat to fight would in fact have deterred the Soviet Union from intervention must remain uncertain. The evidence so far available does not point unambiguously either way, but at the very least it can be said that there is no certainty that such a threat would have been effective, or that it would have been an advisable course of action on which to embark in the period from June to August 1968. In any case, when the Warsaw Pact forces did eventually intervene in Czechoslovakia (in clear breach, incidentally, of the Warsaw Treaty) there was evidence from their preparations, deployments and movements, that they had made some allowances for the possibility of military resistance.[4]

Problems of Fighting in Czechoslovakia

As far as the possibilities of actual armed combat were concerned, Czechoslovakia's position in 1968 was extremely difficult. Its military position *vis-a-vis* its adversaries was desperate. The number of Czechoslovakia's opponents, their great military strength, and their close proximity, made the Soviet invasion far more overwhelming than the American intervention in Vietnam. It was unlikely, to say the least, that Czechoslovakia would have received the supplies of arms and other external assistance which are the *sine qua non* of any protracted guerrilla warfare in a small country against a powerful opponent. Czechoslovakia's geography, with its extensive road system, would have provided a sound base for counter-insurgency activities; the country's advanced economy, and its numerous urban centres, would have been vulnerable targets for the reprisals which are an almost universal feature of counter-insurgency efforts; and the easy-going, unfanatical national character would have been ill-suited to the rigours of a prolonged guerrilla struggle.

The difficulties of Czechoslovakia's position were such that there was bound to be some doubt about the credibility of any threat to fight, either by frontal military resistance or by a defence in depth throughout the national territory and using mainly guerrilla forms of resistance. There is at the present time a strong tendency to romanticize guerrilla warfare, and of course it is often an effective weapon for the Davids of the world to use against the Goliaths. But not always.

Many Czechoslovaks who advocated fighting have implicitly admitted that it would have been little more than a moral gesture. As Kamil Winter, a former editor on Czechoslovak Television, said in a letter to *The Times* in June 1969.

> I have been convinced, since 11 p.m., August 20, that the Czechoslovak people should have been allowed to take up arms against the foreign invaders, regardless of the outcome of armed resistance.[5]

There is no doubt that, even if it had ended in an inevitable defeat, embattled resistance would have imposed substantial costs on the country's invaders. A heroic gesture would have been made, and a price in blood extracted for the crime of unprovoked aggression. But other consequences of armed resistance would have been more damaging to the cause of the Czechoslovaks. The fearful retaliations that they would have had to suffer were obvious enough. But there were three other dangers in military resistance which the Czechoslovaks also, in varying degrees, avoided. The first was the danger—perhaps in any case not a very great one—that any war in central Europe would have carried with it great danger of spilling over national frontiers and turning into a more serious conflagration. The second danger was that a Czechoslovak armed resistance might have made Soviet propaganda easier, by reinforcing the claim that the Czechoslovaks were counter-revolutionaries and disloyal to the Warsaw Pact. The third danger was that the demands of military struggle in the open and vulnerable territory of Czechoslovakia would have been so impossibly high that many people would have felt compelled to engage instead in a collaboration even more direct, more complete, and more irrevocable than that which has actually been pursued.

The Effects of Czechoslovak Civil Resistance

It is indeed one of the tragedies of Czechoslovakia in 1968 that the the statement of the Communist Party Praesidium on the night of 20-21 August 1968, rejected the option of armed struggle. Instead they stumbled on the weapon of civil resistance. Strikes, arguments with tank-crews, obstruction of supplies, defiance of orders and threats, and a refusal to collaborate all emerged in the first few days of occupation in a slow and in many respects spontaneous process. These methods were used despite, or perhaps because of the massiveness of the invasion and the evident willingness of the invaders to use force: in the event some seventy Czechoslovaks were killed in August by the invading forces, and many more injured. Were the resistance methods bound to fail, or were there special and particular reasons for the failure?

It is perhaps one of the tragedies of Czechoslovakia in 1968 that the resistance was not thought out in advance, and was not planned in any way.[6] If it had been, some weaknesses and mistakes might possibly have been avoided. In the event, the civil resistance was more of a gesture, a means of self-expression, than a thought-out policy. Even so, this spontaneous opposition did extract some price from the invaders, and it did delay for eight months the achievement of the principal Soviet objectives.

That the civil resistance was regarded more as a means of self-expression than as a strategy was indicated to me by many of those who in one way or other took part in it. Many Czechoslovak Communists, who have since had to adjust to a new and harsh political climate, say that even at the height of the civil resistance to the Soviet occupation they knew of the slow retreat that would follow. They knew that the spontaneous resistance would not last, that a path of compromise would be accepted by Czechoslovakia's leaders in Moscow and implemented in Prague. Nevertheless they felt, and still feel, that the August resistance was their country's finest hour. Not only did it afford the chance to express the nation's character and to show the Czechoslovaks' contempt for the invaders; it also raised substantially the price the Russians had to pay for the occupation, and prevented them from achieving their objectives as quickly as they had intended.

The Russians knew, of course, that there would be a price of admission to Czechoslovakia, and they were prepared to pay it. They knew that their invasion would incur a good deal of odium in the international communist movement and in the world at large. Many Czechs and Slovaks feel that they raised the price. What the Russians hoped would be a quick surgical operation turned out to be a protracted affair. Some signs of sympathy with the Czechoslovaks appeared in all the European socialist countries, and there was some evidence of demoralization among the invading forces. The industrial go-slows and general Schweik-like behaviour in many sectors of the economy for well over a year after the occupation cannot have been welcome to the Russians, whose economy is integrated with that of Czechoslovakia in several sectors.

The price of the invasion, paid as it was in such intangible currency, is hard to calculate; but even after the Czechoslovak defeat it is unlikely that the Russians look on their side of the affair as a complete and unqualified success. The 'low profile' adopted by the Soviet leaders during the Polish convulsions in December 1970 and January 1971 suggested a desire to avoid incurring once again the odium which they suffered as a result of the invasion of Czechoslovakia.[7]

In the first months after the invasion, however, it looked to many as if the Czechoslovaks had done more than demand a price for a Russian victory. The resistance, after all, had clearly defeated the various attempts made by the Russians in the first few days of the invasion to form an openly collaborationist government. Even if Alexander Dubcek and his colleagues did make serious compromises in Moscow in August 1968, the resistance saved them at least temporarily from probably imprisonment or execution. It had been an effective demonstration of non-violent power. A famous battle was won. But, to adapt a saying of de Gaulle's, the Czechoslovaks won a battle but lost a war. By 17 April 1969, when Dubcek was replaced as First Secretary of the Czechoslovak Communist Party by Dr. Gustav Husak, it was evident for all to see that the Prague Spring was finally at an end.

The extent of the Czechoslovak failure has been made manifest in the period since Dr. Husak became First Secretary. The Soviet-led invasion has been blessed by its victims as an act of fraternal aid; and the essential elements of totalitarian dictatorship have been restored. However, to say that the resistance failed is not to say that Czechoslovakia is a political corpse. Dr. Husak's rule may in some essentials be Stalinism, but it is, as they say in Prague, 'Stalinism with a human face'. And it is just conceivable that in the future some Czechoslovak leaders may try to revive the democratization process. The resistance may have had some effect as a demonstration of the national will or as a punishment for aggression, but it did not succeed in the medium term in preserving Czechoslovakia's territorial integrity, its political policies, or its party leadership.

There have of course been some people who have persisted, in face of all the evidence, in describing the civil resistance as a success.[8] Few Czechs or Slovaks would agree with such judgement. But it is legitimate to quetion whether the defeat which undeniably occurred was due to civil resistance itself, or to a more complex set of factors of which the decision not to offer military resistance was only a small part.

It is after all a curious paradox of the Czechoslovak crisis that whereas in August 1968 the Czechoslovak people refused to submit in the face of a brutal use of military power, in April 1969 Czechoslovakia's leaders submitted, without overt resistance, to a much less visible threat. The change in leadership which the Soviet leaders failed to achieve by illegal means in August 1968 they succeeded in achieving in April 1969 with at least the appearance of constitutional and legitimate process. It is true, if banal, to say that the April 1969 defeat occurred because of the lack of civil resistance, not because of its practice. The underlying question about civil resistance in Czechoslovakia remains: why did the civil resistance end?

Causes of the Czechoslovak Defeat

One of the main reasons for the ending of the resistance was its wholly spontaneous and unplanned character. It grew up in the first hours and days of the invasion as the response of an impotent and outraged nation to an inexcusable crime. Many sectors of Czechoslovak society took little or no part in it, and were uncertain how to act. It came to be regarded as something of a seven-day wonder, about which such adjectives as 'unbelievable' and 'incredible' were frequently used. It was a phenomenon, a child of crisis, and not a deliberate national defence policy. As Lord Chalfont has said: 'There was a general lack of preparation, principle, theory, doctrine. I think all that was partly the reason for the apparent failure of this kind of defence.'[9] It may have been partly because of all these factors that few people in Czechoslovakia regarded civil resistance as something for which plans could be made, or which it might be possible to repeat. In the eight months following the Moscow 'agreement' of 26 August

1968 there was surprisingly little discussion in Czechoslovakia of the possibility of repeating the August resistance if the situation again deteriorated, and if the tanks again returned to the cities, or pro-Soviet elements attempted a *coup d'etat*.

A second reason for the ending of the resistance was that it was not only unplanned, but essentially leaderless. The principal party and government leaders in Czechoslovakia never really led the Czechoslovak resistance, and after August they gave no hint whatever that it might be necessary to repeat the resistance if Soviet pressure continued. Instead, the Czechoslovak leaders attempted a policy of limited concessions to the Russians which they conducted with remarkable dignity and even for a while, with comparative success. Controversy naturally surrounds, and will continue to surround, the whole policy of concessions to the Russians; and the willingness of Dubcek, both before and after the invasion, to discuss Czechoslovakia's internal political developments with its Russian neighbours is likely to be seen as a dangerous precedent by any future Communist reform leaders. It resulted in too many concessions, too many promises, and perhaps too much faith in negotiations in a situation where many Czechs and Slovaks felt that a firmer policy, and possibly even some kind of active political struggle, was necessary.

A third reason for the ending of the resistance was that the phenomenon of political unity which as so marked a feature of Czechoslovakia in August 1968 was a somewhat brittle weapon. The fact that unity was Czechoslovakia's main weapon meant that the people could not resist where their leaders had conceded. In the secret part of the Moscow 'agreement' of 26 August 1968 the Russians secured some important commitments from the Czechoslovak leadership; and in subsequently demanding the implementation of all promises that had been extracted the Russians played an astute game. Like almost all occupation powers, the Russians sought to work through local political leaders if at all possible. They could use Czechoslovak unity against Czechoslovak aspirations. The absolute necessity of unity explains why, despite numerous threats from students and workers to strike if concessions went too far, none of these threats was ever really carried out. To make the threat made perfect sense; to execute it would have ended the unity it was meant to preserve.

Czechoslovak unity was in any case never total. The Russians were perfectly right to calculate in August 1968 that they still had many loyal pro-Soviet supporters in all levels of the party and state bureaucracies. Indeed, with the benefit of hindsight many people now bitterly regret that Dubcek never purged the conservative elements from their positions of power in the spring and summer of 1968. The Russians clearly calculated that August 1968 was the last chance to invade before such men were dismissed from their posts—a process which might well have followed the imminent Slovak and Czechoslovak party congresses, scheduled for the end of August and early September 1968. In this respect the invasion was regrettably well-calculated, as developments in subsequent months indicated.

It is said that all resistance movements against foreign occupations are in a sense civil wars as well. This was particularly true in Czechoslovakia, where the Soviet invasion was essentially intended to reinforce one political faction in its battle with another. This internal struggle in Czechoslovakia was often invisible to the outside observer because the conservatives were by nature quiet *apparatchiki* and bureaucrats. However, the inner political battle was no less real for that, and its existence was a special and peculiarly Czechoslovak cause of the defeat of civil resistance.

As well as the more obvious pro-Soviet elements in the Czechoslovak Communist Party there were several leading figures who, while appearing to be loyal to the national cause, were clearly prepared to introduce conservative policies which would in fact be acceptable to the Soviet Union. Dr. Gustav Husak in particular advocated such a path. As First Secretary of the Slovak Communist Party he was in a strong position to advocate a course of 'realistic' compromises. From September 1968 onwards he staked out a position as the man who might resolve the differences with the Russians.

In the months after the invasion, and at the same time as these political manoeuvres, there was still a good deal of opposition to the Soviet demands. Although after the Moscow 'agreement' of 26 August 1968 many of the more open forms of resistance were called off, some defiance of the invaders continued. Despite a nominal censorship, the press was remarkably free right up to April 1969. For a brief period in early 1969 the trade unions emerged as an independent force with an independent role. Occasionally great public demonstrations were held with obvious anti-invasion implications. The funeral of Jan Palach, the philosophy student who burned himself to death on Prague's Wenceslas Square on 16 January 1969 in protest against the Soviet invasion, was an impressive, though completely unofficial, display of national unity. None of these developments can be considered as an initiative emanating from the

Party, where the key battle was being fought. But all of them were permitted by the Party leadership, which remained in the hands of Alexander Dubcek.[10]

The chain of events which triggered off Dubcek's replacement by Husak was started by a Czechoslovak act of violence—not by its absence. On the night of 28-29 March huge crowds gathered in many Czechoslovak cities to celebrate the Czechoslovak ice hockey team's victory in Stockholm over the Soviet Union. Numerous incidents occurred, including, in Prague, a certain amount of damage to the Aeroflot airline office in Wenceslas Square. Naturally, many people suspected that these incidents were provoked by the Russians in order to provide a pretext for applying new pressure against Czechoslovakia's leaders. My inquiries, however, lead me to believe that the incidents on the night of 28-29 March were probably the natural and instinctive expression of a nation's revenge and contempt. The demonstrations on that night were that dangerous phenomenon—public mass protests without either leadership or specific aim. Such activities can easily get out of hand, even among people as politically disciplined and mature as the Czechoslovaks. The Czechoslovak government, the police, and the radio employees bear some responsibility for the incidents, which they could have foreseen. Hockey matches against the Soviet Union had been followed by demonstrations at least twice before. No appeals for calm and order were made on the night of 28-29 March.[11]

It was the hockey match incidents, grotesquely inflated by the Kremlin and by the Moscow *Pravda* in its issue of 31 March, which led to the most serious Czechoslovak capitulation since the invasion. The Soviet defence minister, Marshal Grechko, put intense pressure on the Czechoslovak leaders to clamp down in all spheres, particularly on the press: and indeed vicious new censorship regulations were introduced by the Czechoslovak Communist Party praesidium on the evening of 1 April 1969. It was probably at that moment that the real Czechoslovak defeat occurred. Indeed, Dubcek's dismissal on 17 April was a logical culmination of what was decided on 1 April. The things for which Dubcek stood had already been conceded, and he was no longer the man for the first secretaryship of the Party.

Dubcek's replacement by Dr. Husak, and all the other momentous changes in party life announced after the meeting of the Czechoslovak Communist Party Central Committee on 17 April 1969, were accepted unenthusiastically, but without overt and public acts of resistance, by the people. Once again they were caught in the dilemma of maintaining their unity as well as their aspirations. Most people considered that it would be politically pointless as well as personally dangerous to threaten national unity by openly opposing a decision which had already been taken by high party organs. One of the great problems of civil resistance is that it does depend to a large extent on unity, and it is therefore somewhat vulnerable when heavy pressure is exerted on a key group in society, as when Soviet pressure was exerted on the Czechoslovak leaders.

The remarkable human capacity for adjusting to difficult situations and changed circumstances also played some part in the Czechoslovak defeat. Czechs and Slovaks have a strong belief, born of centuries of bitter experience, that somehow they can muddle through and survive. As the Prague daily paper *Mlada Fronta* said on the first day of the invasion: 'Our history is filled with tragedies. We were often oppressed. But we always lived to regain liberty.' Even after the invasion, life was quite bearable, if unheroic, and the very bearability of life added to the general reluctance to hazard everything on resistance. Clausewitz said it all in Book I of *On War:*

> Even the final decision of a whole war is not always to be regarded as absolute. The conquered state often sees in it only a passing evil, which may be repaired in after times by means of political combinations. How much this must modify the degree of tension, and the vigour of the efforts made, is evident in itself.[12]

What the costs would have been if the Czechoslovak leadership had pursued a more defiant policy in late 1968 and early 1969 has been, of course, a lively matter of conjecture in Czechoslovakia. Particularly after the hockey match incidents, the Russians delivered to the Czechoslovak leadership clear and explicit threats that they might reoccupy the cities ruthlessly; and these threats were reinforced by military manoeuvres during two crucial political crises at the beginning and in the middle of April 1969. Many people naturally argued that the Russians were probably bluffing. Indeed, it must be open to doubt whether the Russians, after the reception which they received in August 1968, wished to send their troops back into the cities, or to attempt to set up a direct occupation government. But the possibility of some new Russian action was one that would have to be faced if capitulation was to be avoided. The possibility was not faced, there was little sign of Czechoslovak planning for such an eventuality, and the leadership did not appear to be prepared to accept the casualties that would have been involved in any defiance of a new Soviet action. In a situation so desparate as Czechoslovakia's, civil resistance, to be effective, might well have involved casualties on a scale comparable to those of war.

There were many indications in Czechoslovakia that the people were more defiant, and more prepared to take risks, than their leaders. Their vast participation in events such as the Palach funeral and the hockey celebrations was proof enough of this.

But even the course that was pursued by Czechoslovakia's leaders up to April 1969—admittedly in some respects an indecisive and inadequate one—does suggest that civil resistance had given them some bargaining strength. For eight months they avoided any complete abandonment of the principles of the Prague Spring, and Czechoslovakia remained, until April 1969, the most free and open society in the Soviet bloc. These achievements proved to be temporary, ending in April 1969 when the Central Committee accepted Dubcek's resignation, but they surprised many observers; and they do suggest that civil resistance in Czechoslovakia, although ultimately it failed, did show some potentialities.

Further reading matter:

The Czech Black Book Littell, Robert (ed.) (Pall Mall Press, London, 1969).

Winter in Prague: Documents on Czechoslovak Communism in Crisis Remington, Robin (ed.) (M.I.T. Press, London, 1969).

On Events in Czechoslovakia Press Group of Soviet Journalists (Press Group of Soviet Journalists, Moscow, 1968).

Czechoslovakia 1968: Reform, Repression and Resistance Windsor, Philip, and Roberts, Adam (Chatto and Windus, London, 1969).

1 This is an extensively revised version of an article originally published in *War-Peace Report,* New York, June-July 1969. The copyright is the author's.

2 For a detailed source of the main events of this initial resistance, which I make no attempt to describe here, see the 'Black Book', published in Prague in late 1968 by the Czechoslovak Academy of Sciences under the title *Seven Prague Days: 21-27 August 1968.* This has also been published in English as Robert Littell (ed.), *The Czech Black Book,* Pall Mall Press, London, 1969.

3 It has sometimes been suggested that Lt. Gen. Vaclav Prchlik, head of the Military department of the Central Committee of the Czechoslovak Communist Party, did prepare some contingency plans in case the Czechoslovak Army should be called upon to defend the country against other members of the Warsaw Pact. (See for

example the reference to this in *The Times,* London, 24 July 1971). It is certainly true that on 15 July 1968, at a time when Warsaw Pact forces were still on Czechoslovak territory after the June manoeuvers, Prchlik held a press conference in Prague at which he criticised certain aspects of the military structure of the Warsaw Pact, and referred to the possible development of 'a Czechoslovak military doctrine.' The Soviet authorities made strong protests about Prchlik's statements, and on 23 July 1968 the Czechoslovak leadership eliminated Prchlik's party post. Although the elimination of this post may in some respects have been an adroit move, it has also been interpreted as marking a clear decision by the Czechoslovak authorities not to embark on the risky course of making military preparations against a Soviet military intervention. In the spring of 1971 Prchlik was put on trial and charged on the basis of his 1968 statements. He was found guilty and, after appeal, his sentence was fixed at twenty-two months. For a text of Prchlik's 15 July 1968 press conference see Robin Alison Remington (ed.), *Winter in Prague: Documents on Czechoslovak Communism in Crisis,* M.I.T. Press, 1969, pp. 213-220.

4 This latter point is put at slightly greater length in Philip Windsor and Adam Roberts, *Czechoslovakia 1968: Reform, Repression and Resistance,* Chatto and Windus for the Institute for Strategic Studies, 1969, pp. 110111.

5 *The Times,* London, 6 June 1969.

6 It is worth emphasising here that the Czechoslovak resistance, because it was spontaneous in character, cannot be described as a case of 'civilian defence'—a term which implies advance preparation on a national level.

7 This point was stressed in a report from Moscow in *The Times,* London, 22 December 1970. Of course, there may also have been a deterring element in the possibility that the Poles might have reacted more violently than the Czechoslovaks to any direct intervention by Soviet forces.

8 See for example the repeated references to the 'success' of the Czechoslovak resistance in V. V. Sveics, *Small Nation Survival.* Exposition Press, New York, 1970.

9 Lord Chalfont in a programme on 'Non-violence', B.B.C. Third Programme, London, first broadcast 19 June 1969.

10 One of Dubcek's advisers, who was still living in Czechoslovakia in 1971, has said of the situation in early 1969: 'At the time of the pro-Smrkovsky campaign, and of the Palach protest, there was still a chance of avoiding defeat (note the trade union congress), but Dubcek failed to appreciate this; on the contrary, he shunned mass actions, broke off relations with most of his former advisers, and thereby paved the way to his own ruin.'—Article by Moravus in *Survey,* London, vol. 17, no. 4, Autumn 1971.

11 In early 1974, however, a defecting Czechoslovak intelligence officer, Mr. Josef Frolik, alleged in a statement that a number of 'anti-Soviet' demonstrations in Prague in 1968 and 1969, including the breaking of windows of the Aeroflot office in the 'hockey riots', were rigged by the regional directorate of state security in Prague. See *The Times,* London, 25 January 1974.

12 Gen. Carl von Clausewitz, *On War,* trans. Col. J. J. Graham, Routledge and Kegan Paul, London, 1962, vol. I, p. 10.

NON-VIOLENCE IN UN PEACE KEEPING OPERATIONS

ANTONY C. GILPIN

Currently Special Advisor/Chief of Division for Southern and Eastern Africa in the Bureau for Africa at the Headquarters of the UN Development Programme in New York.

Previously Regional Representative of the UN Development Programme in South East Africa. Previously Deputy Chief of UN Civilian Operations in the Congo* (1962-5) and Civilian Officer in Kasai Province (1960-1); Deputy Director, UN Technical Assistance Board, New York (1957-60); Economic Affairs Officer, UN Secretariat, Shanghai, Bangkok, New York (1947-57); Senior Research Worker, PEP, London (1943-47).

This chapter describes aspects of the work of the UN peace-keeping forces in the Congo. Mr. Gilpin reflects on the lessons he learnt there while working for the UN.

* Since this chapter covers events in 1960-61, the old names of the Congo (now Zaire) and of various cities have been retained.

When the United Nations Charter was drafted, peace-keeping was envisaged in terms of preventing or dealing with aggression through collective mandatory measures of coercion. In practice, but for the exceptional case of Korea, the existence of the veto has made this kind of approach somewhat theoretical, and United Nations action to keep the peace has been devoted mainly to dealing with the threat or fact of relatively small-scale conflicts which, if left alone, might lead to global war.

Various ways of dealing with such conflicts were developed by Dag Hammarskjöld, usually through sending out some form of UN 'presence' — the Secretary-General himself or his representative, a diplomatic mission, observers, or an armed 'non-fighting' force.[2]

All but the last of these types of presence are unarmed and therefore totally non-violent. Their success depends on their skill and diplomacy, besides the existence of a genuine desire for peace on the part of the States or factions in conflict. This is true also of the 'non-fighting' force, whose presence requires at least the formal consent of the parties concerned.

This chapter will deal with one case of the UN 'non-fighting' force, namely that sent to the Congo in 1960, and, by examining a number of practical examples, will try to throw some light on how far a non-violent approach by an armed peace-keeping force can be effective.

The United Nations Force in the Congo was a collection of national military contingents, brought together with great speed under a Supreme Commander, initially a Swede. It was lightly armed and had instructions that arms should only be used in self-defence. While in the strict sense of the term, it could not therefore be described as "non-violent", its aim was to avoid the use of violence except in the last resort, and it is only in this sense that the expression "non-violence" can be applied. In a military context, this limitation on the use of weapons put the force at a considerable disadvantage.

Apart from the military aspect of the UN Congo operation, more than a thousand experts and technicians were brought into the country under the UN Civilian Operations, to help fill the gaps left by the departing Belgians. They were not armed, although most of them came under the protective "umbrella" of the UN Force until the complete withdrawal of the latter in mid-1964.[3] Aside from accidental deaths, about six of these civilian staff lost their lives as a result of acts of violence during the first five years of the Congo's independence.

In evaluating non-violence in the Congo operation, one must look at the circumstances giving rise to and surrounding the operation and at the differing interpretations of what it was intended to achieve. For example, the Congolese Government's request to the UN was to "protect the national territory against acts of aggression posed by Belgian troops", whereas the Security Council's resolution (13th July, 1960) called on Belgium to withdraw its troops and authorised the Secretary-General to provide the Congolese Government "with such military assistance as may be necessary until, through the efforts of the Congolese Government with the technical assistance of the United Nations, the national security forces may be able, in the opinion of the Government, to meet fully their tasks".

In practice, the first task of the UN Forces was to restore law and order and thus remove any excuse for Belgium to retain troops in the Congo. The departure of Belgian troops in fact took place fairly rapidly from the greater part of the country. However, the task of the UN became immensely complicated by the secessions of the copper-producing province of Katanga and of the somewhat mis-named South Kasai, the region producing industrial diamonds. Belgian and other military "advisers" remained in both these areas. These developments brought the UN face to face with the internal political problems of the Congo, a situation made even more difficult some two months later by the split that occurred between President Kasavubu and Prime Minister Lumumba, followed by the seizure of power by the then Colonel Mobutu.

Apart from President Kasavubu, who managed to regain and retain his position, there was thus no "legitimate" central authority with whom the UN could deal, and only *de facto* relations could be established with the College of Commissioners which Mobutu set up to advise him on the administration of the country.[4] In this respect, the situation outside Leopoldville was somewhat easier because, except in South Kasai, there were legitimate provincial governments.[5]

With the establishment by Antoine Gizenga of a "central authority" in Stanleyville early in 1961, the Congo had two rival central governments, hostile to each other and both hostile in varying degree to the secessionist authorities in Katanga and South Kasai.

Each faction had its own ideas of the role to be played by the UN Force. such ideas usually involving the use of violence to put down its opponents. Lumumba and Gizenga, and later Mobutu, claimed that the UN Force, as part of its mandate to render "military assistance" to the Congolese Government should support the ANC (Armée Nationale Congolaise) in quelling the secessions of Katanga and South Kasai; Mobutu, part of whose army was supporting the authorities in Stanleyville, would doubtless have liked to see the UN help crush the Gizenga government; the Mulopwe (Emperor) Albert Kalonji of South Kasai, whose Baluba had suffered greatly from the ANC's attempts to put down his secession, regarded the UN as offering some protection against any renewal of such action as well as against the hostility of neighbouring tribes, on whose territory he himself had aggressive designs. And even Tshombe, with his numerous foreign advisers and mercenaries, probably saw some value in the UN in keeping the peace between his own people and the Baluba of northern Katanga who actively opposed the Katangese secession.[6]

To those who wished the UN to use force in support of their particular factions, Secretary-General Hammarskjöld had replied in these words (8th August 1960): "I do not believe, personally, that we help the Congolese people by actions in which Africans kill Africans, or Congolese kill Congolese, and that will remain my guiding principle for the future."

The UN Force, rather than receiving whole-hearted co-operation from the Congolese, thus often found itself caught in a critical crossfire. The whole UN Operation was indeed enmeshed in a chaotic complex of conflicting forces. In addition, two events had a direct bearing on subsequent outbreaks of violence in the Congo. The first was the killing of Colonel Kokolo, of the ANC, by UN troops guarding the Ghanaian Embassy in Leopoldville (November 1960). The background to this incident was an order by the Congolese authorities to the Ghanaian Ambassador, Nathaniel Welbeck, to leave the country because (not alone, however, among the diplomatic corps) he had been actively involving himself in Congolese politics; hence the UN guard which he had requested for his protection. Although the guard was Tunisian, the Congolese subsequently blamed the killing of Colonel Kokolo on the Ghanaians. The incident had an adverse effect on the attitude of many Congolese soldiers to the UN Force as a whole, and especially to the Ghanaians.

The second event (January 1961) was the despatch, by the central authorities, of Patrice Lumumba and two of his Ministers to southern Katanga and of several others of his Ministers to South Kasai where, as might have been surmised in view of the hostility of those regions to the Lumumbists, all but one were killed. These were the first acts of political killing since the Congo had become independent, and they were to bear a bitter fruit.

Such was the background to UN efforts to help establish law and order. My own first-hand experience was in the province of Kasai, where I served as a civilian officer from October 1960 till June 1961. For a Quaker and pacifist this was an unusual and illuminating experience, as it involved working closely with the military, in this case primarily the Ghanaian contingent. The commanding officer, Brigadier Joseph Michel, (working closely with the then chief UN civilian officer, Francis Veillet-Lavallée), had a clear understanding of the essentially non-violent role of the UN in the Congo: his first words on visiting tribal chiefs in the course of numerous missions to prevent outbreaks of fighting were: "Our mission is to help you live in peace. My hope is that, when my soldiers eventually return to Ghana, they will not have fired a single shot." Unhappily this was not to be, and a considerable number of Ghanaians were killed in their efforts to keep the peace in Kasai. Michel died in an air crash in Ghana a few days before Dag Hammarskjold met a similar fate in Northern Rhodesia.

There is no doubt in my mind that, had it not been for the active presence of the UN Force, the bloodshed in Kasai due to tribal unrest would have been infinitely greater. This, I believe, was true also of the country as a whole. One has only to look at the recent tragedy in Nigeria to see what might have happened in the Congo.

The UN Force consistently did its utmost to avoid the use of violence. In trying to assess the effectiveness of this limited form of non-violence, one may ask whether the known possession of arms by the Force, for use in self-defence, was a help or a hindrance. In other words, could a completely unarmed peace-keeping force have been more effective? The following incidents, where there were elements of both violence and non-violence, and where non-violence was put to the test, may help to throw light on this question, even though answers can only be hypothetical.

On 8th November, 1960, a UN patrol of eleven Irish soldiers was ambushed by Baluba near Niemba in northern Katanga. The Irish opened fire only after the Baluba had delivered a volley of arrows. They were outnumbered by about ten to one, and only two survived.[7]

This incident perhaps only illustrates the dangers of peace-keeping and shows that friendliness and a wish not to use force are an inadequate defence in such circumstances. According to their leader, Jason Sendwe, the Baluba may have been unaware of the significance of the blue helmets and may have associated the Irish with Tshombe's European mercenaries. In any case, it would be rash to suggest that an unarmed, peace-keeping patrol would not have suffered the same fate.

In February 1961, a small Stanleyville force arrived in Luluabourg. The local ANC Commander sought UN protection and was removed to Leopoldville. Leaders of the two military factions met under UN auspices, and agreement was reached on mutual disarmament under UN supervision. However, the leaders were unable to enforce the agreement, and the ANC arrested their own officers, including Major Mulamba,[8] the only Lulua officer stationed in Lulabourg, who was stripped, beaten and imprisoned. They also arrested most of the provincial ministers, suspecting them of being implicated in the Stanleyville "attack".

General Alexander, Brigadier Michel and Francis Veillet-Lavallée went unarmed into the ANC camp and, after hours of negotiation, secured the release of the ministers but not of the officers. Subsequently, an angry crowd of Lulua gathered outside the UN building demanding UN intervention to obtain Mulamba's release. Another unarmed mission set forth and after further prolonged negotiations, the officers were released, and Mulamba returned with the mission to the UN building. The anger of the crowd dissolved into warm friendship and embraces for the UN troops.

In the meantime the Stanleyville troops withdrew from Luluabourg, having lost a number of their men, killed or captured by the ANC. The same evening, some ANC soldiers, walking through the city, were attacked and killed by civilians. Their comrades then ran wild and, in a night of terror, killed about fifty men, women and children. Order was eventually restored by the UN Force, carrying arms and working with co-operative elements of the ANC.

On this occasion, the unarmed missions to the military camp would have been prejudiced if they had carried weapons. Had they not succeeded, Mulamba and the ministers might well have been killed. The subsequent show of force by the UN troops, on the other hand, brought confidence both to the civilian population, who saw the weapons as a protection against the largely Baluba ANC, and also to the ANC themselves who doubtless feared reprisals from the Lulua civilians.

The Ghana contingent suffered its first losses, in South Kasai, a few weeks later.[9] Here it must be explained that the BCK railway between Port Francqui and Elisabethville could only function if the Congolese engine-drivers and mechanics were changed, according to their tribe, at certain points along the line because, if they had ventured beyond, they would have been killed. As there had been trouble at one of these points, the UN representatives had agreed with the authorities concerned (one of whom was the Mulopwe Kalonji) that a new point should be used. A UN unit was posted there to ensure a smooth change-over. However, when the first train arrived, South Kasai (Baluba) soldiers appeared from the bush and tried to seize the Lulua driver and fireman. The Ghanaians intervened and firing broke out. Two Baluba were killed and one was seriously injured. Peace was restored, and the Baluba requested UN help to get the injured man to hospital. The Ghanaians responded to this plea, and a platoon sergeant and driver volunteered to accompany the injured man in a UN jeep. The two Ghanaians were never seen again.

In this case, the Ghanaian gesture of helping one's injured "enemy" was probably negated by the earlier use of force, and was in any case insufficient to overcome the Baluba desire for revenge. If the peacekeepers had been unarmed, one may theorise that the Lulua railwaymen would have been killed and their fellow-tribesmen would have wrought vengeance on the Baluba elsewhere.

The Ghana contingent suffered much heavier losses at Port Francqui in April 1961, some fifty soldiers and European officers being killed by the ANC. The small UN force in Port Francqui had been keeping an uneasy peace between a Baluba-dominated and undisciplined ANC and a multi-tribal civilian population. The latter included a large number of Lulua, who claimed that they were being victimised both by the ANC and by the other tribes. Both the ANC and the Lulua felt that the UN should give them greater protection against each other. Other factors contributed to a generally tense situation, probably including ANC memories of their popular Colonel Kokolo, whose death had been blamed on the Ghanaians. One evening some ANC soldiers approached the local UN headquarters. The Ghanaians thought they were on a friendly visit but, in the next moment, found themselves held up and disarmed. An incomplete radio message got through to the UN at Luluabourg, and arrangements were made for a patrol to proceed at dawn next day from Mweka to Port Francqui. The patrol started off, unaware that the ANC in Port Francqui had been informed of their movements through the railway communications system. As a result they were ambushed as they approached Port Francqui, and at least one ANC soldier was killed. Word of this got back to Port Francqui before the patrol could get there, and the ANC immediately started on a rampage of killing. Only a few Ghanaians escaped.

With the benefit of hindsight, it is easy to argue that if, instead of a patrol, a small, unarmed mission had proceeded by air to Port Francqui and had been allowed to land (as in fact happened, at probably greater risk, after the killings), the reactions of the ANC might have been different. In the event, the use of force in self-defence by the patrol had led to greater violence. This demonstration of a classical pacifist argument still leaves the pacifist with important unanswered questions. The extremely complex situation in Port Francqui was not one that would have lent itself to a cut-and-dried non-violent solution.

The most serious outbreaks of violence involving the UN Force occurred in southern Katanga. This is not the place to examine these in detail.[10] What happened was that which Dag Hammarskjöld had aimed to avoid in the "guiding principle" quoted above. Since then, however, the continuance of the Katanga secession, coupled with the murder of Lumumba and his colleagues, had prompted the Security Council to adopt a further resolution (21st Feb. 1961) urging the United Nations "to take immediately all appropriate measures to prevent the occurence of civil war in the Congo, including the use of force, if necessary, in the last resort". Thus an element of "enforcement" as distinct from "peace-keeping" was introduced into the UN mandate; this was strengthened by a subsequent resolution of 24th November 1961. Without these resolutions, the UN Force would have remained a strictly "non-fighting" one, authorised to use force only in self-defence.

The Katangese secession presented a continuing threat of civil war in the Congo. The support of Tshombe's regime by outside powers and the presence of mercenaries gave Tshombe the confidence he would otherwise have lacked to continue the secession.

In each case, the outbreaks of fighting in southern Katanga were sparked off by provocation on the part of the mercenaries and Katangese gendarmerie. In each case, the military effectiveness of the UN Force was limited by its basic peace-keeping role as well as by the restraint urged by certain interested powers who feared that the great industrial installations in Katanga might be destroyed. Nevertheless, after the third round of fighting, at the end of 1962, the secession was at last brought to an end.[11]

Tshombe's propaganda apparatus, supported by the overseas "Katanga lobby", succeeded in greatly exaggerating the extent of the actual fighting and loss of life and property. Nevertheless, the events in southern Katanga clearly illustrate the danger of a UN peace-keeping force becoming involved in even a small war, especially if it cannot count on the wholehearted support of all member states.

The presence of mercenaries in the Congo, apart from their incidental rescue of missionaries and others in 1964,[12] was a disruptive and evil influence. Many of them openly gloried in the chance to kill Africans. Most of them merely wanted adventure and money. A few, including their commander, Mike Hoare, had a naive belief that they were "fighting communism." My only personal experience with mercenaries was in and around South Kasai, where they formed part of Kalonji's army. Here, they often actively hindered UN efforts to keep the peace. On one occasion the Baluba officer, with whom Brigadier Michel was discussing means of stopping an outbreak of inter-tribal fighting, was a friendly and reasonable man, but his mercenary adviser, a Frenchman, was hostile to the UN and did his best—in the event, unsuccessfully—to cause the talks to fail. Previously a young British mercenary had been captured while leading Baluba tribesmen in an attack on a neighbouring tribe. It is a matter for speculation how the species of mercenary that found its way to the Congo would have reacted to an unarmed, non-violent international peace-keeping force.

In most of these incidents the basically non-violent approach of the UN peace-keeping force failed to prevent bloodshed and killing. The successes of non-violence were less newsworthy and, just because violence was avoided, most of them have gone unrecorded. A few examples may be cited.

On 18th August 1960, two UN officials, while delivering a letter from Dr. Bunche, were arrested by gendarmes at Prime Minister Lumumba's residence and threatened with death. It required the personal intervention of Brigadier Rikhye (the Secretary-General's military adviser), unarmed, to secure their release. In this case, what probably carried most weight with the gendarmes was the fact that Rikhye's uniform showed him to be of high military rank.

In 1961-62, Major Lawson, of the Nigerian contingent, carried out several unarmed missions to rescue nuns and priests in remote parts of Kasai and northern Katanga. Like Rikhye, he wore uniform, and this could be said to represent the ultimate sanction of force. However, the killers of nuns and priests were perhaps not much influenced by the thought of ultimate sanctions.

In referring to the unarmed character of such missions, Major-General Alexander[13] wrote of the Ghanaians: "When in small parties we always did the same, because even if you had a weapon you were so severely outnumbered that the weapon was not much use to you. What is more, the Congolese seemed to trust you much more if you did not carry a weapon. If you did, there was always the danger that they would assault you in order to take your revolver or whatever it might be."

In my own experience, when accompanying both large armed and small unarmed UN military missions, I had a definite sensation of greater security without the "protection" of weapons, and I was interested to read this military confirmation of my own, pacifist-oriented reactions. On the other hand, in highly tense circumstances, like those in Luluabourg during the episode of the Stanleyville troops, one was inclined to take for granted the carrying of weapons by the UN soldiers. In any case, the atmosphere on such occasions was not conducive to dispassionate consideration of the pros and cons of carrying arms in a peace-keeping operation.

In March 1961, at Banana in the Bas-Congo, Sudanese UN troops were surrounded and shelled by the ANC. Tensions were reportedly reduced by the arrival of a Nigerian police band which marched through the lines and, under cover of martial music, led out the beleaguered Sudanese.

In Luluabourg, in April 1961, after the killing of the Ghanaian soldiers at Port Francqui, the ANC took up positions throughout the town, expecting reprisals from the UN. Major (later General) Joseph Ankrah, then commanding the Ghanaians, went unarmed to the ANC headquarters where he found the officers, headed by Major Mulamba, in battle array. He quietly reasoned and joked with them: "Why are you dressed up like this? We have no quarrel with you. It was the Congolese soldiers in Port Francqui, not you, who killed my men." Eventually he convinced them that their fears were groundless, and Mulamba went unarmed around the town persuading the reluctant and fearful Congolese soldiers to return to camp. Thus, through the courage and non-violent approach of two men, one Ghanaian and the other Congolese, a threat of much greater bloodshed was averted.

In November 1961, two senior civilian officials, George Ivan Smith, Acting UN Representative in Elisabethville, and Brian Urquhart, were assaulted by Katangese gendarmerie in Elisabethville, and Urquhart was taken to the military camp where he was further beaten up. A move to send UN troops to rescue him was the subject of second thoughts and, instead, representations to Tshombe secured his eventual release. In the course of the same incident a UN Gurkha officer and soldier were killed. Urquhart would almost certainly have suffered the same fate if an attempt had been made to secure his release by force.

Starting in March 1962, a series of "air liaison" missions was initiated by UN to visit parts of the Congo where, in the main, there were no UN military units. Their object was to deliver medical supplies and bring technicians to determine other urgent needs. A uniformed UN officer accompanied each mission, but it was an explicit rule that no weapons should be carried. Another rule was that adequate notice should always be given to the places to be visited by the mission. The importance of this second rule was underlined on the first such mission, when an unscheduled second visit was made to Boende to pick up a doctor who was seriously ill and take him to Leopoldville. A telegram was sent to Boende, but it proved later that the receiving station there was out of order. On arrival, the mission's plane was surrounded by armed Congolese soldiers, probably the same who had welcomed it a few days earlier, and, in spite of a round of friendly handshakes by members of the mission — the best and only possible non-violent approach in the circumstances — an atmosphere of sullen suspicion persisted. Members of the mission were questioned for about an hour, during which they were accused of being "Tshombe agents coming to kidnap our doctor." But the atmosphere slowly improved, and the mission was eventually allowed to leave with the doctor. It was fortunate that the plane was not searched since, if it had been, some weapons would have been discovered which, contrary to instructions, had been brought on to the plane by a member of the crew; this episode might then have ended less happily.

It would be unwise to generalise, but one may still try to draw a few tentative conclusions, bearing in mind the very different groups —

undisciplined Congolese soldiers, panic-stricken civilians, warring tribesmen, and white mercenaries — with whom the UN Force had to deal.

While only the last incident described above is of a purely civilian character, it is clear that the extensive technical aid provided by the UN was part of the basically non-violent approach of the entire UN peace-keeping operation. By and large, the Congolese respected and appreciated the work of the UN civilian technicians. Doctors, in particular, were held in high esteem. During the massacre at Port Francqui, the life of the UN military doctor was spared, as was that of a British soldier wearing a white coat who was also taken to be a doctor. With one or two exceptions, the respect for doctors ensured their safety throughout the troubles in the Congo although, on at least one occasion, a doctor had to carry out an operation at gun-point, fervently hoping that it would be successful; it was.

From time to time, the UN Force itself became involved in action in support of the civilian population. A notable example was the large-scale famine relief operation in South Kasai in 1960-61, when the military assisted the UN civilian personnel responsible for the distribution of food and medical supplies. Co-operation with the civilian population in constructive action on their behalf, for example, road-building and improvement of public services, is indeed one of the non-violent techniques open to a peace-keeping force that will help it gain the confidence and goodwill of the local population and thus reduce any danger of outbreaks of violence.

There are elements in most of the other examples which demonstrate on the one hand, the value and effectiveness of non-violent techniques in reducing tensions and, on the other, the danger in carrying weapons of increasing tensions and perhaps provoking outbreaks of violence, especially in tense situations involving ignorance and misinformation. In at least one case where UN civilian staff were killed, it was found later that, contrary to instructions, they were carrying weapons. The example of the Nigerian band assisting in the release of the Sudanese soldiers shows how non-violence may bring peace to a situation where there has already been violence and killing.

It is sometimes argued that the effectiveness of the UN troops in the Congo depended on the moral authority of the "Blue Helmet" and that, once the troops were involved in fighting, this moral authority was weakened. There was, perhaps, a sentimental tendency to attach a mystique to the blue helmet. Wearing a blue helmet did not necessarily turn a soldier into a saint, even though some people, especially critics of the UN, apparently thought it should have done. The fighting in Katanga did not weaken the moral authority of the UN *within* the Congo; on the contrary, except in southern Katanga itself, its moral authority was, if anything, strengthened. It was *outside* the Congo, fed by skilful and unscrupulous propaganda for which the UN information services were no match, that opinions tended to harden against the UN. So long as a peace-keeping force possesses weapons of any kind, one may *hope* that it may prove unnecessary to use them, but it is unrealistic and sentimental to believe that, in no circumstances, will they be used or that their use will in some way reduce the moral authority of the Organisation.

In circumstances where there was a fairly continuous undercurrent of violence, I often asked myself the question, posed earlier, whether a totally unarmed force, skilled in the techniques of non-violence, would have been more effective than the hastily gathered, makeshift armed force to which the UN in fact gave the job of keeping the peace.

While acknowledging the successes of non-violence, I could not find my way to a straight, affirmative answer. In the first place, to recall for a moment the initial task of the UN Force, it is scarcely conceivable that Belgium would have agreed to withdraw its troops in favour of an unarmed international force. Indeed given the alarming and chaotic situation in the Congo, and making due allowance for exaggeration and rumour, Belgian opinion, both at home and in the Congo, could hardly have been expected to rely on such an untried instrument. Politically, therefore, any such solution would have been a non-starter. At a slightly later stage, when a large part of the Congolese civilian population stood in fear of the undisciplined ANC, they too would almost certainly have shared Belgian doubts on this score. As for the ANC, the Katangese gendarmerie and the mercenaries, it is fanciful to think that, in their varied feuds and struggles, they would have been much influenced by a completely unarmed international force; in the event, the knowledge that the UN Force possessed arms undoubtedly exercised a restraining influence on these armed groups.

Moreover, on the side of the peace-keeping force itself, weapons, even when not actually carried, give confidence to the soldier. General Alexander, for example, when arguing that the carrying of weapons by small groups created more danger than going unarmed, added the qualification that "as a rule we did have a platoon or so within easy call".[14] Whether or not this confidence was justified, it was a fact.

One may thus conclude that, especially in seeking to keep the peace between armed military factions, a peace-keeping force is likely to be more effective if it possesses the ultimate sanction of weapons than if it is, and is known to be, completely unarmed. This is not far from the position of the British police, who possess arms but very rarely carry or find it necessary to use them. Most pacifists tacitly accept this.

Accordingly even pacifists should, I think, be prepared to flex their thinking to accept the idea of a peace-keeping force, using non-violent methods to the greatest extent possible, but nevertheless possessing arms in reserve. On this basis, one can recognise the value of military discipline and of military uniform. This may seem a far cry from pure pacifism, but we are a long way from a completely non-violent peace-keeping force of self-disciplined saints. Moreover, experience has shown that most pacifists, saintly or otherwise, tend to be individualists who react adversely to the idea of discipline, especially discipline imposed from above. A peace-keeping force must be a more worldly instrument. In fact, this need for discipline is recognised by many pacifists; hence the emphasis they place on preparation and training in the use of non-violent techniques.

The effectiveness of a lightly-armed force of this kind must depend on the *will* of the opposing factions to stop fighting and to seek an acceptable, peaceful solution to their quarrel. If this will does not exist, an international force would have to *enforce* peace; in that case, it would have to be greatly superior militarily to the warring parties and be ready to fight, not necessarily only "in the last resort." This raises issues beyond the scope of this chapter, although, even in such circumstances, non-violent techniques could still have a place in limiting the extent of violence.

It must also be recognised that peace-*keeping* is likely to amount only to first-aid unless it is accompanied by effective peace-*making*. The UN Emergency Force in the Middle East helped to keep an uneasy peace for over ten years, during which efforts to remove the causes of tension in that region were not sufficient to prevent a further outbreak of violence — and with it the removal of UNEF — in 1967. Indeed, there is some danger that the mere presence of a UN peace-keeping force may encourage the parties in conflict to relax their efforts to find a peaceful solution. It was one of the strongest features of the UN Congo operation that, along with the military presence, the UN promoted continuous, patient and prolonged negotiations with and between the conflicting factions. These efforts at peace-making, while admittedly leaving many internal problems unsolved, at least brought the secessions of South Kasai and Katanga to an end and laid the foundations of the relative stability which the Congo (now Zaire) has enjoyed since 1965.

Once one accepts the idea of an international police force, possessing though not normally carrying arms, to help in situations where there is a will towards peace, there can be wide agreement on both the desirability and effectiveness of non-violent methods. The occasions when weapons have to be actually carried will depend on the judgment of those in the field.

Every call on the United Nations to provide a peace-keeping force will involve different circumstances, to which the UN response must be adapted. There is much to be said for a permanent international force, lightly armed, highly disciplined and trained in non-violent methods. A force of this kind could also stand ready to rush to any part of the world to help in natural disasters such as floods and earthquakes; besides its intrinsic value, this secondary function would help to maintain morale between peace-keeping assignments. The force would have its own logistical support, which could be supplemented, as necessary, from national sources.

A practical alternative — already envisaged in certain countries such as Sweden — would be for a number of countries to earmark units of their national armed forces for international peace-keeping service when called on by the United Nations. Training would be the same as for a permanent force, but it would be supplemented by exchanges of personnel, especially officers. An international staff training college might also be established.

Teaching of languages would be an important element, and the United Nations itself, learning from the lessons of the Congo, should prepare its information services to cope effectively with hostile propaganda.

Training in non-violent techniques would be an essential feature. Indeed, faced with the total destructiveness of modern weapons, some military thinkers are already looking seriously at the power and effectiveness of non-violent methods of resistance. The introduction of training in non-violence to military courses, however paradoxical this may seem, might well bring nearer the day when the initial military response to situations threatening violence will be to use every technique of non-violence before resorting even to the threat of armed force.

Many, perhaps most, pacifists may find this an unsatisfactory conclusion, in that the individual, who is not prepared to use violence himself, would feel unable to serve in a force that held armed force in ultimate reserve, however strong its emphasis on the initial use of non-violent methods. No-one would claim infallibility for non-violence. At the risk of a "holier than thou" attitude, it may perhaps be argued that a basic difference between the pacifist and the regular soldier lies in their respective attitudes to the greater element of sacrifice that may be involved in the use of non-violence as opposed to violence.

I hope this chapter has shown that, in spite of differences of principle, there can be in practice an increasing area of common ground between the pacifist and the military in international efforts to maintain peace in situations which threaten violence. Tensions are a part of human progress. International peace-keeping, using non-violent techniques to the utmost, and accompanied by untiring efforts at peace-making, can prevent tensions from turning into uncontrollable violence and can help direct them into creative channels consistent with a dynamic and peaceful world order.

1 The author is at present Special Advisor/Chief of the Division for Southern and Eastern Africa in the Bureau for Africa at UN Development Programme in New York. He served the United Nations in various capacities in the Congo between October 1960 and December 1965. The views expressed here are entirely his own and do not necessarily reflect those of the United Nations.

2 See Sidney Bailey, "Some Reflections on the Use of Force", Friends Quarterly, April 1969. The term 'non-fighting force' was one introduced by Dag Hammarskjöld.

3 An appreciable part of this civilian programme, containing a large element of training, continued under the auspices of the UN Development Programme.

4 In August 1961, a goverment with Mr. Adoula as Prime Minister was approved by both Houses of Parliament, meeting with the help and protection of the United Nations. This made possible *de jure* as well as *de facto* relations with the UN.

5 The UN thus dealt with Mr. Tshombe as the legitimate President of the *province* of Katanga.

6 The Baluba of northern Katanga were anti-Tshombe and pro-Lumumba, while the Baluba of Kasai were bitterly anti-Lumumba, and well-disposed to Tshombe.

7 For a full account, see "The Peacemakers of Niemba" by Tom McCaughren (Browne and Nolan Limited, Dublin).

8 Later General Mulamba, Prime Minister of the Congo in 1965-66, under President Mobutu.

9 See "African Tightrope" by Major General H. T. Alexander (Pall Mall, 1965).

10 A vivid, highly subjective, and in parts controversial account of the first outbreak of fighting in southern Katanga will be found in Conor Cruise O'Brien's "To Katanga and Back" (Hutchinson, 1962). For a more balanced account, the reader is referred to Brian Urquhart's "Hammarskjöld" (1972).

11 In 1964, Mr. Tshombe, by then Prime Minister of the Congo, wrote to UN Secretary-General U Thant to express appreciation of the successful efforts of the UN "in preserving the integrity of the Congo".

[12] See "Congo Mercenary" by Mike Hoare (Robert Hale), 1967.
[13] Op. cit., page 72.
[14] Op., cit., page 72.

A SEARCH FOR WORLD ORDER
JAMES AVERY JOYCE

Dr. Joyce is Visiting Professor of International Relations at several United States Universities and Colleges. He has written a number of books on the United Nations and is also a Consultant at U.N. Headquarters in New York. Barrister-at-law and Senior Research Associate, Fletcher School of Law and Diplomacy, Havard and Tufts, he now lives in Geneva as I.L.O. Consultant.

This chapter gives some of Professor Joyce's recollections of the League of Nations at the time when, as a staff member of the League of Nations Union in London and special correspondent in Geneva, he closely followed the events which he makes the subject of the following comparative study of the League of Nations then and the United Nations now.[1]

In the mid-1930's, Mrs. H. M. Swanwick wrote a remarkable book, which was not too widely noticed at the time, entitled *Collective Insecurity*.[2] A Cambridge graduate and formerly editor of *Foreign Affairs,* Mrs. Swanwick was no insignificant personality in her time. She had been a member of the British Government delegation to the Fifth and Tenth Assemblies of the League of Nations in Geneva and was created a Companion of Honour for her public work.

We are taking her book as the starting point of this discussion on world order because it carries an interpretation of those turbulent inter-war years far different from what the present generation has been led to believe and it offers a devastating commentary on what passes as "collective security" today. Helena Maria Swanwick believed strongly in the League and she held that the League had an essential work of peacemaking to perform, but she insisted that it was a fundamental error in world constitution-making to attempt to bind sovereign states to impose on other sovereign states military sanctions which might at any time draw them into a League war.

The 1930's had been marked by a double race among the nations of Europe: a race for "security" and an arms race away from it. Mrs. Swanwick saw that this double race was its own contradiction: armaments and "security" were incompatible and self-cancelling. Her book, *Collective Insecurity,* was her rationale against a world order which rested on armaments—collective or otherwise. Armaments could never be stopped by making them "collective". Mrs. Swanwick has gone. The League has gone. But the United Nations, a quarter of a century later, is indeed with us. Yet the same problem remains: can world order be based on collective security—on collective arms? Can, with hindsight, we learn anything from the mirror that Mrs. Swanwick held up to the League during her lifetime?

The first thing we notice about this almost forgotten book is that, although Mrs. Swanwick was "peacenik" herself, her strongest criticisms were directed against her fellow "peaceniks". Why was this? Let her speak for herself. She says: "If a machine breaks down, the only sensible course is to inquire the cause of the breakdown. We must not, like savages, beat the machine. We must ask: was it adapted to the work it was expected to do? In the case of a new, even revolutionary institution like the League, can we think that the men who undertook to co-operate in it were themselves revolutionary enough to make it a success?"

To be specific, was it wise, she asked, when constructing an organization, as the Covenant declares, "to promote international peace and security", to attempt to arm that association with coercive and destructive force, before it had been armed with ordinary goodwill? Her grievance was thus directed against the basic assumption of the League, backed as it was by her own close friends in the League of Nations Union, namely that military sanctions could keep the peace. The League of Nations Union (L.N.U.) was the national organization that, however reluctantly at times, advocated collective warmaking operations to stop aggressors when all the other mediatory provisions of the League Covenant had failed. There can be no doubt that this was the essence of the League policy, though the League had many other important jobs to do and did them with varying degrees of success. Nor is there any doubt that it was the sanctions requirement of the League which kept the United States out of it. In any case, during twenty years sanctions never even got off the drawing board.

Mrs. Swanwick declared quite bluntly: "Between sovereign states, sanctions can never work." In taking this line, she was going against the policies of the organized peace movement itself. The 1930's had built a broad-based organization in the L.N.U., as one of the most representative voluntary policy-shaping bodies in Britain. The L.N.U. had, moreover, focused public opinion on this central issue by initiating in 1935 the famous Peace Ballot, in which co-operated a considerable range of other voluntary bodies. Some eleven and a half million citizens eventually voted in this nation-wide popular referendum in general support of the League of Nations—a unique and magnificent effort in itself. Of this total nearly seven million voted in favour of military sanctions, the specific question being:

"Do you consider that, if a nation insists on attacking another, the other nations should combine to compel it to stop by, if necessary, military measures?"

Two and a half million voters abstained on this issue. (Incidentally, there was a separate Christian Pacifist vote also recorded on this particular question which came to a bare seventeen thousand, out of the overall eleven and a half million votes.) So the L.N.U. had done its work well.

In building her case against collective military action, Mrs. Swanwick pointed out that the "good" (i.e. peace loving) members of the League were never in a moral (or even legal!) position to punish the "bad" members. For example, it was necessary, she said "to take into account the French view, which was that the only way to secure France was to hold Germany down forcibly for ever and ever. There were a good many Frenchmen who doubted whether this was a feasible policy; there must have been few indeed who reflected that with the passage of time, as Germany was treated, so she would react."

France's occupation of the Ruhr was soon followed by Hitler's occupation of the Rhineland—both were a breach of the Versailles Treaty. We need well pause at this point to reflect on how the containment of Germany by France was as unsuccessful *then* as the containment of China by the United States has proved to be in our time.

Mrs. Swanwick insisted that France never had any confidence in the security provided by the League Covenant, nor the least appreciation of the fact that it was her treatment of Germany, more than anything else, which menaced her own security. "Security in France's opinion—and a very tenacious opinion it has been—could be attained only by the possession of preponderant military force, available at short notice. Germany was still the only Power to be feared, and France was determined to run no risk of her ever becoming preponderant again." This may be forgotten history to this generation, but not a word need be changed today, except to substitute USA for France and Soviet Russia for Germany. This abject reliance on a "preponderant military force" outside the U.N., rather than within it, will be the subject of the second part of this discussion, for "collective security" is still the offical mythology of NATO. Times have changed, but not minds.

The United States never even belonged to the League's Collective Security system, yet Secretaries of State since World War II have not hesitated to sermonize about the League's failure to stop "aggression" in Manchuria and Ethiopia, and Britain's alleged failure at

"Munich", as examples-in-reverse to justify America's military ventures in Vietnam and elsewhere.

The League was expected to implement the immoralities of the peace treaties in terms of military force. "What is intolerable," Mrs. Swanwick states, "is the pretension that, though pre-League diplomacy may have been black and bloody, post League diplomacy is so radiantly pure that it can be trusted with the sword of the Lord and of Gideon; in other words, with the threat and use of starvation, incendiary bombs, high explosives, poison gas, and — doubtless in time—a death ray." Mrs. Swanwick's imagination could hardly have conjured up the obscene abominations of the H-bomb; yet, at the recent meeting of NATO war-lords in Brussels, actual deployment of unlimited megatons of nuclear "death-rays" was unanimously voted as guarantee of collective insanity in the 1970's.

Under the pretext of implementing the League's Covenant the military men of Europe were then steadily building their primitive NATO system against possible aggressions—while the arms race accelerated. The Draft Treaty of Mutual Assistance, the Geneva Protocol, and so on, were all doomed to futility. She calls these outside League alliances a "House of Cards". Analyzing the Draft Treaty of Mutual Assistance, for instance, she says:

> "These measures included the summoning of all the signatory States . . . to provide naval, air and land forces and to organise priority of communications, financial co-operation and the appointment of the Higher Command. In the event of actual hostilities breaking out, the Council was to decide in four days which parties were the objects of aggression. So, on the mere suspicion of aggression, or 'menace of aggression', the Council of the League was entitled to wage war in the completest sense and was also given the task of deciding within four days which Power was the aggressor, although there was no definition of aggression."

More important, perhaps, than these promises to act were the actions of the military compulsions behind the scenes. "When the military got going on these provisions," she pointed out, "they naturally declared that if the assistance is to be immediate and effective, it must be given in accordance with a pre-arranged plan and this plan must be made an integral part of the Treaty. Moreover, as the methods of attack and defence are constantly changing, the Treaty will have to be periodically revised." That, of course, is where NATO is today. And she concludes: "Although at that time perhaps the conception of 'possible aggressors' was not as extensive as, owing to bitter experience, it is now, these intensive studies would have kept the League happily employed for an indefinite period on planning League war." (NATO again!)

The crowning tragedy of our own time is not that the Treaty of Mutual Assistance (like its successors) never produced peace in their time, but that the more sophisticated planning of NATO in our time has practically reduced the United Nations to impotence in terms of peace-making and mutual disarmament. The military men have taken over at a cost of 170,000 million dollars a year, and ABMs are succeeded by MIRVs. The U.N. Secretary General has gravely warned that less than ten years remain to reverse the process and replace collective insecurity under NATO by collective co-operation under the U.N.—or, as Mrs. Swanwick called it: Collective Neutrality.

It would take us too far from our present purpose to follow Mrs. Swanwick's rejection, which she skillfully argues, of the false analogy between soldiers and police. Figurative language, she states, "hampers clear thinking. There is no such thing, for instance, as a criminal nation; but there are criminal individuals against whom police measures may be both necessary and practicable. Police measures are not practicable against a nation, which is composed largely of decent citizens, whom war welds into a whole." But her startling new thesis on "Collective Neutrality" takes on a new dimension in the 1970's. We might well apply it to the U.N. for a number of specific reasons.

The first reason is the main role of the United Nations as (to use U Thant's frequent words) "a centre for harmonizing the actions of nations." The second is the emergence of a Third World, which we call the unaligned. The third is the fact that World Law, as a basis of World Order, must by its nature be collective *neutrality* between sovereign states.

We shall take each of these points in turn. The relevance of Mrs. Swanwick's novel thesis to the present crisis can be seen in her vision of the League's real purpose over three decades ago:

> "If Collective Neutrality could be secured, it would be one of the chief duties of the League to offer continuous mediation and at the same time to do all in its power to broadcast the facts so far as they were ascertainable; not merely the facts concerning the progress of the war but the facts relating to its alleged causes and

objects and also to the mediation proposals. It would be of in calculable benefit if there were some centre from which something resembling truth could radiate."

Firstly, Mrs. Swanwick, calling for a "neutralized" fact-finding body, acting impartially amid the disputes of its members, was a prophetic voice preparing the way for U Thant's constant emphasis on "harmonizing the actions of the nations". She estimated correctly that, "if the League itself were involved in the war, that would be good-bye to truth. Every type of peaceful settlement should be offered, not once for all, but at frequent intervals: conciliatory, arbitral, judicial. The neutral world should stand solid behind the League in approving this."

It is significant that, for whatever reason, the military sanctions embodied in the present U.N. Charter—Chapter VII—have never been used and presumably never will. Chapter VII "Action with respect to threats to the Peace, Breaches of the Peace, and Acts of Aggression", was carried over from the League Covenant; but Mrs. Swanwick's thesis still runs true, the U.N. cannot wage war on a sovereign nation. The Korean War, where a U.N. Command was (and still is) technically in operation, due to the unjust rejection of Peking's legal claims to representation in 1950 and, thus, the non use of a Soviet Union veto on that occasion, is no exception to the rule. In fact, the inconclusive and ruinous Korean War proves just how right she was.

Since that unsettling experience of "collective security" under the U.N. flag, the slowly emerging peace keeping functions of the U.N. have been developing techniques of world "police" very different in motivation and character from the war-making functions of sovereign states, who still like to parade as world policemen. The Congo, Suez, Kashmir, and Cyprus have varied in their origins and purposes; but each of these local growing points of world order has had its base in those chapters of the Charter calling for peaceful procedures, *not* collective security. It is noteworthy that, after preserving the delicate balance of peace for eleven years, it was the very *withdrawal* of the U.N. peacekeepers which led to the outbreak of hostilities. There were 64 meetings of the Security Council in 1969 alone.

The writer has described elsewhere how the U.N. has saved the peace as well as the face of the world's most powerful nation in its military confrontations in Lebanon, Cuba and San Domingo.[3] But no-one would deny that the U.N.'s principles and resolutions are still treated with impunity and hostility by its members time and time again, thus delaying the expansion of world law. There are, under the U.N. Charter, as under the League Covenant, no "private wars" any more. War anywhere is a threat to peace everywhere. That is the true meaning of collective security. But military sanctions against sovereign states are never the answer to intransigence, however rigid.

The defiance of the U.N. Charter by the United States in South-East Asia (note, again, its pretended reliance on a South-East Asia "Pact of Mutual Assistance") and of the Government of Israel's repeated evasion of the unanimous proposals of the Security Council of 22 November 1967, are but two different but blatant instances of how U.N. members, big or little, are crippling its peace-keeping functions by insisting on their right to wage *private* wars. Since military sanctions are so obviously not the answer, in both South-East Asia and the Middle East, the central mediating and peace-keeping operations of the U.N. will ultimately prove to be the means by which "collective neutrality" will oust private wars, where one or the other parties now reject the way of the Charter.

Secondly, the Third World, unknown to the League of Nations, brings a stability to World Order of many promising dimensions. For one thing, the Third World has little or no use at all for the Cold War. Its leaders in Africa, Asia and Latin America are saying so plainly. For another thing, the Third World is bridging the ideological gap between the Western and Communist factions: it is drawing both factions together in sharing their common primary needs for training and technology, for trade and economic development.

The insane arms race between the Big Powers is becoming increasingly irrelevant to the interests of the developing countries, who make up 80% of U.N. membership. Incidentally the voting at the 1969 General Assembly revealed that, on issue after issue, this growing segment of small and middle powers are pressuring the Big Powers to revise their assumptions on the nuclear arms race and much else. Again, the "collective neutrality" ideas expressed in the original Rapachi plan for a neutralized zone, running from Finland and across central Europe, Austria and Switzerland, to Yugoslavia, has more recently been supplemented by tentative proposals to bring the NATO and Warsaw antagonists into an All-European Non-Aggression Treaty. Collective Neutrality may not sound positive in its terminology, but it is a positive step to European security; it does what neither League military sanctions nor NATO nuclear "capacity" could ever do, and that is stop European war before it begins.

Thirdly, and finally, the new areas of World Law that are emerging out of the peaceful pursuits of mankind are not based on military force, but on what modern international lawyers have come to call the "law of co-operation."[4] The old "laws of co-existence" between states which became the bedrock of diplomacy since the days of Grotius, have been yielding rapidly to a global law touching millions of individuals as world citizens. Within the U.N. family, for example, functional agencies are building daily a permanent structure of legal relationships which although still mostly framed within the traditional treaty-making concepts of sovereign states, are covering a vast range of true law-making from the Antarctic wastes to Cosmic Space, from air-line operations to working conditions in the world's coal mines, from locust control in the Middle East to protein production in the Indian Ocean, from urban planning in South America to freight and insurance facilities for African shipping.

Never has World Law had a broader or more positive meaning for the future of the earth's billions. World order is meaningless without world law; but the real question is: what sort of law is it to be? Is it to be law between states or law between men? We have only just begun to answer that question. If it is the former, backed by "collective security", we know what the end results will be. If it is the latter, man in his global village is only at the beginning of a New Age of Discovery—the discovery of World Order centred not on soveriegn states but on Sovereign Man.

1 A fuller treatment of the ideas expressed in this chapter is to be found in *The League of Nations (Dilemma of Peace 1919-39)* James Avery Joyce. New York 1973.

2 *Published by Jonathan Cape (London) in 1937. Collective Insecurity* was republished in 1939 as a selection of the Peace Book Club, of which the present writer was then Literary Editor.

3 See J. Avery Joyce: *End of an Illusion* (Allen & Unwin), 1969.

4 See Wolfgang Friedmann: *The Changing Structure of International Law* (Columbia) 1966, and Part II of J. Avery Joyce: *End of an Illusion* (Allen and Unwin) 1969.

5 This article was written in 1970.

HUMAN RIGHTS AND THE RULE OF LAW
SÉAN MacBRIDE

Séan MacBride, of the Republic of Ireland, was Chairman of the International Committee of Non-Governmental Organisations for Human Rights Year. An eminent international jurist, he was President of the Committee of Ministers of the Council of Europe (1949-50) and has been a sponsor and signatory of a number of international treaties, including the Geneva Convention for the protection of War Victims (1949) and the European Convention of Human Rights (1950). He is a former member of the Irish Parliament and was Minister for External Affairs for Ireland from 1948 to 1951. From 1963 to 1970 he was Secretary-General of the International Commission of Jurists. Mr. MacBride is also Chairman of the International Executive of Amnesty International and Chairman of the International Peace Bureau.

What is needed is a radical new conception of the right to wage war.

1. THE PROTECTION OF HUMAN RIGHTS

Both the Charter of the United Nations and the Universal Declaration of Human Rights reflect the universal reaction to the horrors which had taken place before and during the Second World War. The world leaders were determined to ensure that the world should never again witness the mass violations of human rights, the genocide and the brutality that had engulfed humanity in an unprecedented neo-barbarism.

Thus the Charter declared one of the stated purposes of the United Nations to be the "promoting and encouraging respect for human rights and for fundamental freedoms for all". The Universal Declaration recognized that human rights "should be protected by the Rule of Law" and specified the rights in detail.

The Universal Declaration of Human Rights is, and remains, the most important instrument and landmark in the recent history of mankind. It is the Charter of liberty for the oppressed and downtrodden. It defines the limits which the all-mighty state machine should not transgress in its dealings with those it rules. In the twenty-seven years since its adoption it has acquired a moral and political authority which is second only to that of the Charter itself. As a legal catalyst, its impact may be partly measured by the international conventions which it has inspired, the national constitutions in which its provisions have been embodied, and the occasions on which its provisions have been used for the purposes of judicial interpretation in different jurisdictions. Indeed, there is a growing view among international lawyers that some of its provisions, which are justiciable, now form part of Customary International Law; this conforms with the definition of customary law contained in the oft-forgotten

Martens clause in the Preamble to the Hague Convention 1907:

"... the law of nations, derived from the usages established among civilized peoples, from the laws of humanity and from the dictates of the public conscience".[1]

In one sense one might say that the Universal Declaration does now represent in written form the basis for the law of nations, the laws of humanity and the dictates of the public conscience as accepted in the twentieth century.

Yet, despite the standards to which lip-service is paid by world leaders and the general public alike, the fact remains that over twenty years after the adoption of the Universal Declaration, humanity is witnessing the same destruction of human rights and acts of brutality which in 1948 the world had wished to render impossible. Massacres, tortures, inhuman treatment, and individual and collective acts of brutality are common currency; such acts create a momentary horror which shocks the human conscience, but they are all too easily relegated to a "lost property compartment" of the public conscience. Moreover, cruelty, and brutality are contagious, and the fact that they are so easily tolerated and easily forgotten tends to encourage further resort to them.

There is a paradox in human nature. Many will condemn warfare or cruelty when faced with the stark reality portrayed in photographs or on the television screen; yet, the same people often condone the existence of a dictatorial regime, known for its intolerance and cruelty to its opponents. Many scientists will discuss the advantages of one or other weapon of mass destruction, yet claim its use to be "unthinkable". Many soldiers who would recoil from killing a defenceless child will not hesitate to drop bombs from hundreds of feet in the air, knowing that this action will result in the killing of a great number of defenceless people. This capacity which men have to abstract the content of their acts saves them many embarrassing and difficult problems of conscience. But are their acts to be tolerated nevertheless?

Clearly there is an urgent need to re-awaken the moral, ethical and social responsibility of mankind. This is no easy task and would require great effort on the part of the leaders in all fields of human activity. Unfortunately, however, there is little awareness of the gravity of the problem, and so far no overall philosophy of the future organisation of man and his world has been formulated with any success. It may be that the world will have to destroy itself before it will be willing to save itself.

The apathy towards the destruction of human rights is equally evident in regard to the construction of adequate machinery to assist their protection. It is not sufficient to enunciate or define human rights: it is essential to provide a real remedy easily accessible to those affected. Thus, it is in the field of the practical application of the provisions of the Universal Declaration that efforts should be concentrated.

Such "implementation" machinery must exist on two levels, the national and the international. First priority must be given to the protection of human rights at national level. This involves the existence of an independent and objective judiciary, the guarantee by law of fundamental human rights and freedoms, restriction on and control over the assumption of emergency powers, a free press, free elections, and so on. An institution such as the Ombudsman is a valuable adjunct to existing judicial safeguards, especially in countries which do not have a system of Administrative Courts.

However, experience has shown that purely domestic remedies are not always adequate. In times of political turmoil or ideological passion, governments, and even judges, readily impose their views without regard to the rights of the individual or of minorities. With the continued advance in technocracy it has also been found that bureaucrats may tend to ride roughshod over the rights of those they dominate. For these reasons, international supervision of the domestic mechanism for the protection of human rights is essential. This can be provided at a regional international level and at a universal level.

2. INTERNATIONAL JURISDICTIONS

It is interesting to note that, for the most part, the progress of international law is expressed by an increase in the number of institutions of a jurisdictional nature. There are a growing number and a variety of international jurisdictions: the International Court of Justice, for example, may adjudicate between all States, while the Court of the European Economic Community is limited to the nine States of the Community, and "conciliation commissions" under various treaties generally only have bilateral competence. International jurisdictions may be of a general nature, such as the International Court of Justice, an economic nature, such as the Court of the European Economic Community, or an administrative nature, such as the Administrative Tribunal of the United Nations or of the International Labour Office. In regard to the law of human rights, however, the only international jurisdiction which exists is that of the European Court of Human Rights: some machinery of an extra-judicial nature has been provided in the two International Covenants on Human Rights adopted by the United Nations in 1966, and in the International Convention on the Elimination of all Forms of Racial Discrimination in force since 1969.

(a) *The International Court of Justice.*

The International Court of Justice is probably the most widely-known international tribunal. It is the principal judicial organ of the United Nations whose jurisdiction is partly contentious and partly advisory. The contentious jurisdiction comprises all cases which the parties refer to it and all matters specially provided for in the charter of the United Nations or in treaties and conventions in force (Art. 36 (l). However, except for a general reference to the desirability of referring legal disputes to the Court, the Charter does not specifically provide for adjudication in disputes between States, and confines itself to provisions relating to advisory capacity. The advisory jurisdiction of the Court arises under Article 96 of the Charter which provides that the General Assembly or the Security Council may ask the Court to give an advisory opinion on any legal matter. Other organs of the United Nations and specialised agencies may also request opinions if authorised by the General Assembly on questions arising within the scope of their authority. Judgments in contentious cases are formally binding; advisory opinions are not.

The great defect of the Court stems from the provision in its Statute which provides the only States may be parties in cases before it. Thus no individual can file a complaint with ultimate appeal to the Court, and, since States themselves are loth to bring human rights problems to an international tribunal the court does not adjudicate on matters relating to human rights. In disputes between States, the foundation of the Court's jurisdiction is the consent of the parties, given either ad hoc for the purposes of the particular dispute, or generally and in advance under a Treaty or by means of a Declaration in relation to one or more categories of disputes. No State can be compelled to come before the Court unless it has given its consent in one of these forms. As a matter of fact the Court has not decided much more than one contentious case a year since it was founded, a fact that indicates both that the length and cost of cases encourage resort to other means for the settlement of disputes and that there is a lack of faith in the Court's ability to adjudicate contentious issues.

An attempt was made in 1960 by Liberia and Ethiopia to have the Court adjudicate on "the continued existence of the Mandate for South West Africa and the duties and performance of the Union as Mandatory thereunder" — a case of direct significance in regard to the protection of human rights in South West Africa. The protection from intervention which the Charter affords on matters of purely domestic policy had made it extremely difficult to mount effective international opposition to apartheid in South Africa. But because of the specific international obligations attached to the South West Africa Mandate, the possibility of creating an inroad into the whole question of apartheid was opened. The institution of litigation over South West Africa presented the African states with an opportunity of being supported by a judicial order to desist from the practice of apartheid.

However, this hope was not to be realised. The judgment of the Court was eventually handed down in 1966, and did not in fact provide any answers to the substantive issues raised by the parties. Instead the Court found that States which brought a case before the Court had to show some special, national interest before they were entitled to a pronouncement of the Court, and that neither Liberia or Ethiopia had such "special" interests. The Court thus declined to adjudicate on the merits of the case.

Both the legal merits and some very unfortunate judicial events related to the case have cast grave doubts not only on the objectiveness of the International Court of Justice in the South West Africa case, but on the Court itself. However, in 1971 by means of a request by the Security Council for an Advisory Opinion the whole matter was reopened before the International Court. The Court on this occasion found against the Republic of South Africa and held that its continued occupation of Namibia (South West Africa) was illegal.[2]

(b) *The Machinery of United Nations Conventions and Covenants.*

The extra-judicial machinery provided in three of the human rights instruments recently adopted by the United Nations represents a step forward in the effective protection of human rights. Unfortunately, however, it illustrates a dangerous tendency to deal with human rights in a piecemeal and disjointed manner.

The International Convention on the Elimination of all Forms of Racial Discrimination, is in force. It was adopted by the General Assembly in 1965, and by 1969 there were sufficient ratifications to bring it into operation. The Convention provides for the setting-up of a Committee on the Elimination of Racial Discrimination "consisting of eighteen experts of high moral standing and acknowledge impartiality" to whom the State Parties undertake to submit reports dealing with all measures adopted by them to give effort to the provisions of the Convention within their national systems. The Committee in turn will report annually to the General Assembly and make recommendations based on these reports. The Committee is also empowered to hear disputes between the States Parties on matters relating to the interpretation and carrying out of the provisions of the Convention. For the settlement of a dispute, the Committee may appoint an ad hoc "Conciliation Commission" whose good offices shall be made available to the States concerned with a view to a friendly settlement of the matter. Further, the Convention provides for the right of individual petition in that a State Party may at any time declare that it recognises the competence of the Committee to receive and consider communications from individuals or groups of individuals within its jurisdiction claiming to be victims of a violation by that State Party of any of the Rights set forth in the Convention. The Committee will only be competent to exercise its functions in regard to the right of individual petition however when at at least ten States Parties have bound themselves by declarations to the effect that they recognise the competence of the Committee.

The International Covenant on Civil and Political Rights, adopted in 1966 but not yet in force, contains similar machinery as the above Convention for the implementation of its provisions. It provides for the establishment of a "Human Rights Committee" also consisting of eighteen members, the submission by the States Parties of reports indicating the factors and difficulties affecting their implementation of the Covenant, and the hearing of disputes between States Parties. The right of individual petition is contained in an Optional Protocol to the Covenant which was adopted at the same time. By Protocol, the States Parties recognise the appropriateness of enabling the Committee to receive and consider communications from individuals claiming to be victims of violations of any of the rights set forth in the Covenant; by becoming a party to the Protocol, a State thus binds itself to recognise the competence of the Committee in this respect.

A different form of implementation machinery is to be found in the *International Covenant on Economic, Social and Cultural Rights*, also adopted in 1966 but not yet in force. The States Parties undertake to submit reports on the measures adopted and the progress made in achieving the observance of the rights recognised in the

Covenant; such reports may indicate factors and difficulties affecting the degree of fulfillment of obligations under the Covenant. The reports shall be transmitted through the Secretary-General to the Economic and Social Council, which may bring to the attention of other organs of the United Nations any matters arising out of the reports which may assist such bodies in deciding what international measures should be taken for the progressive implementation of of the Covenant.

It can be seen that the right of individual petition in these instruments depends on the specific recognition of this right by states which have ratified the Convention on Racial Discrimination or the protocol to the Covenant on Civil and Political Rights. Given the attitude of most states at present to the international protection of human rights, it will probably be a very long time before the right of individual petition could become operative in any effective manner. No doubt, these recent instruments will improve the overall situation to the certain extent, but they will never be capable of meeting the urgent need for comprehensive judicial machinery to stem the widescale destruction of human rights so prevalent today.

As will be appreciated the existing United Nations machinery, in so far as it exists at all, is ineffective and quite unco-ordinated. It also suffers from the major defect of being political rather than judicial. The various United Nations Committees that deal with Human Rights are politically subjective and make no pretence to be judicially objective. Even the Committees composed of experts suffer sometimes from these defects; there is no criterion as to what qualifications, if any, an "expert" should have.

(c) *The European Commission and Court of Human Rights*

There is thus only one judicial organ specially designed to protect human rights on an international level, the European Commission and Court of Human Rights. Article 19 of the European Convention for the Protection of Human Rights and Fundamental Freedoms (signed at Rome in 1950 by the Member States of the Council of Europe, and coming into force on the 3rd September, 1953) set up the European Commission of Human Rights and the European Courts of Human Rights. Only two states of the Council of Europe have not ratified the Convention; they are France and Switzerland.[3]

The Convention is based on the Universal Declaration of Human Rights; the Members of the Council reaffirmed "their profound belief in those Fundamental Freedoms which are the foundation of justice and peace in the world and are best maintained on the one hand by an effective political democracy and on the other by a common understanding and observance of the Human Rights upon which they depend", and resolved "to take the first steps for the collective enforcement of certain of the Rights stated in the Universal Declaration".

The Guarantees are set out in detail in Section 1 of the Convention: the right to life, the prohibition of torture and of inhuman or degrading treatment or punishment, the prohibition of slavery, the right to liberty and security of person, the right to the fair administration of justice, the prohibition of retroactive criminal legislation, the right to respect for private and family life, home and correspondence, the right to freedom of thought, conscience and religion, the right to freedom of expression and opinion, to freedom of assembly and association, the right to marry and found a family, the right to an effective remedy when these rights are violated, the right to property, the right to education, and the prohibition of discrimination in the enjoyment of the rights and freedoms in the Convention.

Limitations on the exercise of the rights and freedoms are in some cases stated, but are only permitted when prescribed by law and necessary in a democratic society on grounds such as public order, public safety and the protection of the rights and freedoms of others. Measures derogating from the obligations under the Convention may only be taken by the parties "in time of war or other public emergency *threatening the life of the* nation", and only to the *extent strictly required* by the exigencies of the situation, provided that such measures are not inconsistent with other obligations under international law. In any case, *no* derogations from the articles protecting the right to life and those prohibiting torture or inhuman treatment, slavery or retroactive legislation are permitted.

Allegations of a breach of the provisions of the Convention must primarily be referred to the Commission through the Secretary General of the Council of Europe and be made either by a High Contracting Party or by "any *person, non-governmental organisation or group of individuals*" claiming to be the victim of a violation by one of the High Contracting Parties . . . "

The right of individuals to lodge complaints with the Commission is undoubtedly the cornerstone of the structure set up by the Convention. It is also the original feature of the entire mechanism. Here, virtually for the first time in the history of human rights, the individual's right to take his complaint directly to an international body of a partly judicial nature is recognised. The right does not yet exist in relation to all European States. Nevertheless, it provides a most effective shield for the defence of human rights, and it is this procedure rather than that of inter-state complaints which has in practice made possible the effective implementation of the European Convention.

Under Art. 25 and 46 of the Convention, the right of individual petition and the jurisdiction of the European Court must be expressly recognised by the States Parties. This has now been done by Eleven States. However, any other Contracting Party may accept the jurisdiction of the Court for a particular case.

Before applying to the Commission, a State or an individual must first exhaust all domestic remedies available for the effective redress of the alleged violation. Secondly, the application must be lodged within six months from the date of the final domestic decision. In regard to individual petitions, the Commission must reject those which are anonymous, or which have already been dealt with by the Commission, and it must consider inadmissible any petition which is incompatible with the provisions of the Convention, is manifestly ill-founded, or constitutes an abuse of the right of individual petition.

The main function of the Commission is to investigate the facts of a dispute and to seek a friendly settlement; its only judicial function is to determine the admissibility of petitions. By the end of September 1967, the Commission had registered 7 cases brought by one member State against another, and 3,350 complaints brought against States by individuals or groups of individuals. About 95% of the total of the individual complaints have been declared inadmissible; inevitably many complaints emanate from people with an imaginary grievance or mentally-deranged persons, and the Commission has finally felt that their non-admissibility was so clear as not to require any comments from the Government complained against. However, in the remaining 5%, or about 140 cases, about 90 cases were rejected only after the Government concerned had been requested to present written and/or oral observations.

Where a case has been neither rejected nor settled by conciliation, the Commission draws up a report and gives its opinion as to whether the facts found disclose a breach of the Convention. This report is transmitted to the Committee of Ministers of the Council of Europe, after which two things may happen: the case may be referred to the European Court either by the Commission itself or by a State concerned, or, if it is not referred to the Court within three months, the Committee of Ministers must take a decision on the case. There are thus two bodies empowered to take decisions under the system set up by the Convention; a judicial authority, the European Court of Human Rights, and a political authority, the Committee of Ministers of the Council of Europe.

Proceedings before the Court are normally in two parts, written and oral. At the oral stage, the case is examined at a hearing in the presence of the Parties and the delegates of the Commission. An individual applicant may not bring a case before the Court itself, and thus may never be a party to the proceedings. He must rely on the Commission to inform the Court of his views, although certain provisions in the rules of the Court do make it possible for the individual to be heard. The normal conclusion of an action which reaches the Court is by a judgment of the Court, when there is a decision as to whether or not there has been a violation of the Convention and the reasons are given. The judgment of the Court is final. It is binding on the parties who have accepted its jurisdiction, and its execution is supervised by the Committee of Ministers.

Decisions of the Commission and the Court have, on the whole, been fairly conservative, as the pioneers of a new and revolutionary jurisdiction they have felt it wiser to "crawl before walking". They are also probably conscious that Governments which have not adhered to the optional clauses in the Convention would form their future policies in regard to adherence in the light of the jurisprudence of the Court. Not a valid legal consideration, this may have been a wise one. Several of the States which did not iriginally accept the right of individual petition and the jurisdiction of the Court have now done so. Other states are still considering the question.

The European Convention has indeed provided the sort of implementation machinery that is required for the effective protection of human rights, and the operation of this machinery has provided the world with an important precedent. The Convention, of course, suffers from some defects. The failure of all Member States to recognise the right of individual petition is one. There should also be an Attorney General who should have power to draw the attention of the Commission to obvious public breaches of the Convention; he should also have the function of guiding and assisting individual complainants.

3. THE FUTURE PROTECTION OF HUMAN RIGHTS

Machinery on a regional level for the protection of human rights is under consideration in the Americas, in Asia and the Pacific Region, in the Arab world and in Africa.

By far the most advanced of these projects is the Inter-American Convention on Human Rights. The Inter-American Commission on Human Rights which was set up in 1960 has drawn up a Convention setting out the human rights to be protected and establishing implementation procedures for their enforcement. The Draft Convention is much more modern in spirit than its European predecessor in that it gives substantial emphasis to economic, social and cultural rights, which form a new and genuine dimension of human rights today. The organs responsible for implementing the provisions of the Convention will be the Inter-American Commission on Human Rights and the Inter-American Court of Human Rights. As the Commission has already been in existence for some time, the only new body will be the Court. The Draft Convention retains the present structure and functions of the Commission and gives it new powers. The most important of these is the right to receive individual petitions, and unlike its European counterpart, the Commission's competence to hear individual petitions does not depend upon acceptance by the countries concerned and its decisions are binding. This provision is a gigantic step in the evolution of implementation machinery and an extremely valuable safeguard for the individual. Before a case can be submitted to the Inter-American Court of Human Rights, however, both parties must have recognised the Court's jurisdiction.

Developments in regard to the Inter-American Convention will be watched with interest by all those interested in the effective protection of human rights; it is hoped that ratifications will be forthcoming so that the Commission and the Court may put their mandate into operation without delay.

In Asia there has been a proposal promoted mainly by Asian jurists in the International Commission of Jurists for a *Council of Asia and the Pacific* analogous to the Council of Europe. So far there has not been specific reference to a Convention on Human Rights for the region; it is rather a machinery for debate, consultation and co-ordinated action at Parliamentary and Governmental level that has been envisaged. The Council would discuss questions of common concern and by agreement and common action on economic, social and cultural matters would further the Rule of Law and the fuller realisation of human rights and fundamental freedoms. The establishment of such machinery clearly merits full consideration and every encouragement.

The League of Arab States, which already provides a machinery for debate and discussion of problems in the Arab world, has established a *Commission on Human Rights* under the aegis of the League of Arab States. A Commission is also under active consideration for Africa as a whole.

These developments are of tremendous significance, and the examples cited above could well be followed in other areas of the world. But, however well human rights can be protected at the international level by regional juridicial machinery, the ultimate aim should be for implementation machinery at universal level. Just as national judicial processes would be more effective with international regional supervision, so regional processes require the supervision of a universal Court. The time has come to envisage the establishment of a *Universal Court of Human Rights* analogous to the European Court with jurisdiction to pronounce on violations of human rights. The jurisdiction of such a Court could be two-fold: in areas where there already exists an effective international regional court, its functions could be that of an appellate court; in areas where there is not yet an effective regional machinery, it could have original jurisdiction to hear complaints from governments, groups or individuals. It is true that the creation of a Universal Court would inevitably involve a degree of supra-national jurisdiction, but the extent of such acceptance could be regulated by optional clauses. But in fact the conception of national sovereignty is completely out-dated since every convention, treaty or even trade agreement involves a limitation on national sovereignty.

Independently of any international judicial machinery for the protection of human rights, there is a vitally important proposal before the United Nations for the establishment of a *United Nations High Commissioner for Human Rights* with a status somewhat analogous to the High Commissioner for Refugees. When established, this institution will provide the United Nations with a modest but useful instrument for the fulfillment of its mandate under Article 13 (1) of the Charter, to assist "in the realisation of human rights and fundamental freedoms for all". The High Commissioner for Human Rights is not intended to form part of the machinery for the implementation of existing or future international instruments relating to human rights, he is rather intended to be complementary to such machinery. He will have power to give advice and assistance to United Nations organs which request it, and will be of considerable value to bodies such as the Commission on Human Rights which is not organised in

EX-OFFENDERS

Church Army

Law Courts - "see Probation & After-Care"

Margery Fry Memorial Trust (Birmingham & West Midlands)

Prison Welfare Department (Part of the Birmingham Probation & After-Care Service)

Probation and After-Care Service (West Midlands County)

Rotary Club of Birmingham

Stonham Housing Association Limited (Formerly St. Leonard's Housing Association Limited)

Women's Royal Voluntary Service

such a way as to enable it to undertake detailed examination of particular problems and has no independent authority to which it could entrust such a task. The High Commissioner for Human Rights could also render assistance to governments in regard to problems affecting human rights when requested to do so, and through his report to the General Assembly, he could play an important part in encouraging the better protection of human rights at all levels and in securing the ratification of international conventions relating to human rights.

The proposal for the institution of a High Commissioner for Human Rights is most worthy of the support of those anxious to promote the cause of human rights. It would make a useful contribution to the protection of human rights which would be acceptable to a large majority of the member states of the United Nations, since in no way can it be said to encroach on their national sovereignty and, while providing them with an institution to which they may turn for assistance, refrains from any unsolicited interference in their domestic affairs.

4. MASS DESTRUCTION OF HUMAN RIGHTS AND INDIVIDUAL RESPONSIBILITY

What is the reason for the lack of real progresss in the effective protection of human rights? Delay is, of course, partly due to governmental inertia and hesitation, a phenomenon which hampers almost every international endeavour, and is largely based on an outdated conception of national sovereignty. However, a major problem to which not enough attention has been paid is the increasing number of incidents of mass violations of human rights in armed conflicts and the recurring resort to armed conflict as a means of settling international and internal disputes. Repression, brutality and armed conflicts, engendering as they do violations and counter-violations of human rights, are a distinctive feature of our time and display recognisable symptoms of a civilisation in process of decay. Even on a purely scientific and sociological basis, these problems require urgent attention; from the point of view of the protection of human rights, their overall effect is to generate a sense of futility at any attempt to provide protection against violation, and disillusion at the relative ineffectiveness of any machinery actually in operation.

In my opinion, war and armed conflicts present the greatest obstacle to the protection of human rights. Each war sets in motion a process of moral erosion. It produces hatred, bitterness and fear; it leads to the abandonment of moral scruples and restraint and traces a path of moral descent. Moreover, the present refinement of weapons of mass destruction threaten the actual survival of a large part of the human race.

In this context, the elimination of warfare is desirable, though probably utopian, as can be seen from the lack of progress in the United Nations Disarmament programme. A recent development which may lead to a lessening of the horrors of warfare is a move to revise the laws and customs relating to armed conflicts in order to harmonise them with technological advances and new methods of warfare; the necessary studies are at present being undertaken by the United Nations and the International Committee of the Red Cross.

It should be remembered that the Charter of the United Nations virtually outlaws war and certainly forbids "the threat or use of force against the territorial integrity or political independence of any state or in any manner inconsistent with the purposes of the United Nations".

It is, however, time that *criminal* sanctions for acts of war, aggression and brutality were applied to individuals, and that a permanent international criminal tribunal were established for this purpose. A bold new concept of international jurisdiction was adopted under the Charter of the International Military Tribunal which dealt with war crimes at the end of the Second World War. This jurisdiction affirmed "the existence of fundamental human rights superior to the law of the State and protected by international criminal sanctions even if violated in pursuance of the law of the State".[5] The one major defect was that this was a jurisdiction to try the vanquished by the victors. Nevertheless it reflected a universal reaction against the atrocities committed before and during the war, and a determination to punish those guilty of such atrocities. Later, in 1950, the principles on which the jurisdiction was based were confirmed in the *Nuremberg Principles* formulated by the International Law Commission following a directive of the General Assembly of the United Nations.[6]

The Principles constitute highly authoritative guides as to the character of the legal obligations of citizens and leaders in regard to war crimes, crimes against humanity and crimes against peace; *they place criminal responsibility on individuals for the commission of any of the crimes defined.*

Principle I which provides that "any person who commits an act which constitutes a crime under international law is responsible therefore and liable to punishment" emphasies that international law may impose duties directly in individuals. Moreover, the fact that the internal law of a country does not impose a penalty for an act which constitutes a crime under international law does not relieve the person who commits the act from responsibility under International law (Principle II). Superior orders do not relieve an individual from his responsibility, provided that a moral choice was in fact possible (Principle IV). The Nuremberg Tribunal has declared that killings or torture under orders in violation of the international law of war had never been recognised as a defence for such acts of brutality, although the order of the superior could be urged in mitigation of punishment.

The crimes punishable as crimes under international law were defined by the International Law Commission under three headings in Principle VI, crimes against peace,[6] war crimes[7] and crimes against humanity.[8] In its definition of crimes against humanity the Commission omitted the phrase 'before or during the war' contained in Article 6 (c) of the Charter of the Nuremberg Tribunal, because this phrase referred to the particular war of 1939. The omission reflects the opinion of the Commission that crimes against humanity may take place even before a war in connection with crimes against peace.

Criminal responsibility is placed on both governments and individuals by the Genocide Convention of 1948. Article 4 provides:

"persons committing genocide or any of the other acts defined in Article 3 shall be punished, whether they are constitutionally responsible rulers, public officials or private individuals."

It emerges clearly from these developments that there should be established a permanent international tribunal to deal with all crimes defined in the Hague and Geneva Conventions, the Nuremberg Principles and the Genocide Convention. Such a permanent judicial tribunal would not suffer from the defect of being set up on an ad hoc basis to deal with a particular situation. Its decisions might remain temporarily unenforceable in some regions, but the individual offender could at least be identified and branded as an outlaw. Such a sanction would have a restraining influence and would reduce the trend towards the brutalisation of mankind.

A further aspect of this new approach to the right to wage war is the individual's right to refuse to participate in a war, which derives logically from the criminal liability described above. The combined effect of Articles 6 and 8 of the Charter of the International Military

Tribunal was to make every soldier liable for crimes against peace, war crimes and crimes against humanity. The fact that he was acting "pursuant to the order of his Government or of a superior shall not free him from responsibility". This liability having been confirmed by the Nuremberg Principles each individual therefore must make a value judgment before participating in any war or obeying certain military orders if he is not to incur the risk of becoming a war criminal. The question of *refusing* military service and orders is thus no longer a question of pure conscience (the classic conception of "conscientious objection"); it is also in many cases a legal obligation under international law.

In fact there would seem to be four categories of 'conscientious objectors' accepted today, even though all are not yet recognised by law. There is firstly the 'classical' objector whose objection to participation in a war or related activities is derived from religious or moral conviction. The right of such persons to refuse military service has been recognised by the Consultative Assembly of the Council of Europe which has produced the best modern definition of the classical objector.[9] The Assembly declared that "Persons liable to conscription for military service who, for reasons of conscience or profound conviction arising from religious, ethical, moral, humanitarian, philosophical or similar motives, refuse to perform armed service shall enjoy a personal right to be released from the obligations to perform such service. This right shall be regarded as deriving logically from the fundamental rights of the individual in democratic Rule of Law States which are guaranteed in Article 9 of the European Convention on Human Rights". The second category, whose number has increased steadily in recent times consists of those who object to participation in a particular war because they regard that war as unjust or illegal. Thirdly, there are those who object to performing military service in a country which is bound by a military alliance which may involve the country in a war which is not of its own choosing. Finally there are the objectors who, not objecting to military service as such, do object to fulfilling certain orders which are against their conscience, or which quite simply, they regard as illegal.

The modern conception of the 'right to wage war' is not only based on the sovereign right of states; the right of the individual to be protected from inhuman treatment and his correlative right to refuse to participate in the infliction of suffering on his fellow-men has at last to be acknowledged.

The religious leaders of the world have now recognised the right of people to refuse to participate in wars. This right was enunciated first at the Baden Consultation of Christian Churches in 1970 and was subsequently enunciated by the World Conference on Religion and Peace held in Kyoto at the end of 1970. These important religious conferences reached the same conclusions:

> "We consider that the exercise of conscientious judgment is inherent in the dignity of human beings and that, accordingly, each person should be assured the right, on grounds of conscience or profound conviction, to refuse military service, or any other direct or indirect participation in wars or armed conflicts. The right of conscientious objection also extends to those who are unwilling to serve in a particular war because they consider it unjust or because they refuse to participate in a war or conflict in which weapons of mass destruction are likely to be used. This Conference also considers that members of armed forces have the right, and even the duty, to refuse to obey military orders which may involve the commission of criminal offenses, or of war crimes, or of crimes against humanity".

I have tried to outline briefly the major problems connected with the protection of human rights and to suggest some possible solutions. For the sake of world peace and freedom for all men, indeed for the sake of the very survival of mankind, new and dynamic thinking is now urgently required on a world-wide basis.

1 These words are taken from the Preamble to the Hague Convention No. IV of 1907. It is known as the "Martens Clause" after its author, Professor F. F. De Martens. The same words are also to be found in each of the Geneva Conventions 1949 (First Convention Art. 63; Second Convention, Art. 62; Third Convention, Art. 142; Fourth Convention, Art. 158).

2 For more detailed consideration of this case, see the JOURNAL of the International Commission of Jurists. Vol. VII. No. 2 and Vol. VIII, No. 2.

3 The States that have not adhered to Article 25 (the right of individual petition) are: Cyprus, France, Greece, Italy, Malta, Switzerland and Turkey.

4 Sir Hersch Lauterpacht in the 7th edition of Oppenheim.

5 G.A. Resolution 177 (II) par. (a).

6 (i) Planning, preparation, initiation or waging of a war of aggression or a war in violation of international treaties, agreements or assurances;
(ii) participation in a common plan or conspiracy for the accomplishment of any of the acts mentioned under (i).

7 Violations of the laws or customs of war which include, but are not limited to, murder, ill-treatment or deportation to slave-labour or for any other purpose of civilian population of or in occupied territory, murder or ill-treatment of prisoners

of war, of persons on the seas, killing of hostages, plunder of public or private property, wanton destruction of cities, towns or villages, or devastation not justified by military necessity.

[8] Murder, extermination, enslavement, deportation and other inhuman acts done against any civilian population, or persecutions on political, racial or religious grounds, when such acts are done or such persecutions are carried on in execution of or in connection with any crime against peace or any war crime.

[9] Resolution 337 adopted on 26th January 1967.

COERCION OF STATES AND WORLD PEACE
MULFORD Q. SIBLEY

Professor of Political Science in the University of Minnesota. Quaker. Author of *The Quiet Battle,* an anthology of writings on the theory and practice of non-violent resistance.

This Chapter explores the proposition that if coercion is to play any role at all in the establishment of world peace it must be coercion of individuals under law, never coercion of States.

It has often been said that the only lesson history teaches us is that it teaches us nothing. While this is doubtless an exaggeration, when we turn to the history of futility in world organization, we are tempted to conclude that the statement does not distort the truth in any considerable degree.

For the history of world organization is in part that of the attempt to build "peace" structures on the principle of coercion of States; and experience shows that such attempts have produced only confusion, war and interference with peaceful progress. Yet we continue to repeat those attempts, as if we were oblivious of past failures.

The League of Nations had its principle of "collective security" and the United Nations apparently has envisioned some kind of military staff organization which would, on orders of the Security Council, carry out the instructions of the UN to coerce recalcitrant so-called aggressive States. Even today, certain writers seem to argue that if only we could get the Great Powers together, they could effectively control other States in the name of a kind of world order. And some western thinkers apparently believe that if only the "democratic" powers could be organized on the principle of coercion of States, they could prevent aggressive Russia from making war (which it is assumed that the Soviet Union is always eager to do).

This paper briefly explores propositions of this kind and finds them wanting. The gist of our argument will be that, if coercion is to play any role at all in the establishment of world peace, it must be coercion of *individuals* under law and never coercion of States.

In developing the argument, we make three points: (1) in terms of theory, the notion of coercion of States is fallacious; (2) historical experience suggests that the theory is correct; and (3) if we reject coercion of States, the possibilities of world peace—given certain non-coercive measures, which we suggest—are enhanced and not reduced.

1

The theory of coercion of States is built on the proposition that certain States are "aggressors" and that if there is previous agreement to proceed against these bad States, aggression will be discouraged and some kind of world order will ensue. The theory has a ring of plausibility about it and, as a matter of fact, deserves fuller attention than we are able to give it here.

It reposes on the notion that national States, with sovereignty, are the stuff out of which world organization must necessarily be created. In the past, the argument goes on, States have acted freely, each pursuing its interests and each asserting the right—in the absence of an adequate world organization—to defend its own borders by military force. But this freedom of States in effect means that each is to be the judge of when aggression has taken place and when it is essential, in the name of national honour and vital interests (conceptions usually left rather vague), to resist aggression. Under such circumstances, however, it is obvious that those who plan aggression will always have an advantage—they will prepare their aggression beforehand and there will be no world organization to say them nay. Because each State is on its own, international "anarchy" and war are the inevitable result.[1]

If, the argument continues, men could agree before the event took place that non-aggressor States would immediately proceed by military force against aggression, the aggressor would be stopped in his tracks; and thus the principle of non-aggression would be upheld. The threat of force against the aggressor would be enough to hold him at bay, in most circumstances, and when it was not adequate, the pooled military forces of the non-aggressors could certainly stop the armies of the aggressor before they had inflicted much damage.

Is it not obvious, it has often been asked, that if the world had been organized along these lines Hitler's attempts to dominate the world would have been frustrated and World War II averted? Is it not clear, the question would proceed, that had a general system of "collective security", with a military staff empowered to call on States for assistance, existed at the time of the "rape" of Ethiopia, the rape would never have occurred? These are often regarded as rhetorical questions.

It should be noted, however, that the usual arguments for coercion of States proceed on the assumption that each national State will retain its own national army. Thus the wherewithal for aggression exists, as well as the resources for "collective security" which will presumably either prevent aggression or frustrate it after a slight battle. Most schemes for coercion of States do not make a plan of complete disarmament an integral part of their proposals, although they usually look forward, to be sure, to a day in which national armaments will be reduced. On the whole, most plans assume a continued latitude on the part of each national State for its manoeuvres and manipulations of armed forces.

Now what is wrong about such a world organization, in principle? On the surface it would appear to have much merit, and it still seems to be the predominant image of universal order which most persons have in mind.

Assuming that "aggression" can be clearly defined—and so far we have been unsuccessful in doing so—there would seem to be two clear and powerful objections to the theory of coercion of States. In the first place, it could be implemented only with a very serious risk of war. Secondly, the very existence of the threat of coercion, or the use of armed forces, would tend to disrupt the world organization.

The first objection was developed at length by the founders of the American Federation during the Constitutional Convention of 1787 and in the years immediately following.

Thus James Madison, often called the "father" of the American constitutional system,

> "observed that the more he reflected upon the use of force, the more he doubted the practibility, the justice and the efficacy of it when applied to people collectively, and not individually . . . A Union of the States containing such an ingredient seemed to provide for its own destruction. The use of force against a State, would look more like a declaration of war, than an infliction of punishment".[1]

And Alexander Hamilton, speaking before the New York State Convention called to ratify the Federal Constitution, asked

> "If you make requisitions, and they are not complied with, what is to be done? It has been observed, to coerce the states is one of the maddest projects that was ever devised. A failure of compliance will never be confined to a single state. This being the case, can we suppose it wise to hazard a civil war?"[2]

In the *Federalist Papers,* written to defend the new constitutional system, several numbers were devoted to a vigorous attack on any system of federation which might be built on the notion of coercion of States.[3]

Other figures associated with the rise of American federalism were equally outspoken. One of the plans submitted to the Constitutional Convention—the so-called New Jersey Plan—embodied a scheme for coercion of States. It said, in part,

> "that if any State, or any body of men in any State shall oppose or prevent ye carrying into execution such acts or treaties, the federal Executive shall be authorized to call forth ye power of the Confederated States, or so much thereof as may be necessary to enforce and compel an obedience to such Acts, or an observance of such Treaties".[4]

Commenting on this proposal, Edmund Randolph said that it "tended . . . to habituate the instruments of it to shed blood and riot in the spoils of their fellow Citizens . . ."[5]

Dr. L. P. Jacks, a modern scholar, has thus finely and correctly characterized the opposition of the American constitutionalists to coercion of States:

> "What Hamilton opposed and dismissed as impossible was a *coercive union* of States endowed, under the terms of the union, with the right to make war *on one or any of its own members,* and armed with a collective preponderance of strength for that purpose. Such a union, he argued, would be a contradiction not only in logic but in fact. It would contain the seed of internal conflict and therefore no union at all . . ."[6]

In essence, then, what the leaders of American federalism were saying was that the proposed cure—coercion of States—because it could only be carried out by war, was worse than the disease it was supposed to correct.

But even if war did not ensue, they continued, the very threat of force would be an instrumentality of division rather than of harmony. Perhaps there would be no armed resistance, to be sure, but the possibility of using federal forces against a State as such would be deemed unjust and would stimulate and encourage rebellions in the future. Force threatened under such circumstances—when whole communities as corporate bodies were deemed "guilty"—would always sow the seeds of discord. All this was well reflected in the words of Oliver Ellsworth, who, speaking to the Connecticut convention called to ratify the Constitution, said:

> "I am for coercion of law—that coercion which acts only upon

delinquent individuals. This Constitution does not attempt to coerce sovereign bodies, states, in their political capacity. No coercion is applicable to such bodies, but that of an armed force. If we should attempt to execute the laws of the Union by sending an armed force against a delinquent state, it would involve the good and the bad, the innocent and guilty, in the same calamity".[7]

Running through the whole argument is, of course, the idea that while it might be necessary, legitimate, and possible to coerce individuals effectively, the same could not be said of States as such. A whole community cannot be placed in prison. Morally, it is doubtful whether it is ever legitimate to condemn a large body of persons; for surely all are not equally "guilty". But even if we could assume their guilt, to attempt to coerce them would always require military force, the use of military force under those circumstances would often lead to war, and yet war supposedly was what coercion of States was designed to eliminate.

Thus far, to be sure, we have been dealing with the theory of the American federation. Is that theory, in its condemnation of coercion of States, applicable to the international arena? The answer would seem to be a resounding "Yes". And the reasons are similar to those offered by the founders of the American Federation. Coercion of States through military force is impracticable and almost always leads to results worse than the situation it is designed to correct.

Communities are held together not primarily by force or threat of force but by such intangibles as tradition, emotional bonds, cooperative activities of a positive nature, acceptance of common legal standards through usage and debate, and factors of a similar type. Even coercion of individuals through "police" force can be effective only when it is very marginal, limited, and administered in a context of law. To be sure, we are all familiar with governments which attempt to rule by terror and apparently succeed for long periods of time. But the price paid is enormous—disruption of community, fear, inefficiency, and disintegration of personalities—and always greater than any benefits it may produce.

All this was said very well by the American philosopher John Dewey, when, at a time during which many were proposing that the League of Nations establish some kind of an army, he said:

"I think no reasonable person will hold that the coercive force of the federal government of the United States is chiefly or in any large degree that which keeps the various states together; or that it is a factor of any great importance as compared with the bonds of common tradition, habit of mind, beliefs, information, intercommunication, commerce, etc., which tie the people of the states together. Nor can I imagine any sensible person today who, when he looks at rivalries of interest and latent friction between sections which still exist, would urge as a remedy the strengthening of coercive force exercised from above upon them . . . I cannot imagine such a person proposing anything but means which will positively intensify the bonds of common interest and purpose which exist among sections . . . Laws that are enforced are enforced because there is a community consensus behind them. The threat of force does not bring about that consensus".[8]

If we are to have world peace and world order, then, they will not come if we build into the structure of the world framework the principle of coercion of States. That principle can only lead to war or, at best, to disintegrating tendencies, fear, and injustice to individuals.

Does experience with political organization support this theory? By and large it would seem to do so.

It should be noted that in modern federal systems that have been most "successful"—Switzerland, the United States, Australia, Canada, and several others—the principle of coercion of States was deliberately rejected. General law is applied directly to individuals. If disputes between and among States arise, they are taken to the courts, and, generally speaking, the decisions of the courts are amazingly well observed by the States involved.[9]

Looking at the matter from the perspective of history, it would seem that those federations which seek to hold their members by force of arms either, if successful, create more misery than would have existed had they not so acted, or, if unsuccessful, cause utterly needless bloodshed. Someone may ask about the American Civil War in this connection. It is a prime example of an allegedly "successful" war to hold States in a federation. Yet a powerful case can be made for the contention that it proves our point. The South, as a result of the war, was antagonized for three generations, so that even in our day the wounds have not healed. The black man, while formally "emancipated", was really placed under another form of slavery; and it has only been in relatively recent years that he has begun to see the light of day. In many respects, the war postponed true emancipation for a century or more. Had the war not occurred, it can be persuasively argued, legal emancipation would inevitably have taken place in any event and under conditions far more conductive to the healing of wounds. To be sure, the southern States were held in the Union; but at what price? And was not the price too high? This is not even to mention the fact that the Union was violating its own central principle: that coercion of States as such ought not to be undertaken. To be sure, the notion was that it was "conspiracies" of individuals who carried out the secession, and not States; but this was a fiction only and the fact remains that the war was against large bodies of men organized corporatively.

Commenting on exactly such points, the well-known student of federation, A. E. Freeman—who studied the problem of federal government in Greece and Italy and attempted to relate his findings to the American Civil War—had this to say:

> "A Federation, though legally perpetual, is something which is in its own nature essentially voluntary: there is a sort of inconsistency in retaining members against their will. What is to be done with them when they are conquered? They can hardly be made subjects of the other States: are they then to be compelled at the point of the bayonet to recognize their conquerors as brethren, and to send, under the penalties of treason, unwilling Senators and Representatives to Washington? Either alternative is utterly repugnant to the first principles of a Federal Union. Surely the remedy is worse than the disease. The revolted State, as a foreign power, may become a friendly neighbour; as an unwilling Confederate, it will simply be a source of internal dissension and confusion. A State will hardly think of Secession as long as it is to its manifest interest to remain in the Union. When it ceases to be its manifest interest to remain there may at least be grave doubts as to either the justice or the expediency of retaining it by force. The Achaen League was weakened, indeed we may say that it finally perished, by nothing so much as by the attempt to retain members in the Confederation against their will.[10]

One might add that coercion of States is usually adopted as a principle in international organization when a victorious alignment of Powers desires to maintain the *status quo* and to prevent peaceful change. This was certainly true after the Napoleonic Wars, with the Holy and Quadruple Alliances; and much of the argument for coercion after World War I came from those who hoped to freeze power relations as they had emerged after the conflict. World peace depends on our finding forms of organization which will encourage those intangible bonds of unity so essential for any order; yet at the same time it must be an organization which will not only permit but even at points stimulate social, political and economic change. A framework of coercion of States is highly unlikely to do this.

2

But, it may be said, if you reject coercion of States as a principle, what would you do? How do you propose to organize the world in such a way that the danger of war will be minimized and peaceful change be encouraged? These are fair questions, but our answers, because of space limitations, will have to be sketchy ones and will merely suggest the lines along which progress might possibly take place.

We have to disabuse ourselves of the near-idolatry with which we tend to view military force. Despite all our experiences, we still seem to believe that military force can defend something worthwhile. This faith has to be shattered and we must come to see that just the reverse is true, particularly in the modern world: arms, whether used for "collective security" in the form of coercion of States or as nationally administered "national defence" are utterly worthless if the objective be the protection of human life. Until our whole attitude to this subject changes, we are unlikely to make progress. Until States stop regarding reduction of arms as a "sacrifice" they are unlikely to reach agreement to reduce the burden of armaments drastically.

Once they do see the light, so to speak, and agree to scrap military forces completely—and nothing less than this will do—the kinds of institutions needed are apparent. We need to encourage world organizations through which men can co-operate for positive ends—health, labour regulation, distribution of food, and countless other objectives which are today reflected in the so-called "functional" agencies of the UN. We have to build a network of co-operation so strong that it will be to the obvious interest of every State to support it. We have made considerable progress in this direction already; but even so, we have just begun.

As a completely disarmed world builds institutions of this kind it will be gaining the only kind of "security" that is possible. It will be a security, to be sure, that is not perfect; but then no system of security is without flaws. If in the process of building co-operative institutions, it is deemed desirable to provide for coercion of world law—by which we mean coercion of individuals—this can be done to a limited degree. But the world police force must always act on *individuals* and not on States as such; and the "force" used must be peripheral and essentially non-violent. If there are world laws to be implemented, the basic enforcement must rest on a widespread opinion that they are rational and that they contribute to the welfare of men everywhere. If a relatively few men reject them, only mild forms of coercion should be employed to put the laws into effect. Anything more than this will run the risk that a psychology of fear will once more arise.

Fundamentally, what we require is a revolution in our thinking. Negatively, this entails a complete rejection of the principle of coercion of States and the idea that nations can be defended by arms. Positively, it implies a firm understanding that the enhancement of human life can come about only through the painful building and expansion of institutions promoting co-operation for positive ends.

Any attempted short-cuts, any effort, that is to say, to impose peace by force, are foredoomed to failure. This is the clear lesson both of theory and of experience.

1 Max Ferrand, ed. *The Records of the Federal Convention of 1787* (New Haven: 1923), I., 54.
2 Jonathan Elliott, ed., *The Debates of the Several State Conventions on the Adoption of the Federal Constitution* (Philadelphia: 1901), II., 232-233.
3 See *The Federalist,* Nos. 15 through 22.
4 Ferrand, *op. cit.,* I., 245.
5 Ferrand, *op. cit.,* I., 256.
6 L. P. Jacks, "Alexander Hamilton and the Reform of the League", *International Conciliation,* No. 325, December 1936, p.616.
7 Jonathan Elliott, *op. cit.,* II., 197.
8 John Dewey in Raymond Leslie Buell and John Dewey, *Are Sanctions Necessary to International Organization?* Foreign Policy Association Pamphlet No. 82-83 (New York: 1932), 32-33.
9 On the history of Switzerland, see Welhelm Oechsli, *History of Switzerland, 1499-1914* (Cambridge: 1922). On the theory and practice of Swiss federalism, see William Bross Lloyd, Jr., *Waging Peace: The Swiss Experience* (Washington D.C., 1958).
10 A. E. Freeman, *History of Federal Government in Greece and Italy* (New York and London: 1893), 119.

UNITED NATIONS PEACE KEEPING: AN ASSESSMENT

GEOFFREY CARNALL

Reader in English Literature, University of Edinburgh. Friends' Service Council worker in India and Pakistan from 1948 to 1950, and author of *To Keep the Peace*, a *Peace News* pamphlet on United Nations forces, published in 1965.

Should the UN have used tanks in Cyprus, and did the UN action in Korea make the UN impotent in Vietnam? Just what are the essential conditions for any successful UN action?

A few years ago, with the success of the UN Emergency Force on the frontiers of Israel and Egypt, and the large-scale intervention by the UN in the Congo, international peace-keeping was a live political issue, at least in some western countries. Were we witnessing the early stages of an instrument of world government? And how could these untidy, improvised enterprises be put on a more regular footing? Was UN action likely on balance to be a conservative or a revolutionary influence? What kind of strategy and tactics were appropriate to such forces? UN peace-keeping was debated in both Houses of Parliament in Britain, and considered in elaborate semi-official research projects in the USA. There was (perhaps there still is) an international organization to register Volunteers for a World Police Force, with headquarters in the Netherlands.

But as the world moved into the 1970's this degree of interest came to seem rather remote. Many were disheartened by the failure to reach international agreement on the financing of peace forces—the issue that, having paralysed the General Assembly in 1964-65, was resolved only by acceptance of the Franco-Soviet refusal to pay. Since that time the UN has had one notable success, that of helping to foster the slow, unsteady, but unmistakable improvement in the situation in Cyprus. Unhappily, this is the kind of success which is indicated chiefly by the absence of Cyprus from the newspapers, so that its publicity value is slight. The publicity, on the other hand, attending Egypt's expulsion of UNEF from its borders on the eve of the June war in 1967 was glaring and ignominious. Equally conspicuous has been the failure of the UN to find a peace-making role in Vietnam. An impression of ineffectiveness has virtually destroyed popular faith in the possibility of the UN's developing an alternative to war.

This faith may always have been too much bound up with the notion that peace-keeping was dependent on powers of enforcement. The role of the Emergency Force was often seen as that of "keeping Nasser in check"— although, if anything, its purpose, stationed as it was exclusively on Egyptian territory, was rather to check Israel. Seen in this way, for anyone taking the Nasser-checking view, UNEF's precipitate dismissal looks mortifying in the extreme. It becomes less mortifying if one recognises U Thant's acceptance of this dismissal as the price that had to be paid to keep open the possibility of a renewed UN presence in the Arab-Israel area. But the mere fact of a presence will be small consolation to those who hanker after a collective system of security in the Middle East which would give all parties actual defence on the ground against any attack.[1]

In the early stages of the UN intervention in Cyprus, much dissatisfaction was expressed at the apparent feebleness of its tactics. UN officers might insist that they could get a lot done by talking, and that if you asked someone to stop firing he usually would, for a while at least—an achievement that would not be possible after pumping bullets into the people you wanted to talk to. But Mr. Harold Wilson, for one, felt that these forces had been put in a vulnerable and humiliating position, reluctant and passive spectators in a civil war. He wanted to have Greek and Turkish strong points forcibly dismantled, if necessary sending heavy tanks to do so. In a similar vein, Dr. D. W. Bowett, the author of a massive legal study of UN forces,[2] suggested that if the UN were not prepared to take enforcement action in Cyprus, there might well be little point in its embarking upon or continuing with any military operation at all.[3] Subsequent events have shown that this was too gloomy a view: the presence of a third party, actively concerned to intervene in situations where open fighting threatened to break out between Greeks and Turks, has been a critical factor in preventing the bitter—and still unresolved—conflict from getting out of hand. The more forceful approach favoured by Wilson and Bowett, so far from being more effective, might actually have precipitated disaster by engendering a war atmosphere in which the Greek and Turkish governments would have found it impossible to stand, as the phrase goes, idly by.

In retrospect (though not in 1964) Cyprus may seem to have been a good place to try non-violent tactics. The dispute between Greeks and Turks was bitter, but it was at least possible to envisage the outline of a settlement that both parties might acquiesce in. When, however, one turns to the conflict between the Arabs and the State of Israel, conditions are obviously far worse. The very foundation of Israel involved the displacement of around a million Arabs, who became refugees, many of them in appalling poverty. An upheaval on this scale was bound to leave a legacy of hatred and violence on the Arab side, while the Israelis might well feel that, given the violent birth of their state, its one hope of survival lay in an unrelaxed militancy. The UN's various armistice arrangements have attempted to inhibit resorts to force, but it has been almost impossible to work towards an acceptable long-term settlement. A glimpse of such a settlement emerged in 1955, when Jordan, Egypt, and Syria were beginning to take a serious interest in Mr. Eric Johnston's plan for joint Arab-Israeli exploitation of the Jordan waters. It was becoming at least conceivable that the Arab States might consider recognition of Israel in return for substantial concessions to the uprooted Palestinians, but the project was killed by one of Israel's massive retaliation raids (on Syria, December 1955). It is difficult not to be overcome by a fatalistic sense that any move towards peace in this area will be overwhelmed one way or another.

None the less, the pressure to keep the peace in the Middle East, and to work towards a settlement, has been remarkably persistent. Although the Great Powers are involved in the Arab-Israel conflict, with much western support for Israel and a substantial Soviet backing for the Arab cause, they seem united in anxiety that they should not themselves be drawn into large-scale fighting, with the consequent peril of world war. Since both Arabs and Israelis depend for much of their resources on their outside backers, these pressures towards caution are not entirely unavailing. They serve to reinforce the tenuous physical presence of the UN, which is the visible expression of the outside world's anxiety. How unequal the conflict is, however, between external influence and the intrinsic explosiveness of the situation becomes painfully evident in the memoirs of General E. L. M. Burns, the Canadian who headed both the UN Truce Supervision Organisation and the Emergency Force in the Sinai Peninsula. His book[4] gives one a vivid idea of the temper in which peace-keeping has to be carried on: the rigorous concern to maintain existing agreements; the cool concentration on what is actually happening, attending to but never being deflected by the keen animosities of the opposite sides; the untiring watchfulness for any chance to nudge people in a more peaceable direction. But in spite of this dedication, the near-impossibility of the task comes through time and time again. Once, when General Burns went off to New York to attempt some negotiation at the General Assembly, he obtained an assurance from senior officials of the Egyptian and Israeli Foreign Offices that nothing would be done to aggravate the situation while he was away. On arrival in New York he received news that the Egyptians had mounted a raid on Israel in the particularly sensitive area that he was negotiating about. "It was", says Burns, "another proof of the lamentable fact that in the Israel-Arab conflict, the fair and reasonable promises of the diplomats can be set aside by the action of some irresponsible or irreconcilable person within the echelons of the military command" (p.97). Frustrating though such incidents were, however, it is clear that if there had been no UN presence the fighting would have been on a larger scale, and the chances of major war much higher. General Burns obviously regrets that stronger pressure was not brought to bear on the situation from outside, and notes with pleasure such examples of direct sanctions as occurred: for instance, when Israel carried out her raid on Syria in December 1955, negotiations with the US to secure arms to balance Egypt's supplies from Czechoslovakia were broken off; and when, after the Suez adventure of 1956, Israel refused to withdraw from some of the conquered areas, the US cut off all aid to Israel from governmental sources. The physical presence of a UN force, moreover, itself complicates the calculations which the strategists affected have to make. General Burns makes this clear when speaking of the danger that the Israelis might still have come back to Gaza after their agreement to withdraw early in 1957, because of their objections to the setting up of an Egyptian administration there. The UN troops could not possibly have withstood an attack, but Burns' chief anxiety was that the Israelis might simply walk around the UN posts on their way to reoccupying Egyptian territory. "The Israelis would never attempt to force the UNEF lines if to do so they had to fire on UNEF and cause casualties, which would bring the anger of the whole of the United Nations and most powerful sanctions down upon them at once" (p.273). Whether because of this consideration, or simply because of direct American pressure, Burns' anxiety proved unnecessary, and there was no attack.

Even from this brief account, enough has been said to show that peace-keeping, the organised effort to damp down violent modes of conflict, exploits forces which cannot be reckoned up by simple arithmetic. People actively committed to a conflict are likely to perceive these pressures as something that paralyses their leader's capacity for strong action, subtly corrupting an original purity of resolve. This paralysis is induced, not so much by specific sanctions (though these are indispensable), as by uneasy calculations of the unspecified benefits and penalties that may follow from acquiescing in or flouting the wishes of an outside power or powers. Such manoeuvring amid conjectural assessments of the international situation is, of course, a commonplace diplomatic activity, and can stoke up conflict as well as damp it down. But on balance the effect is likely to be pacific. In the post-Hiroshima world, the international community as a whole has never judged any particular conflict to be worth a nuclear holocaust. Greeks and Turks, Arabs and Israelis, Hindus and Muslims, partisans of Mr. Lumumba and Mr. Tshombe, may throw caution to the winds; some Americans still think it better to be dead than red, and many Chinese take comfort from their country's supposed ability to survive a nuclear war. But although an exalted disregard of consequences is normal in anyone whole-heartedly engaged in the defence of vital interests, no world-wide consensus is likely on what constitutes the proper occasion for displaying such exaltation, if this entails going over the nuclear brink. The problem of peace-keeping is that of translating into positive action this unwillingness to be blown up in somebody else's quarrel.

The crucial difficulty was noted by General Burns when he said that the fair and reasonable promises of diplomats can be set aside by irreconcilable military officers. The diplomats are aware of the full extent of the sanctions, solid or imponderable, which can be brought to bear on them. Soldiers in the field, or orators at a mass rally, will have other things on their mind. Between these two extremes there are a variety of social elements which may be induced to support either militant or pacifying policies. A peace-keeping presence can serve to make the notion of an agreed settlement more salient than it would otherwise be, counteracting the effect of the clear-cut aims of those bent on all-out victory.

It is in this context that one must examine the question of the composition of a peace-keeping force, and of the tactics it should adopt. It is premature to think at present in terms of a permanent supernational force, if only because the nationality of troops employed can be an important factor in their acceptability to both sides in a given conflict. Soldiers are conspicuously representative of their nation, and their presence dramatises the nation's commitment to a settlement acceptable to the international community as a whole. This commitment is not a military one in the usual sense of the word. UN troops are normally either not armed at all, or lightly armed. In theory, weapons are used only in self-defence, and the full weight of national armed forces could be encountered only in the unorthodox way suggested by General Burns, when he wanted to be sure that any Israeli attack on Gaza would have to fire on his own troops. The case of the Katanga secession from the Congo provided an awkwardly marginal escalation towards full-scale war, though even here the theory behind the operation was that UN troops were assisting in the expulsion of foreign mercenaries from the region, and great pressure was exerted by the formidable diplomatic combination against secession, including both the USA and the USSR. Where an attempt is made to hold a position without a comparable diplomatic consensus—as happened in Korea in 1950—a peace-keeping role is impossible.

A temporary incapacity to act is disheartening but not fatal to a peace-keeping enterprise. The one thing it must avoid at all costs is loss of its mediating role. The UN has paid a heavy price for the claim that the Korean War was a properly accredited enforcement action: in the Far East the UN is virtually indistinguishable from the USA. This has prevented it from playing any significant part in dealing with the war in Vietnam. Since in any case the role of mediator is not easy to combine with that of a combatant, it is of special importance to study the situations where the UN has contrived to assert its presence by non-combatant means. Brigadier Harbottle's book *The Impartial Soldier*[5] is helpful in this context. It is an account of his two years of service with the UN force in Cyprus, and provides some vivid examples of the vigorous initiative and patient diplomacy needed to keep the peace in conditions of sustained communal tension. There is obviously much to be learnt from the Cyprus experience, and it is depressing to find Harbottle complaining that the British Ministry of Defence appears to show little or no interest in it. A counterpart to the detailed studies undertaken by the Swedes and the Canadians might, after all, have come in very useful in Northern Ireland.

Peace-keeping techniques have been conspicuously employed under the auspices of the UN but there is no necessary connection between these techniques and any particular international organisation. A body of what was in effect peace-keeping experience was built up by Gandhi in the last two or three years of his life, when the Indian subcontinent was ravaged by fierce communal strife. Lord Mountbatten and General Sir Francis Tuker both described his peace missions to Bengal in 1946-7 in terms of a striking military achievement.[6] What he did was to act as a focus for conciliatory moves, directing the minds of anxious, angry, and apparently unpersuadable people towards a state where Hindus and Muslims could again think in terms of peaceful co-existence.

While engaged in this work, Gandhi admitted that he felt himself to be in great darkness, his non-violence not sufficient to make an impact on the violence around him. A subjective sense of ineffectiveness must be recognised as a routine hazard of even the most successful peace-keeping work. The nearest that anyone has ever got to a non-violent equivalent of *Blitzkreig* is the Gandhian fast, and as Gandhi himself pointed out, when embarking on his Calcutta peace fast in September 1947, fasting makes no direct impression on 'goondas' (hooligans), the actual participants in rioting. But, he insisted, "the conflagration has been caused not by goondas but by those who have *become* goondas. It is we who make goondas. Without our sympathy and passive support, the goondas would have no legs to stand upon. I want to touch the hearts of those who are behind the goondas".[7]

The apparent simplicity of Gandhi's approach concealed a shrewd assessment of the latent political forces that could be evoked on behalf of a peaceful settlement. He was also willing to accept distasteful political arrangements (in this case the partition of India) if that was the alternative to unceasing conflict. The making of such assessments, and willingness to act on them, is an indispensable factor in the work of peace-keeping, and one that is intractably difficult to generalise about. The nature of the problem, however, is well illustrated by British responses to the Northern Ireland troubles from 1969 onwards. The province is in the grip of a typical communal conflict, with the minority community owing at most only a qualified allegiance to the United Kingdom. Britain's denial that the conflict is anything but a matter of internal law and order is the conditioned reflex that all governments similarly circumstanced invariably make. Unfortunately it is a reflex that makes the British army into a force occupying hostile territory. To acknowledge the essentially international dimension of the conflict would make the majority community feel deeply menaced and, indeed, betrayed—with a consequent danger of heightened violence. But a joint policy pressed by Britain, Ireland, and outside powers would be in a stronger position to damp down intransigence, and reinforce the very considerable elements working for peace within the province. An international presence, perhaps from the Council of Europe rather than the UN, might well form part of that pressure.

All along I have been making the assumption that bloodshed and social breakdown are evils. This is an assumption that many will be indisposed to make. Angry protests at what looks like weak-kneed acquiescence in intolerable wrong will meet any argument in favour of the peaceful resolution of conflict. The protests tend to become louder when the costs of violence are not seen to be immediate and overwhelming. Rightly or wrongly, the fear of nuclear war has tended to become less intense in recent years, and this has some bearing on the failure of UN peace-keeping to stir the interest it once did. Still, as Mr. Alan James has pointed out in *The Politics of Peace-Keeping,*[8] a repertory of techniques for containing and patching up conflicts is undeniably useful. Its usefulness resembles that of the informal international arrangements that now exist to cope with natural disasters. An international disaster relief organisation has often been mooted in recent years, and it could prepare the ground for a more systematic international presence in disastrous conflicts.

With recent memories of intransigence and massacre in Biafra and East Bengal, one hesitates to attribute much influence to that elusive entity 'world opinion'. The fact remains that modern means of communication have made it more difficult than it used to be to carry out ruthless policies on the quiet; and the mere fact of observation has something of a deterrent effect. These humane tendencies find their most explicit institutional expression in the agencies of the UN. Its headquarters is the place where conflicts can most naturally be looked at as problems to be solved rather than battles to be won. As long as the blue helmets of its forces represent, no matter how clumsily and inadequately, an attempt to bring this mentality to bear upon actual areas of conflict, then we have achieved something which it would be irresponsible to underestimate. It may be utopian to talk of UN peace-keeping forces as though they were an embryonic world police force; but they at least foreshadow a world order in which the war system can be undermined, if not dismantled altogether.

Further Reading:

The Politics of Peace-Keeping Alan James.

The Blue Berets Michael Harbottle. London: Leo Cooper, 1971.

The United Nations: Sacred Drama Conor Cruise O'Brien. London: Hutchinson, 1968. A survey of the field from a very different point of view: the author's suggestions for future research into the role of the UN are particularly useful.

Soldiers Without Enemies Larry L. Fabian. Washington D.C. The

Brookings Institution, 1971.

International Peacekeeping at the Crossroads David W. Wainhouse. Baltimore: The John Hopkins University Press, 1973.

[1] E.g. The Observer, London in an editorial published on 28 May 1967.
[2] *United Nations Forces* (London, Stevens, 1964).
[3] *The Listener* (London, 20th August, 1964).
[4] *Between Arab and Israeli* (London, Harrap, 1962).
[5] London, Oxford University Press, 1970.
[6] See V. P. Menon, *The Transfer of Power in India* (London, Longmans, 1957)), p.434, and F. Tuker, *While Memory Serves* (London, Cassell, 1950), p.426.
[7] *Non-Violence in Peace and War,* Vol. 2 (Ahmedabad, Navajivan Press, 1949), pp.300-2. From *Harijan,* 14 September, 1947.
[8] Chatto and Windus, London, 1969.

Conclusion

The reader will probably ask, what conclusions has the editor arrived at, after living for so long with these chapters. Does he really believe there is an alternative to war as a means of controlling and resisting aggression? The answer must be "Yes", an affirmative answer based on a search for, and discovery of a natural basis for a legal and moral non-violent authority. This search has also revealed an assumption; held by most people, about power and authority, which is not only false, but is one of the main reasons why we cannot live at peace.

The assumption is, that an aggressor must be curbed, controlled or prevented by force in one form of another. If a nation such as Russia, the U.S.A., or even a small nation, commits a crime, most people feel that if the U.N. takes no action against that nation, or fails whilst taking action, then the U.N. fails and its prestige is diminished.

The falseness of this assumption is illustrated by the failure of the League of Nations. The League of Nations failed to achieve its aim of collective security based on armaments because the nations of the world would not trust each other; they instinctively distrusted, giving excessive power into fewer hands, and this distrust made it even more difficult to disarm. Trust and confidence are the essential foundations for any international authority, and the belief in collective military security strikes at the heart of these foundations. Nevertheless this false assumption about collective security continued into the early days of the U.N. and is written into his charter. After the Korean war, however, the idea of military collective security was quietly dropped as being impracticable, but the underlying idea was not, and it still lives to haunt us today.

If this idea of collective security is found to be impracticable then what is the alternative? Here the role of the police force, as in Britain, may help us to understand the problem. A truly effective police force is one which relies upon the support of the public, and, unlike the soldier, the policeman is not judge, jury and executioner all rolled into one. His actions must be within the laws laid down by parliament, and must conform to a minimum code, recognised by all as being fair, if they are to be acceptable. If the police are given excessive personal powers to use violence, or intimidation, then their authority is soon diminished, and replaced by fear and mistrust. See chapters by C. H. Rolph and David Wills.

Why not emulate this rule of law, as applied by the police force in Britain and elsewhere, and relate it to international affairs?

A police force, however, needs a written code under which to operate, and the U.N. is fortunate in having already agreed on the Charter of Human Rights. We must now translate this Charter into specific Covenants, confirmed by governments and supported by International Courts. We need to relate Human Rights directly to the individual, and in particular to the individual who actually orders, or commits crimes, crimes already defined in the Nuremburg Principles as "against peace", "against humanity" and as "war crimes". The Nuremburg Principles were formulated by the International Law Commission following a directive given by the General Assembly of the U.N., and as such they already represent international law. But although much of the legal framework has already been agreed, the institutions and the *will* to support the law are sadly lacking. Much of this book is written outlining the steps needed to be taken to correct this condition. The important need is to create procedures whereby individuals can no longer shelter behind others, on the pretext that they were ordered to commit crimes. The Nuremburg Principles rest on the belief that the individual has to make a moral choice.

The chapter by Professor Mulford Q. Sibley confirms the practicability of individuals being made responsible for their own actions, with an illustration describing how the unity of the U.S.A. came into being. Further support for this concept is given by the psychiatrist, Dr. Jerome Frank, and by Dr. James Avery Joyce in his comparative study of the League of Nations with the U.N.

Much more progress towards implementing human rights has been made than most people realize, and the reader is asked to study Mr. Sean MacBride's chapter, in which he gives us a brilliant account of human rights and the rule of law. Few people seem to recognise the importance of the Charter of Human Rights as a means for ensuring a peaceful world, and it is vital for this understanding to be made clear, so that the resources of will and material may be used more effectively.

The European Commission and Court of Human Rights deserve special mention because it shows the world what can be done towards safeguarding human rights. Although it has only been in existence a short time, the fact that it *is* working and that nations have *already* agreed to accept the verdict of an international court in advance, is very encouraging and the answer to the sceptics who say such an idea is impossible. (It probably would be impossible if the Court ever attempts to enforce its authority by force of arms!) Other regions are also contemplating similar action to the European Court, some far more advanced. The time has now come for the establishment of a Universal Court of Human Rights, and a United Nations High Commissioner for Human Rights acting as the distribution centre, to advise individuals and governments, about Human Rights.

Another aspect of international law is seen to be that which directly arises when nations agree to co-operate. Some important areas for co-operation are discussed by Gordon Evans. Since this book was compiled, there have been other issues which have demanded world conferences, and which will probably lead to further international agreements, if the world is to avoid catastrophe and remove many of the economic causes of war. These include, for example, measures to control the population explosion, and sharing the world's food and mineral resources. International agreements of this kind will need machinery for dealing with disputes, and therefore the growth in importance of international courts, such as the Court at The Hague, will become even more important.

Underlying all laws, however, is seen to be the need for *natural justice* and this important subject is discussed by Professor D. V. Cowen. It is essential for us to be clear about this subject because it does determine our attitudes to all other matters relating to peace and freedom. All laws must be grounded on an understanding of natural laws which, over the years, has given rise to the much misunderstood concept of Natural Law.

One way of learning more about natural laws is to learn directly from primitive peoples, especially those who have learned to live peacefully with each other. Professor Ruth Finnegan in her chapter tells us of how non-industrialized primitive peoples have learnt to "ritualize" their conflicts, and the clear lesson for us is not only to seek to remove the causes of war, but to recognise that there will always be conflict, and we too must learn to ritualize. We have learnt this lesson within individual countries and established courts of law, the need now is to ritualize conflict at international level with international courts.

But it is of little use setting up international courts if the foundations of their authority is lacking. One of the central problems to overcome is that of controlling excessive power. For example, the question we should be asking ourselves today, is whether the Common Market is going in the right direction? If the Common Market countries co-operate fully until they become virtually one big power bloc, gaining more and more centralized power, especially if they pool their military power, then surely this must be in the wrong direction. If, on the other hand, the Common Market countries decentralize and co-operate within a world wide framework, acting as a regional arm of the U.N., and all its policies integrated with the other areas of the world, then the Common Market countries will be taking the path of peace. The important need is to be clear about our long term objectives.

Unfortunately the world suffers from the assumption that evil can cast out evil; that aggression must be met with superior force. The fact is that, although the threat of war may deter, it cannot make for a lasting peace; indeed the preparations for war stand in the way of peace. The presence of armaments encourages fear and suspicion in other nations, which in turn encourages fear and suspicion, and consequently nations spend more money on so-called defence expenditure. For instance, Britain alone has spent £30,000 million on defence since the last war, money which, if it had been spent supporting the many institutions of peace, including peace studies, would have gone a long way towards transforming our sick world into a healthy one, and Britain could have gained for itself economic prosperity and the moral leadership of the world. Above all, such acts would have instilled trust and confidence amongst the nations, dispelling much of the fear, hatred and poverty in the world, and going a long way towards providing the basis for the rule of law.

But the redirecting of £30,000 million by Britain is not as important for the peace of the world as the *will* to seek, understand, and build on the natural basis of a peaceful world order, and it is interesting that few of the chapters in this volume make demands for large sums of money. They demand something more difficult, which is a change in our sense of values and necessity to relate these values to long term planning.

One of the long term subjects must include education. Not education for academic achievement, or material gain, important though they are, but education for living; education to encourage co-operation and the flowering of the human spirit. This is essentially what Peter Manniche, Professor Elvin and Fr. Eric Doyle are calling for from their respective chapters on the Danish Folk High Schools, UNESCO, and through the teaching of Teilhard de Chardin.

But no matter how much we educate or co-operate, if the social and political power structure is unbalanced, the peace we seek will be impossible to find. The need for power to be decentralized to small units is seen to be of paramount importance, and Dr. Kohr, Dr. Schumacher and John Papworth all discuss this matter. Only small units can be self-regulating and lead to the psychological needs of individuals being satisfied, and thus lead to permanent solutions. This problem of small units within the U.N. contains many similarities to that of the Roman Empire and Professor John Ferguson provides us with a fascinating chapter on some of the reasons for the long period of peace the Romans gave us. Important was the concept of double citizenship. A City State loyalty was encouraged together with a loyalty to Rome, but regional loyalties were discouraged. The Romans, it seems, were obeying the natural laws of harmonizing unity with diversity.

Small units are seen to be essential if individuals are to be given a sense of meaning and purpose. The reason is that a healthy world order demands that we consider the whole complex of people's thoughts, feelings, senses, impressions and values, as of more importance than our material needs. It is of little use communicating with people's minds unless we communicate also with their feelings, and sensations. We need a constant flow of sights, sounds, knowledge and information, all within a structure in which these things re-enforce and invigorate each other. We all need to be wanted by others, yet at the same time to express our individuality. Much of this book is devoted towards helping the seeking reader to find the spiritual, material and factual guidance needed to achieve this result.

In a book of this kind the idea of non-violence is a subject which must be discussed. No attempt is made to discuss the general phiosophy of non-violence, but two case studies are made. The first, by Adam Roberts, discusses non-violent resistance in Czechoslovakia against the Russians in 1968, and the second by Antony Gilpin, about U.N. peacekeeping operations in the Congo and the lessons of non-violence he learnt there.

One important lesson I draw from their writings is that it is important, if non-violence is to succeed, for the nations' economy and power structure to be decentralized, and for the planning of non-violence to be undertaken in times of peace, in much the same way as we now plan for war.

Another lesson is that we need to understand more fully those forces which generate *the will* to act against injustice.

The beauty of non-violence is that, unlike war, it does not undermine the basis of law; on the contrary the same forces which go towards strengthening the forces of non-violence, as outlined above, are the same forces which go towards strengthening the bases of law.

Perhaps the most hopeful feature about today's world is that many new dimensions have been opened to us. The world is a very different place from that of only twenty-five years ago. Today, with modern means of communications, information and facts freely available, we are all near neighbours and the world a very small place. All this has changed attitudes considerably, and much more is known about poverty, for instance, to awaken our awareness as never before. Because of new knowledge and quick communications many injustices are clearly seen, and if steps are not taken to deal with the many problems facing us there will be an explosion. Fortunately these new dimensions of the modern world can be harnessed to create a peaceful world order and the proposals in this book outline the steps needed to be taken. We have to make a radical change in our thinking, and today the time is ripe for such a change.

Index

A

B

J

K

L

O

P

Q

T

U

V

W

Y

Z